Race and Contention in Twenty-First Century U.S. Media

This volume explores and clarifies the complex intersection of race and media in the contemporary United States. Due to the changing dynamics of how racial politics are played out in the contemporary United States (as seen with debates of the "post-racial" society), as well as the changing dynamics of the media itself ("new vs. old" media debates), an interrogation of the role of the media and its various institutions within this area of social inquiry is necessary. Contributors contend that race in the United States is dynamic, connected to social, economic, and political structures that are continually altering themselves. This book seeks to highlight the contested space that the media provides for changing dimensions of race, examining the ways that various representations can both hinder or promote positive racial views, considering media in relation to other institutions, and moving beyond thinking of media as a passive and singular institution.

Jason A. Smith is a PhD Candidate in Public Sociology at George Mason University, currently working on his dissertation involving media policy and diversity. Jason's primary research interests lie at the intersection of race and the media. He recently completed a co-edited section in the *International Journal of Communication* (2015) entitled, "Communication in Action: Bridging Research and Policy." Past work has been featured in the *Journal of Black Studies, International Journal of Media and Cultural Politics, Sociation Today*, and the edited volume *Agenda for Social Justice: Solutions 2012*.

Bhoomi K. Thakore is a visiting Assistant Professor and Director of the Sociology Program at Elmhurst College (IL). Her research interests broadly cover structural inequality, with particular focus on race/ethnicity/gender and media. In her forthcoming book, *South Asians on the U.S. Screen: Just Like Everyone Else?* (Lexington Books, 2016), she examines the ways that South Asian characters and actors in popular entertainment reinforce a racialized hierarchy on Screen and in society.

Routledge Transformations in Race and Media

Series Editors: Robin R. Means Coleman *University of Michigan, Ann Arbor*
Charlton D. McIlwain *New York University*

1 Interpreting Tyler Perry
   Perspectives on Race, Class, Gender, and Sexuality
   Edited by Jamel Santa Cruze Bell and Ronald L. Jackson II

2 Black Celebrity, Racial Politics, and the Press
   Framing Dissent
   Sarah J. Jackson

3 The Cultural Politics of Colorblind TV Casting
   Kristen J. Warner

4 The Myth of Post-Racialism in Television News
   Libby Lewis

5 Representations of Black Women in the Media
   The Damnation of Black Womanhood
   Marquita Marie Gammage

6 Race and Contention in Twenty-First Century U.S. Media
   Edited by Jason A. Smith and Bhoomi K. Thakore

Race and Contention in Twenty-First Century U.S. Media

Edited by Jason A. Smith
and Bhoomi K. Thakore

NEW YORK AND LONDON

First published 2016
by Routledge
711 Third Avenue, New York, NY 10017

and by Routledge
2 Park Square, Milton Park, Abingdon, Oxon OX14 4RN

First issued in paperback 2018

Routledge is an imprint of the Taylor and Francis Group, an informa business

© 2016 Taylor & Francis

The right of the editors to be identified as the authors of the editorial material, and of the authors for their individual chapters, has been asserted in accordance with sections 77 and 78 of the Copyright, Designs and Patents Act 1988.

All rights reserved. No part of this book may be reprinted or reproduced or utilised in any form or by any electronic, mechanical, or other means, now known or hereafter invented, including photocopying and recording, or in any information storage or retrieval system, without permission in writing from the publishers.

Trademark notice: Product or corporate names may be trademarks or registered trademarks, and are used only for identification and explanation without intent to infringe.

Library of Congress Cataloging-in-Publication Data

CIP data has been applied for.

ISBN 13: 978-1-138-59950-5 (pbk)
ISBN 13: 978-1-138-93715-4 (hbk)

Typeset in Sabon
by codeMantra

Contents

Acknowledgments — vii

Introduction: The Contours of Race and Media — 1
JASON A. SMITH AND BHOOMI K. THAKORE

PART I
Structures and Contention

1 Failure to Communicate: The Critical Information Needs Debate — 15
RANDY D. ABREU

2 Courting Minority Commodity Audiences: Bounce TV in the Age of Media Conglomeration — 26
LEAH P. HUNTER AND JENNIFER M. PROFFITT

3 New Media and New Possibilities: The Online Engagement of Young Black Activists — 41
NATHAN JAMEL RIEMER

PART II
Navigating Contention Behind the Scenes

4 Black, Asian, and Latino Directors in Hollywood — 59
MARYANN ERIGHA

5 Is Carlos Mencia A White Wetback?: *Media*ting the (E)Racing of U.S. Central Americans in the Latino Imaginary — 70
MARITZA CÁRDENAS

6 Sofía Vergara: On Media Representations of *Latinidad* — 85
SALVADOR VIDAL-ORTIZ

vi *Contents*

  7 Color-Blind Racism in the Media: Mindy Kaling as an
"Honorary White"   100
SHEENA SOOD

PART III
Visual Representations of Contention

  8 Drifting for Whiteness: Hollywood Representations
of Asian Americans in the Twenty-First Century   117
JOHN D. FOSTER

  9 Consuming Black Pain: Reading Racial Ideology
in Cultural Appetite for *12 Years a Slave*   131
JENNIFER C. MUELLER AND RULA ISSA

10 Racial Ideology in Electronic Dance Music
Festival Promotional Videos   148
DAVID L. BRUNSMA, NATHANIEL G. CHAPMAN, AND
J. SLADE LELLOCK

PART IV
Perpetuating Contentious Ideologies

11 The Rise of the Racial Reviewer, 1990–2004   165
BIANCA GONZALEZ-SOBRINO, DEVON R. GOSS, AND
MATTHEW W. HUGHEY

12 Successful Immigrants in the News: Racialization,
Color-Blind Racism, and the American Dream   182
JORGE X. BALLINAS

13 Black Studies in Prime Time: Racial Expertise and
the Framing of Cultural Authority   198
SENECA VAUGHT

14 The Good, the Bad, and the Ugly Muslim: Media
Representations of 'Islamic Punk' through a Postcolonial Lens   214
SAIF SHAHIN

Conclusion: Looking Ahead   231
BHOOMI K. THAKORE AND JASON A. SMITH

Editors and Contributors   235
Index   239

Acknowledgments

We would be remiss if we did not acknowledge the many people who have helped us see this project through to the very end. First, we would like to thank our series editors, Robin R. Means Coleman and Charlton D. McIlwain, for the opportunity to publish this volume under the Routledge Transformations in Race and Media series. We would also like to thank our Routledge editors along the way—Felisa Salvago-Keyes, Katie Laurentiev, and Christina Kowalski—who offered immeasurable advice and support during this process. Special thanks to Rutledge Dennis, whose advice and guidance early on helped lay the foundations and efforts for this edited volume. We also thank and appreciate our many contributors, all of whom were a pleasure to work with. Finally, the editors would like to thank their friends, families, and loved ones for their unconditional support now and always. We dedicate this book to #blacklivesmatter, and all of the people of color who have suffered and died under these social systems built on inequality.

Introduction
The Contours of Race and Media

Jason A. Smith and Bhoomi K. Thakore

The term *contention* implies disagreement, dispute, or claims toward a particular topic. For the purpose of this volume, we see contention as rooted in conflict and intimately tied to issues surrounding race/ethnicity in society. In this volume, we apply contention to specifically examine the intersection between race and media. Perhaps one of the most important institutions in a post-industrial society, the media are more than just gatekeepers or messengers, but sites for political, civic, and social upheaval. This idea of contention is not necessarily a new concept, but rather an extension of current projects that highlight the struggles of various racial groups with the media, both historically and contemporaneously (e.g., Classen, 2004; Craig, 2014; Gonzalez & Torres, 2011). Our use of it here is meant to investigate current projects within media spaces and demonstrate the complexity that exists in the contemporary United States at the beginning of the 21st century. With regard to the media as a contentious space in relation to race, we must also address the concept of "power"—particularly given the importance of the concept with regard to racial inequality in other institutions. Our broad notion of power, and as it is implied in the chapters in this volume, relies on highlighting the unequal distribution of both material and social capital throughout society. Important, and ongoing, changes have occurred in the United States with regard to race and our media system (both of which will be discussed in the following sections), which influence society as a whole.

A majority of the contributors to this volume are sociologists by training, as are the editors of this volume, whose disciplinary focus tends to emphasize the influences of structure and the inherent political forces within. This focus on the structural perspective of the media grounds our volume within critical race scholarship and its efforts to highlight how racial categories are embedded within the patterned interactions of various media organizations. Additionally, it seeks to contribute toward a subfield of media sociology, which has lagged behind in its own theoretical and empirical formulations (Benson, 2004; Katz, 2009; Peter & Pooley, 2012; Pooley & Katz, 2008). Our overarching goal with this volume is to critically assess the ways media and race intersect, with particular attention to the ways that the media is a multimodal institution that overlaps with other areas within society.

Media in the Twenty-First Century

Although a complicated institution, one can view the media at minimum as a mediator that conveys messages, images, and information from one subject to another. With regard to media outlets, many earlier approaches to media studies took this perspective. In the latter half of the 20th century, Todd Gitlin (1978) critiqued the "dominant paradigm" of media sociology as wedded too much toward behaviorist inquiry, administrative viewpoints, and a marketing orientation. His critique highlighted the tensions that existed within the field in its inability to critically examine notions of power that justified the existing system of media ownership and control. Gitlin's response to the field of *mass* communication (as expressed through the commercial media) centered on the focus that social scientists paid toward limiting the concept of the media. Shortly following Gitlin, Denis McQuail (1985) highlighted the renewed sociological approaches used to understand mass communication and, in particular, its interdisciplinary nature, which blends scientific expertise with insights from areas in both cultural studies and the humanities. Apart from the dominant paradigm from before, these new approaches brought with them a renewed focus on power, as well as integrating the study of the media into other institutions. Moving into the 21st century, scholars within the fields of sociology, communications, media studies, political science, and others, have greatly expanded on how we study and understand the media, particularly in areas such as media policy (Craig, 2014; Lloyd, 2004; Pickard 2014a), media industries (Decherney, 2005; Mayer, 2015), political economy (Mosco, 2009), and media use (Jenkins, 2006; Lange, 2014).

Similar to Gitlin and McQuail, we recognize the media as a complex and multifaceted institution made up of various organizations and actors. Although acts of communication occur through mediums, the organization of those mediums into a larger media structure are what distinguish the media from everyday acts of face-to-face conversation or individualized correspondence—such as letters, epistolary novels, or conversations on the telephone. Additionally, the media generally refers to how communication from one source resonates to large groups, often through a centralized system. To further clarify, the distinction between "medium" and "media" is related to their socially defined positions. Whereas mediums are the material components of communication or the tools in which people use to communicate (the telephone, television, Internet, print newspapers, or literary genres like novels and pamphlets), media are the organized systems of mediums for the purpose of sending specific messages to an individual or group. Assessing the media purely as a monolith, or merely a mediator, undermines the complexity of the institution. Thus, participation in the media landscape can be assessed in a number of ways—anywhere from the creator, consumer, or critic of a media product. For the purposes of this edited volume we center our focus on the media as encompassing a variety of mediums (popular television, popular film, newspapers, news channels, magazines, YouTube, and Twitter), which are used for both information and entertainment that are organized under a given set of practices, norms, and values. Additionally, these organized media structures are differentially linked to specific social, economic, political, and cultural positions within the U.S.

Differentiating itself from the 20th century, media in the 21st century has been driven by the technological innovations of the Internet over the past 30 years (Castells, 2000, 2009; Kovarik, 2011). Manuel Castells (2009) noted this in what he called the "network society": "a society whose social structure is made around networks activated by microelectronics-based, digitally processed information and communication technologies" (p. 24). Castells elaborates on this for media institutions in how forms of "mass self-communication," expressed through the medium of the Internet, both challenge and are captured by established media networks on a global scale (2009, pp. 58–99). As others have noted in regard to the concentration of media ownership in the U.S. (see Baker, 2007; Lloyd, 2006; Noam, 2009; Pickard, 2014b; Schiller, 1989), the public suffers from organizational practices that undervalue providing localized information and diverse viewpoints to maintain a robust democracy. In relation to the rise of the Internet as a means of expression outside established media networks, the promise of disrupting this power dynamic is often lost due to issues surrounding the control of and access to the Internet—in which it has, at the time of this writing, been relatively locked into a market-oriented economy as a service to be sold rather than seen as a public good (Crawford, 2013; McChesney, 2013; Meinrath, Losey, & Pickard, 2011). However, the need for established media networks to adapt to newer forms of "mass self-communication" (Castells, 2009) brings about contention within various media organizations.

These contentions find themselves practiced in various ways, as different actors within the media vie for control or instances to highlight new opportunities of expression toward particular issues or goals. The introduction of the Internet into media studies at the turn of the 21st century has shifted scholars, and the public as well, to reevaluate their view of the media. The "new media" field of study has highlighted the breakup of the one-to-many flow of mass communication and has sought to understand this new media environment in more nuanced ways (Jenkins, 2006; Lister, Dovey, Giddings, Grant, & Kelly, 2008). As mentioned earlier, although structure plays an important role in shaping both access to and the content of various media, the cultural dynamics that take place within media spaces are never as clear-cut. The engagement with media by various individuals and groups creates unique opportunities for values and beliefs to be adhered to, challenged, or transformed within the media environment. This focus on connecting structure and culture within analyses of the media highlight the practices that are carried out within particular socially based contexts and historical moments that represent media as a "modality" (Brouwer & Asen, 2010), rather than a decontextualized component of everyday life.

Contemporary Racial Theories (and Their Implications)

In the 21st century, the U.S. is becoming the most diverse and multicultural that we have ever been. It is projected that by the mid-2030s, people of color will become the majority in the United States. While Hispanics/Latinos currently comprise most of the racial diversity, and Asian Americans will also continue to grow, there will be an increasingly projected segment of the population who will identify as multiracial. These changes to the social fabric will become increasingly important for the future of society. Racial identities will also be influenced by gender identities across the spectrum. The intersections of these myriad identities will uniquely inform one's experiences with social class and her relationship to and within the U.S. power structure. For example, we have extreme pockets of inequality sprinkled throughout the country in both urban and rural localities. On the other hand, our society's role in consumerism and falling in line with social decisions made without regard for human rights illustrates how much control the ideologies of a "power elite" have on our social structures (e.g., Coates, 2007; Mills, 1999; Turner, 1993).

As previously mentioned, our relationships with social institutions are strongly informed by race (e.g., Bell, 1992; Blauner, 1972; Bonilla Silva, 1997; Feagin, 2001; Mills, 1997; Pager & Shepard, 2008; Winant, 2000). In relation to race theory at the beginning of the 21st century, Howard Winant (2000) noted that scholars must take seriously the current social context in which they lived, the continued presence of racial signification/identity, and the ongoing structural salience of race in society. More recently, in the classroom, Non-White students are treated in unequal ways that maintain unequal education and the school-to-prison pipeline (e.g., A. E. Lewis, 2004; Alexander, 2012). In real estate, Non-Whites face discriminatory loan practices and redlining (e.g., Squires, 2003). In the employment sector, Non-Whites face limitations in promotion and salary, and even have trouble getting their foot in the door with ethnic-sounding names (e.g., Bertrand & Mullainathan, 2003). In everyday interactions, Non-Whites face microaggressive comments and slights against them (Feagin, 1991; W. A. Smith, Hung, & Franklin, 2011). These are just a few examples of the salience of race within our social structures.

Further, the racialization patterns that inform our place within the social hierarchy of the U.S. are influenced by overt physical manifestations that are "read" as Non-White (e.g., Bonilla-Silva, 2004; Feagin, 2010; Kim, 1999). As Eduardo Bonilla-Silva argued, the U.S. is developing into a racial hierarchy informed primarily by class and skin color. While this racial hierarchy reinforces ideologies of Whites at the "top" and Collective Blacks at the "bottom," what is not consistent is the hierarchy among Latinos, Arabs, and Asian groups in the "middle." However, as a theoretical approach, discussions of racialization have historically focused on skin color as the primary influence (Banton, 1977; Bonilla-Silva, 2004; Fanon, 1964; Omi & Winant, 2014). In the 21st century, other overt markers of cultural and religious "difference" are becoming increasingly relevant to racialization. For example, religion has long been used in the West to persecute and Otherize people. As Saher Selod and David G. Embrick (2013) argue, this process is a form of racialization unique to Arabs and Muslims, who themselves represent a number of "racial" groups. In this post-9/11 environment of fear and surveillance, religion is becoming a stronger factor in the racialization of Arab and South Asian groups. In the 21st century, Muslim racialization will continue to be important as post-colonial contention rages in the Middle East. At the time of this writing, there are Syrian refugees entering the U.S. seeking political asylum, whose own experiences will be informed by their racialization as Syrian Muslims.

In addition to the effects of racialization for Non-Whites in the U.S., racial ideologies have moved from a system of overt structural racism to a more covert and color-blind racism that encourages individuals to focus less on racial identity and more on individual traits (Bonilla-Silva, 2010; Carr, 1997). While the logic behind these ideologies may be sincere in theory, these perspectives limit the attention on the long-standing racial inequality and White supremacy that maintain a socially unjust society. As Leslie G. Carr (1997) wrote, color-blind ideology minimizes the social importance of affirmative action and integration. Extending this argument, Bonilla-Silva (2010) notes how color-blind racism is reproduced in thought with four frames: abstract liberalism, biologization of culture, naturalization of racial matters, and minimization of racism (frames that are addressed in Chapters 7 and 12 in this volume). These are the ways in which conversations (by Whites about their attitudes toward Non-Whites) reinforces this at the "ground level" in conversations and rhetoric. The experiences of Non-Whites against both levels of inequality—with racialization and with color-blind racism—leave their experiences in the U.S. as highly contentious. This is further informed by how they interact and receive messages through media.

Racial Formations and the White Racial Frame

Two dominant trends in racial theory that shape current research are racial formations (Omi & Winant, 2014) and systemic racism (Feagin, 2006; see also Feagin, 2010, with a particular focus on the White racial frame in regard to issues concerning the media). As Michael Omi and Howard Winant (2014) argued, racial formations are the creation and development of racial categories and classifications over time, based on the social and political ideologies of the day. For example, African slaves were once seen as property (not people), and in the 21st century, Black identity is increasingly blending into the U.S. multiracial category. Race is emphasized as an identity that is a social construction, based on dominant racial ideologies of the day. These social constructions further adapt with changes in the racial landscape and the entrance of new immigrant groups. As discussed by Bonilla-Silva (2010) and others, these changes over time have led to more color-blind racial and post-racial perspectives, despite realities and social phenomena that indicate otherwise.

In a 2013 special issue symposium of the academic journal *Ethnic and Racial Studies*, numerous race scholars contributed to the discussion of the relevance of Omi and Winant's original theory today. First, Joe Feagin and Sean Elias presented, as a counter to racial formation theory, systemic racism theory, which emphasizes the role of the foundational structures, mechanisms, and operations that have shaped the United States over time (Feagin & Elias, 2013). Emphasizing Feagin's analyses of systemic racism and the White racial frame, they argue that Omi and Winant fail to emphasize the role of Whites in the structures that maintain these racial formations. The emphasis on White-dominated social structures and normalized White supremacist ideologies, Feagin and Elias argue, are fundamental to a sociological analysis of race relations. In their response, Omi and Winant (2013) collegially contend that the White racial frame emphasizes a Black/White paradigm, which makes less sense in an increasingly diversifying and multi-racial society. Additionally, emphasizing the possessive investment fails to acknowledge those serious anti-racists who practice what they preach. They also contend that U.S. racial formations are unique historically, considering key social influences like post-World War II integration and immigration policies that contributed to the various racial/ethnic populations of today. Other scholars in the symposium highlighted middle-ground perspectives between these two dominant theories, emphasizing the importance of hegemonic Whiteness (Hughey & Byrd, 2013); the historical influence of social events (Dennis, 2013); intersections of gender, class, and sexuality (Wingfield, 2013); the application of both perspectives on race relations outside the U.S. (Golash-Boza, 2013); and the usefulness of both perspectives as a collective explanatory tool (Banton, 2013). These discussions are important as they preface the presentation of our volume in that, even between these two perspectives, there tends to be a contention between the level of significance given to racial hierarchies and normative White ideologies.

Where Race and Media Intersect

As Oscar Gandy stated, "The role of the mass media in the construction and reproduction of race and racism is to be understood in the context of mass media systems and institutions" (1998, p. 93). This structural perspective has pushed for research to analyze issues of representation in both the production and content of media messages. Such work has highlighted the role that racial minorities play in creating media content, the way content promotes racial ideologies, and the connection that the former has with the latter. Additionally, as critical race scholars would argue, racial ideologies also shape the content production of these media products. This fluid dynamic represents what some would call a "possessive investment in Whiteness" (Lipsitz, 2006) or a dominant "White racial frame" (Feagin, 2010) that perpetuates preexisting racial hierarchies through the media. Within media organizations and industries, this positions scholars to study the ways that everyday practices and norms become institutionalized and perpetuate racial hierarchies.

In studies of the media, scholars have demonstrated the ways racial hierarchies are played out in crafting what we see (Chaisson, 2000; Drew, 2011; Lewis, 2016; Pritchard & Stonbely, 2007; J. Smith, 2013; Thakore, 2016). However, given the complexity of race in the contemporary U.S., such hierarchies and their implications are not as clear-cut as they used to be. For example, Emily Drew (2011) conducted interviews with White journalists who were assigned to produce news series to understand racism in the post-Civil Rights era. Her findings showed that through producing these news stories White journalists began to look reflectively on their own news production processes, leading to a deeper engagement with local communities and reporting of racialized events with more nuance. Conversely, David Pritchard and Sarah Stonbely (2007), looking at a metropolitan daily newspaper, found through interviews and an analysis of news content that race played a key role in the story assignments for journalists. For minority journalists, this was a double-edged sword; being both advantageous for them in acquiring story assignments, yet also contributed to those journalists feeling limited to certain positions at the newspaper. These two cases provide conflicting findings in regard to contemporary news practices and how race plays a role for journalists and the content they create. The power dynamics within the news media frame issues of diversity and racial representation in limited ways, although unique opportunities do arise to challenge racial hierarchies in particular moments. Additionally, recent work by Libby Lewis (2016) articulates these power dynamics in the post-racial era through attention to the ways that racial hierarchies shape the experiences of Black journalists. Her work, although speaking toward one particular racial group, raises attention to the shifting opportunities that are allotted racial minorities in a new media environment and how their efforts to fill the gap in these inequalities are important, but perhaps not useful enough. The same applies for entertainment media that challenge racialized representations (Davis, 2014; J. Smith, 2013), yet still adhere to racialized ideologies (Hughey, 2009, 2014; J. Smith, 2013; J. A. Smith, 2016).

Given the dynamic nature of race and its connection to ongoing struggles within the social, economic, and political spheres of society, its intersection with the media further drives the need for more critical engagement in the fields of sociology, communications, and media studies. Freedman's (2014) paradigms of power within modern media highlight complex and interlocking ways in which various groups, issues, agendas, and institutions become present within the media environment. Freedman articulates the nature of competing relationships that stem from various groups both within and outside the media that shape these paradigms. However, he is not leaving out the fact that access to the media is built from structural disparities that reflect how these relationships are formed and interact. Given the rise of new technologies and the conflicts that are produced from their introduction into established media systems, it leads us to question whether we will have new "power mosaics" (Freedman, 2014) or a "people power" (Schiller, 1989) driven media, in which multiple groups can successfully voice opinions and concerns relative to their lived experiences. Such inquires raise critical questions for the study of race and the media.

New Dynamics in Race and Media

In Part I, "Structures and Contention," the authors focus on the dynamics by which media outlets are created, maintained, and used, based on the inherent political oversight of this domain. Here, we emphasize the structural influences of media as it intersects with institutions based in the state, and is ruled by normative ideologies. In Chapter 1, Randy D. Abreu examines the failed attempt of the Federal Communications Commission to perform its Critical Information Needs Study as it relates to media ecologies, and the importance of critical needs for filling the media gaps in community segregation. In Chapter 2, Leah P. Hunter and Jennifer M. Proffitt discuss the marketability of a Black-owned network (Bounce TV) within this government media structure along with the marketability of this medium to Black audiences. The ability for this network to market directly to the Black community is not only important, but also unprecedented in the history of television. In Chapter 3, Nathan Jamel Riemer emphasizes the importance of new media in the current forms of activism among youth of color. Using a case study of a group of Black youth who use new media to speak out against Black marginalization, Riemer builds upon the concept of "participatory politics" in ways that point to a new generation of politically engaged youth mediating their experiences.

In Part II, "Navigating Contention Behind the Scenes," the authors focus on the role that individual players can navigate "backstage." In Chapter 4, Maryann Erigha emphasizes the lack of diversity among Hollywood directors. Using a variety of data from the 1,700 films produced between 2010 and 2011, including secondary interviews with directors, Erigha identifies the stark inequality in this area of film production. In Chapter 5, Martiza Cárdenas focuses on Carlos Mencia, a Central American (Honduran) man, whose comedy and ethnoracial identity created controversy and crises around definitions of Latinidad, a generalized perception of Latino history, identity, and representation. In Chapter 6, Salvador Vidal-Ortiz examines the Hollywood presence of Colombian-born Sofia Vergara and her use of Latinidad through her celebrity. Using news interviews with and media coverage of Vergara, Vidal-Ortiz presents Vergara as an important Latina in Hollywood. In Chapter 7, Sheena Sood positions Indian American producer and actress Mindy Kaling by way of her mainstream media representations on her show *The Mindy Project* (2012–present), noting differences between Lahiri the representation and Kaling the producer.

In Part III, "Visual Representations of Contention," the authors focus on the visual portrayal of Non-Whites through film and online content, and the limitations of these portrayals through these platforms. In Chapter 8, John D. Foster discusses the lack of options for Asian actors in Hollywood, but also how films reinforce the representation of the "perpetual stranger." In Chapter 9, Jennifer C. Mueller and Rula Issa theoretically analyze the 2013 Oscar-winning Best Picture *12 Years a Slave* and its manifestations of pain and humiliation of Blacks for White-dominated audiences. Couched in a historical narrative, this movie was meant to shock and scandalize audiences, in ways that justified White racial frames within society. In Chapter 10, David L. Brunsma, Nathaniel G. Chapman, and J. Slade Lellock examine the racialized representations in YouTube promotional videos of the Electric Daisy Carnival festival. As the authors present, these videos perpetuate White privilege while reinforcing racialized stereotypes.

In Part IV, "Perpetuating Contentious Ideologies," the authors identify the myriad ways that the news media perpetuates racial ideologies of inequality through their coverage of important people, events, and issues. In Chapter 11, Bianca Gonzalez-Sobrino, Devon R. Goss, and Matthew W. Hughey demonstrate how film reviews of top racialized films, ranging from 1990 to 2004, reinforce dominant racial ideologies. In Chapter 12, Jorge X. Ballinas focuses on U.S. news media coverage of immigrants, using the examples of 11-year-old mariachi singer Sebastien de la Cruz (a Mexican American) and 2014 Miss America winner Nina Davuluri (an Indian American). Ballinas illustrates how the news media perpetuate positive and normative ideologies of good immigrants achieving the American Dream from news coverage in a sample of mainstream television and print news outlets. In Chapter 13, Seneca Vaught interrogates the use of Black Studies scholars in mainstream news. Using news coverage of three recent events, Vaught argues that this type of coverage fails at an opportunity to engage with Black Studies scholars and scholarship in order to critically examine current racial crises. In Chapter 14, Saif Shahin provides insight into the taqwacore subculture of Islamic punk by examining U.S. and U.K. media coverage of taqwacore in newspapers. This subculture not only emphasizes the dynamic nature of racialization (one that is infused with religion), but also points to a media narrative toward a marginalized group that is influenced by racialized ideologies of the Orientalized Other. All of the chapters in this volume aim to address the contentious nature of race within the context of these myriad media institutions.

References

Alexander, M. (2012). *The new Jim Crow: Mass incarceration in the age of colorblindness*. New York, NY: The New Press.
Baker, C. E. (2007). *Media concentration and democracy: Why ownership matters*. Cambridge, UK: Cambridge University Press.
Banton, M. (1977). *The idea of race*. London, UK: Tavistock.

Banton, M. (2013). In defense of mainstream sociology. *Ethnic & Racial Studies, 36*(6), 1000–1004.

Bell, D. A. (1992). *Faces at the bottom of the well: The permanence of racism.* New York, NY: Basic Books.

Benson, R. (2004.) Bringing the sociology of media back in. *Political Communication, 21,* 275–292.

Bertrand, M., & Mullainathan, S. (2003). *Are Emily and Greg more employable than Lakisha and Jamal? A field experiment on labor market discrimination.* NBER Working Paper. Retrieved from http://www.nber.org/papers/w9873.pdf.

Blauner, R. (1972). *Racial oppression in America.* New York, NY: Harper & Row.

Bonilla-Silva, E. (1997). Rethinking racism: Toward a structural interpretation. *American Sociological Review, 62*(3), 465–80.

Bonilla-Silva, E. (2004). From bi-racial to tri-racial: Towards a new system of racial stratification in the USA. *Ethnic and Racial Studies, 27,* 931–950.

Bonilla-Silva, E. (2010). *Racism without racists.* Landham, MD: Rowman & Littlefield.

Brouwer, D. C., & Asen, R. (Eds.). (2010). *Public modalities: Rhetoric, culture, media, and the shape of public life.* Tuscaloosa, AL: University of Alabama Press.

Carr, L. G. (1997). *"Color-blind" racism.* Thousand Oaks, CA: Sage.

Castells, M. (2000). *The rise of the network society.* Malden, MA: Blackwell.

Castells, M. (2009). *Communication power.* Oxford, UK: Oxford University Press.

Chaisson, R. L. (2000). *For entertainment purposes only? An analysis of the struggle to control filmic representations.* Lanham, MD: Lexington.

Classen, S. D. (2004) *Watching Jim Crow: The struggles over Mississippi TV, 1955–1969.* Durham, NC: Duke University Press.

Coates, R. D. (2007). Social justice and pedagogy. *American Behavioral Scientist, 51*(4), 579–591.

Craig, R. T. (2014). *African Americans and mass media: A case for diversity in media ownership.* Lanham, MD: Lexington.

Crawford, S. (2013). *Captive audience: The telecom industry and monopoly power in the new gilded age.* New Haven, CT: Yale University Press.

Davis, K. C. (2014). *Beyond the White negro: Empathy and anti-racist reading.* Urbana, IL: University of Illinois Press.

Decherney, P. (2005). *Hollywood and the culture elite: How the movies became American.* New York, NY: Columbia University Press.

Dennis, R. M. (2013). Convergences and divergences in race theorizing: A critical assessment of race formation theory and systemic racism theory. *Ethnic & Racial Studies, 36*(6), 982–988.

Drew, E. M. (2011). "Coming to terms with our own racism": Journalists grapple with the racialization of their news. *Critical Studies in Media Communication, 28*(4), 353–373.

Fanon, F. (2004). *Wretched of the Earth* (reprint). New York, NY: Grove Press.

Feagin, J. R. (1991). The continued significance of race: Antiblack discrimination in public places. *American Sociological Review, 56*(1), 101–116.

Feagin, J. R. (2001). *Racist America: Roots, current realities, and future reparation.* New York, NY: Routledge.

Feagin, J. R. (2006). *Systemic racism.* New York, NY: Routledge.

Feagin, J. R. (2010). *The white racial frame: Centuries of racial framing and counter-framing.* New York, NY: Routledge.

Feagin, J. R., & Elias, S. (2013). Rethinking racial formation theory: A systemic racism critique. *Ethnic & Racial Studies, 36*(6), 931–960.
Freedman, D. (2014). *The contradictions of media power.* London, UK: Bloomsbury.
Gandy, O. H. (1998). *Communication and race: A structural perspective.* London, UK: Arnold.
Gitlin, T. (1978). Media sociology: The dominant paradigm. *Theory & Society, 6*(2), 205–253.
Golash-Boza, T. (2013). Does racial formation theory lack the conceptual tools to understand racism? *Ethnic & Racial Studies, 36*(6): 994–999.
Gonzalez, J., & Torres, J. (2011). *News for all the people: The epic story of race and American media.* New York, NY: Verso.
Hughey, M.W. (2009). Cinethetic racism: White redemption and black stereotypes in "magical negro" films. *Social Problems, 56*(3), 543–577.
Hughey, M. W. (2014). *The White savior film: Content, critics, and consumption.* Philadelphia, PA: Temple University Press.
Hughey. M. W., & Byrd, W. C. (2013). The souls of white folk beyond formation and structure: Bound to identity. *Ethnic & Racial Studies, 36*(6): 974–981.
Jenkins, H. (2006). *Convergence culture: Where old and new media collide.* New York, NY: New York University Press.
Katz, E. (2009.) Why sociology abandoned communication. *American Sociologist, 40*(3), 167–174.
Kim, C. J. (1999). The racial triangulation of Asian Americans. *Politics and Society, 27*(1), 105–138.
Kovarik, B. (2011). *Revolutions in communication: Media history from Gutenberg to the digital age.* New York, NY: Continuum.
Lange, P. G. (2014). *Kids on YouTube: Technical identities and digital literacies.* Walnut Creek, CA: Left Coast Press.
Lewis, A. E. (2004). *Race in the schoolyard: Negotiating the color line in classrooms and communities.* New Brunswick, NJ: Rutgers University Press.
Lewis, L. (2016). *The myth of post-racialism in television news.* New York, NY: Routledge.
Lipsitz, G. (2006). *The possessive investment in Whiteness: How White people profit from identity politics.* Philadelphia, PA: Temple University Press.
Lister, M., Dovey, J., Giddings, S., Grant, I., & Kelly, K. (2008). *New media: A critical introduction.* New York, NY: Routledge.
Lloyd, M. (2006). *Prologue to a farce: Communication and democracy in America.* Urbana, IL: University of Illinois Press.
Mayer, V. (2015). Media work, management, and greed: A new agenda? *Media Industries, 1*(3), 22–25.
McChesney, R. W. (2013). *Digital disconnect: How capitalism is turning the Internet against democracy.* New York, NY: New Press.
McQuail, D. (1985). Sociology of mass communication. *Annual Review of Sociology, 11,* 93–111.
Meinrath, S.D., Losey, J. W., & Pickard, V. W. (2011). Digital feudalism: Enclosures and erasures from digital rights management to the digital divide. *CommLaw Conspectus, 19,* 423–479.
Mills, C. W. (1997). *The racial contract.* Ithaca, NY: Cornell University Press.
Mills, C. W. (1999). *The power elite.* New York, NY: Oxford University Press.
Mosco, V. (2009). *The political economy of communication.* Los Angeles, CA: Sage.

Noam, E. M. (2009). *Media ownership and concentration in America*. Oxford, UK: Oxford University Press.

Omi, M., & Winant, H. (2013). Resistance is futile?: A response to Feagin and Elias. *Ethnic & Racial Studies, 36*(6), 961–973.

Omi, M., & Winant, H. (2014). *Racial formation in the United States*. New York, NY: Routledge.

Pager, D., & Shepherd, H. (2008). The sociology of discrimination: Racial discrimination in employment, housing, credit, and consumer markets. *Annual Review of Sociology, 34*, 181.

Peter, J. D., & Pooley, J. (2012). Media and communications. In G. Ritzer (Ed.), *The Wiley-Blackwell companion to sociology* (pp. 402–417). Malden, MA: Wiley-Blackwell.

Pooley, J., & Katz, E. (2008). Further notes on why American sociology abandoned mass communication research. *Journal of Communication, 58*, 767–786.

Pickard, V. (2014a). *America's battle for media democracy: The triumph of corporate libertarianism and the future of media reform*. Cambridge, UK: Cambridge University Press.

Pickard, V. (2014b). The great evasion: Confronting market failure in American media policy. *Critical Studies in Media Communication, 31*(2), 153–159.

Pritchard, D., & Stonbely, S. (2007). Racial profiling in the newsroom. *Journalism & Mass Communication Quarterly, 84*, 231–248.

Schiller, H. I. (1989). *Culture, Inc.: The corporate takeover of public expression*. Oxford, UK: Oxford University Press.

Selod, S., & Embrick, D. G. (2013). Racialization and Muslims: Situating the Muslim experience in race scholarship. *Sociology Compass, 7*, 644–655.

Smith, J. (2013). Between colorblind and colorconscious: Contemporary Hollywood films and struggles over racial representation. *Journal of Black Studies, 44*(8), 779–797.

Smith, J. A. (2016). Mutating minorities: White racial framing and group positioning. In C. Bucciferro (Ed.), *The X-Men films: A cultural analysis* (pp. 179–192). Lanham, MD: Rowman & Littlefield.

Smith, W. A., Hung, M., & Franklin, J. D. (2011). Racial battle fatigue and the miseducation of Black men: Racial microaggressions, societal problems, and environmental stress. *The Journal of Negro Education, 80*(1), 63–82.

Squires, G. D. (2003). Racial profiling, insurance style: Insurance redlining and the uneven development of metropolitan areas. *Journal of Urban Affairs, 25*(4), 391–410.

Thakore, B. K. (2016). *South Asians on the U.S. screen: Just like everyone else?* Lanham, MD: Lexington Books.

Turner, B. S. (1993). Outline of a theory of human rights. *Sociology, 27*, 489–512.

Winant, H. (2000). Race and race theory. *Annual Review of Sociology, 26*, 169–185.

Wingfield, A. W. (2013). Comment on Feagin and Elias. *Ethnic & Racial Studies, 36*(6), 989–993.

Part I
Structures and Contention

1 Failure to Communicate
The Critical Information Needs Debate

Randy D. Abreu

It was the summer of 2013 as I embarked upon the historic National Mall of Washington, DC. Walking up to the Lincoln Memorial, I spotted a group of Black youth performing music, poetry, backflips, and more. I approached the organizer of the event, who informed me the youth are part of a local DC church and are out in front of the Lincoln Memorial to promote positive stories from the Black community. I look around the swarm of people videotaping and photographing the performers; something was missing. Not one television crew or camera was on site. This display of positive community involvement went unnoticed, but not for lack of trying. The organizer informed me that he did reach out to local news stations in order to promote the event, but to no avail.

That night, I went home and watched the local news. The headline read "Black Teens Rob Convenience Store." Yes, a robbery is news; but if I am a young person of color watching the news, a narrative can have profound effects. The story that covers progressive youth for change goes much further in promoting a diverse and cohesive society than does a seemingly repetitive story of a Black thief. This is not to say that thievery should go uncovered by news outlets, but people of all colors steal on a daily basis; why do some producers feel the need to run the story of the Black kid who steals over the story of the Black kids who want to make the world a better place?

The power of media is exponential; it can shape opinions and help construct societal interactions. With those powers it is imperative to assess whether all Americans have the abilities to acquire the critical information they need to obtain resources for societal progress. From 2009 to 2013 there was an attempt to garner such assessment by the Federal Communications Commission (FCC), but it was met with criticism from leaders within the United States government and the attempt was halted before it could take off.

The FCC was created through enactment of the Communications Act of 1934 and it mandated the FCC to establish regulations that would connect all Americans to an affordable and reliable communications system. Sixty years later, the Telecommunications Act of 1996 provided a necessary update to the law. The 1996 act included a provision that required the

FCC to report to Congress on market entry barriers in the communications and information service market place along with regulations and practices that would help eliminate those barriers.

Our contemporary media is controlled by a handful of corporations that wield great influence over what we see, hear, and read, everyday (Austin, 2011). Consistent with the FCC's mandate is a call to hold regulated corporations responsible for ensuring that media offers the essential information Americans need to equally participate and engage civically. At the FCC this essential information is referred to as Critical Information Needs (CIN), and it can affect an entire population in a myriad of ways simply through the dissemination or denial of such information (FCC, 2013). In 2014, the FCC's attempt to understand what those needs are, how Americans obtain the information critical to their daily lives, and what barriers exist in our media ecologies to providing and accessing this information was derailed by partisan politics.

The equal ability of all citizens to participate in our democracy must be a compelling interest of the United States government. To ensure that those who provide critical information are held to responsible standards when serving local communities it is prudent to inquire into the operational practices and demographics of those that disseminate the information needs to the public. A White producer of news media from a suburban background is less likely to relate to and disseminate the needs of all residents in diverse and urban communities (Kim, 2011); a study examining media ownership and production found that 70% of minority-owned radio stations aired minority-targeted content (Sandoval, 2011). Therefore, if news media is to assume its optimal role in our society, there must be certainty that those who disseminate critical information needs understand their great powers and responsibilities (Smith, 2009).

This chapter will first take a look at historical and structural racism in the United States, particularly taking a critical look at community segregation and access to material goods that foster social mobility. Second, I will introduce the events leading up to the creation of the Critical Information Needs Study (CIN Study) attempted by the FCC. Third, I discuss the integral parts of the CIN Study as they relate to media ecologies. Fourth, I discuss the argument presented by government leaders in opposition to the CIN Study and provide a counter to the argument. Finally, I discuss the derailment of the CIN Study before it could be administered and the resulting policy implications on race and media in the 21st century.

A Critical Look at Race in the CIN Context

Structural racism and a lack of access to material goods has led to disparate needs and outcomes for different racial groups. Take for instance the desegregation of public schools during the mid-20th century. Derrick Bell (1976) noted the attempts of Civil Rights leaders to establish a racial population at every school consistent with the population demographics of the surrounding district. However, the attempts were flawed as White parents with the accessibility and means sent their children to private schools, continuing a cycle of unequal educational attainment and a lack of cultural diversity. Though notions of an equal education system run through our legal system, people of color still experience negative societal impacts. Low-income students (which far too often intersect with students of color) in public schools lack essential technological tools to succeed. As a result, their opportunities are diminished in our democracy when compared to privileged students in private schools.

Furthermore, access to capital consistently impedes the ability of people of color to succeed. While the Federal Housing Authority (FHA) was instrumental in alleviating home-ownership concerns during the mid 20th century, it was inherent in maintaining the segregation of Whites from people of color. The FHA discrimination policy, known as "redlining," denied loans and financial services to people of color interested in buying a home. As a result, Blacks, and other persons of color were forced into segregated communities that garnered zero interest from investors, perpetuating a cycle of inequality and lack of access for social mobility.

In the communications realm, the story of disparate treatment is all too familiar. People of color are deprived opportunities to purchase spectrum and disseminate critical information through use of the public airwaves. As an FCC commissioned study by William Bradford (2000) showed, even when a person of color achieves educational success, they are shut out of the economic process; they are less likely to receive debt financing in capital markets. And when a loan is approved, a person of color traditionally pays higher interest rates than their White-male counterparts. This cycle of inherent discrimination has an effect on maintaining barriers to obtaining critical information needs, and as such, implores the FCC to fulfill its legislative mandate enabled in the Communications Act.

Low-income and non-English-speaking communities begin in a disadvantaged position. The lack of research that addresses the needs of these communities is concerning. Particularly concerning is the lack of research and data that informs lawmakers how disadvantaged communities are receiving, or not receiving, their critical information needs. For example, in the field of medicine there is a quantifiable gap in health access that can grow exponentially if not addressed (Viswanath & Kreuter, 2007). It is important to garner more research and data that directly address the critical information needs of all communities.

The Knight Commission on the Information Needs of Communities is an organized group of 17 media, policy, and communications leaders that joined to address the critical information needs of communities in the digital age. The Knight Commission (2009) identified four basic critical needs of communities: (1) communities need to coordinate a multitude of activities, ranging from elections to emergency response; (2) communities need to solve problems in health, education, and economic development; (3) communities need to establish systems of public accountability; and (4) communities need to develop a sense of connectedness. These needs are fundamental to disadvantaged communities. Following the Knight Commission, in 2012 the FCC requested the provision of a literature review of research into the critical information needs of all Americans. In furtherance of a Congressional mandate to highlight and address barriers to participation in the communications industry, the literature review would be one in a series of coordinated steps to research, gather, and study data.

This literature review would give way to a historic attempt at gathering necessary data and quantifying the actual critical information needs of different communities. The attempt would be known as the Critical Information Needs Study. The CIN Study aimed to assess the needs of a community within the locality, and not from an "outside-looking-in perspective," by assessing the actual and perceived needs of local residents, as well as the diversity and decision-making within particular news organizations serving that community.

The CIN Study

Beginnings

The CIN study was released May 24, 2013. Following its release, Acting Chairwoman of the FCC, Mignon Clyburn, reiterated the commission's mandate to ensure that FCC-regulated entities serve the needs of the American public regardless of monetary status.

A collaborative group of social scientists, legal scholars, journalists, and communications experts, collectively called the Communication Policy Research Network (CPRN), informed the CIN study at the request of the FCC. Though federal in its establishment, the goal of the CPRN review, and ultimately the CIN Study, was to identify and define the critical information needs of local communities, with a particular focus on low-income and disadvantaged communities.

The CPRN defined "critical information needs" as the "forms of information that are necessary for citizens, and community members to live safe and healthy lives; have full access to educational, employment, and business opportunities; and to fully participate in the civic and democratic lives of their communities should they choose" (Friedland, Napoli, Ognyanova, Weil, & Wilson, 2012). The CPRN review identified eight essential categories of "information" that must be accessed by a particular community via media that is accessible and in a language that is interpretable.[1] Within the review, two distinct characteristics were identified. First, the community a person lives in significantly shapes their critical information needs. Second, the particular group a person falls within (e.g., race, gender, religion, occupation) can shape their own critical information needs. In this push, the CIN Study would be important because it took a critical look at the intersection of the growing diversity in the United States media landscape.

The research plan for the CIN Study included seven essential steps: (1) the development of the study itself; (2) development of research protocols and survey instruments for data collection; (3) obtaining regulatory clearance; (4) development of facilitator recruitment materials; (5) providing relevant materials and training to assist facilitators in applying research protocols; (6) coding, analyzing, and interpreting the extracted data; and (7) preparing a findings report for the study. From this position, the CIN Study was constructed.

A Finished Product

To effectuate its goal, the CIN Study was comprised of two prongs. First, it aimed to establish a "Media Market Census" to identify and determine whether FCC-regulated entities provide for CINs across different platforms to different communities. The Media Market Census would determine whether and how FCC-regulated corporations construct news and public affairs to deliver critical information needs.

Second, the CIN Study aimed to create a Community Ecology Study (CES) to understand the actual and perceived critical information needs of community members; whereas members of the community would participate in voluntary interviews and answer questions about their needs and the information they receive from the news. The CES aimed to construct a database of local content for a constructed one-week period to identify the accessibility, or lack thereof, to critical information needs. An emphasis was to be placed on media ownership/manager characteristics, employment data, demographics of decision makers, and barriers to entry.

Strate (2006) defined media ecology as the study of media environments and their eventual affects on society. The study of media ecologies aims to make implicit descriptions explicit by identifying the roles that media force us to play, how media structures what we see, and why media makes us feel and act the way we do. To accomplish this, the CIN Study was designed to assess the local media ecology at the micro, meso, and macro levels through in-depth individual interviews with community members. Unfortunately, this would never occur.

The CES would determine the critical information needs of a broad and demographically diverse population as they are perceived and individually demanded by residents of the studied area. The foundation for the study was derived from scholars who examined the effects of communication ecologies on diverse communities. The CES was based on the understanding that there is a strong and clear relation between urban structure and media ecology (Friedland, 2013) and that understanding the media ecology of a defined community is a crucial step in identifying factors that promote or hinder access to critical information needs and progress (Kim, Jung, & Ball-Rokeach, 2006). To identify the specific critical information needs of various communities, the CIN Study would identify those who receive them and those who do not, and the reason for these discrepancies. Local residents and media consumers would answer questions to determine whether they perceive the identified needs, and if so, how they are met and whether the resident believes adequate information exists to access such information.

At the start, there were shortcomings in the CIN Study. The Media Market Census, by virtue of its construction, indirectly excluded several foreign language news outlets (Social Solutions International, 2013). And the CES did not take intra-community diversity into account. Another drawback of the Media Market Census was its analysis of no more than 10% of non-English-speaking media content. A study of language use in the United States shows that 20.8% of the U.S. population aged 5 or older speaks a language other than English at home; with just over 12% of the population speaking Spanish at home. The number of Spanish speakers at home ranges higher in U.S. states such as Florida, New York, New Mexico, Illinois, and Texas (U.S. Census Bureau, 2015). Though the CIN Study made an effort to analyze some non-English media, by choosing no more than 10% of non-English media in chosen markets, there was not only the likelihood, but also the expectancy that many CINs of non-English-speaking persons would not be analyzed. This highlights the findings of Subervi (2010), who argued that during emergencies, government agencies may not be fully prepared to reach non-English-speaking populations via broadcast media. Thus it would be imperative to study non-English-speaking media content and determine if critical information needs are met on all non-English-speaking content mediums.

Though notable, the CIN Study's drawbacks were minimal compared to its potential benefits in identifying, highlighting, and remedying barriers to critical information needs. Surprisingly, these drawbacks were of no concern for regulators, lawmakers, and lobbyists that wanted to end the provision of the study. Their main concern was the qualitative analysis of media providers and the claim that the FCC had neither the authority to meddle in the affairs of news media or abridge the First Amendment rights of a free press. Both were flawed arguments aimed at derailing an attempt to gather data and ensure that all Americans would not be barred to critical information needs.

A Conflict of Ideologies

Legislative Mandate

Of the seven essential steps to create the research plan, the CIN Study barely made it past step two before being shut down by federal regulators and lawmakers. One must look no further than the language and history of the Communications Act to determine that provision of the CIN Study was not only necessary, but also legal. The United States Congress penned a comprehensive statutory framework for U.S. communications policy with the

Communications Act of 1934. The 1934 act created the FCC to implement and administer the economic regulation of interstate activities of the telephone monopolies and the licensing of spectrum used for broadcast and other purposes. A purpose of the 1996 Telecommunications Act, which amended the 1934 act, was to promote competition in all communications industries while ensuring a diversity of viewpoints in ownership production and consumption of all communications services.

Before adopting the 1996 act, Congress grappled with the notion of eliminating market entry barriers for diverse groups in the communications realm.[2] In his statement following adoption of the 1996 act, President Bill Clinton (1996) touted the efforts put forth in the bill, noting the 1996 act's effort to support a fair balance between economic viability and diversity.

Section 257 of the Communications Act directed the FCC to initiate proceedings to identify and eliminate market entry barriers for entrepreneurs and other small businesses in the provision and ownership of telecommunications services and information services. The law requires the FCC to submit a report to Congress outlining barriers to entry along with recommendations on how Congress may act to remedy remaining barriers. Though the FCC lacks the authority to directly govern a regulated entity, past federal court decisions held that the FCC has the authority to study how a regulated entity operates.[3] This, however, did not matter to Republican leaders who saw the CIN Study as a violation of the law.

Opposition from Leaders

Anthony Cook (1990) states that the kind of community we live in remains a matter of choice—the important question being who will make those choices. The political derailment of the CIN study was swift and effective. Republican lawmakers in the United States Congress, led by Representative Fred Upton, wrote to the head of the FCC and called for an end to the CIN Study. Republican FCC Commissioner Ajit Pai penned an op-ed in the *Wall Street Journal* criticizing the CIN Study and called for its abolishment. First, those in opposition argued that the FCC lacked the authority to inquire into the practices of the newsroom. Second, they claimed the CIN Study impeded on the rights of a free press guaranteed under the First Amendment of the United States Constitution.

The United States Congress is composed of various committees that address specific issues and propose legislation. One committee, the Committee on Energy and Commerce, has jurisdiction over matters concerning communications and information services such as the FCC. Members of the committee wield great power and authority over the FCC by recommending lower appropriations to the FCC, and influencing FCC decision-making through the power of the purse.

Republicans held the majority position in the House of Representatives at the time the CIN Study was commissioned. The chairman of the committee

(Fred Upton), the vice chair of the committee (Marsha Blackburn), the chairman of the Subcommittee on Communications and Technology (Greg Walden), and other Republicans signed a letter to the FCC detailing their concerns over the CIN Study and calling for its abolishment (Upton et al., 2013). These lawmakers, along with FCC Commissioner Ajit Pai, led the initiative to end the CIN Study.

Proponents for the study were disappointed to find out that the FCC would suspend the initiative. The raised concerns from Republican leaders led to a reversal in policy by the FCC and eventual halt until the study could be revised. At the time of this writing, revisions have yet to be made.

As it stands, the United States government does not have a plan in place to ensure a diversity of viewpoints through use of the public airwaves, nor does it have a plan to eliminate barriers to critical information needs and the marketplace that can deliver those needs.

A Critique of the Republican Argument

The argument from Republican leaders that the CIN Study breached the constitutional rights of the free press was flawed. The rights of a free press are abridged when government interferes in decision-making and/or editorial independence. That was not the case here. The CIN Study aimed at inquiring into the practices of regulated press entities. The purpose of the inquiry was to determine who within the entity was concerned with the provision and dissemination of critical information needs to local communities, and in particular, disadvantaged communities. The argument that the FCC lacked authority to conduct the study was without merit. Language contained in the Communications Act and judicial decisions suggest the FCC possesses authority to conduct the lawful study in order to effectuate its mandated goals.[4]

The purpose of the CIN Study was not to restrain the dissemination of news stories, nor did the CIN Study aim to compel news stations to run particular stories. Rather, the study, including the years of research and analysis that came before it, sought to identify the critical information needs of American communities and sought to answer whether every citizen receives this critical information from the very source it relies on.

Conclusion

The policy relied on by the United States government can have a direct influence on the media. Mark Lloyd (2006) argues that corporate "interests" have historically controlled the most prominent modes of communication. Jacksonian Democrats handed control of the telegraph to Western Union; the Telecommunications Act of 1996 sacrificed the communication tools and needs of the American citizen in favor of investment and innovation within corporate industries. Media policy consistently deprives the needs of the citizen for the interests of corporations. It is counterproductive that the Telecommunications Act provides for surveys of certain corporate practices, but the corporations themselves are tasked with conducting the survey. The power to hold corporations accountable for their great power was handed over to the corporations, perpetuating a cycle of government policy that favors corporate interest over American unity and progress.

Today, media consolidation has left communities of color with few options in terms of where they acquire the information they need to succeed (Turner, 2013). Government inquiries such as the CIN Study would hold news media accountable for providing all Americans with the critical information they need to progress in our society—needs that are often overlooked for disadvantaged communities. They include employment and educational opportunities, such as applying for schools, scholarships, loans, and acquiring training in digital tools to break barriers for future progression. The critical information needs for disadvantaged communities include a necessity to communicate with a primary healthcare physician at all hours on all days. The critical information needs for disadvantaged communities include anything that can help the underprivileged achieve success. The critical information needs of disadvantaged communities do not include news coverage of another robbery by Black youth.

I make connections back to my original encounter with the inspiring group performing outside of the Lincoln Memorial in Washington, DC. If that story was covered during the nightly news, viewers may have a different opinion. The media ecology in the local community could have altered and likely encouraged viewers to reach out to the group and join or participate. Instead, the media ecology of that particular community likely focused on the dangerous correlation between high crime and Black youth.

There is a link between access to information and status in the United States. Years of research on the topic consistently show communities with a lack of access to evolving technologies also lack access to critical information needs. These are the same communities that fall at the bottom of the education and income stratosphere. These are the same communities that the enabling clause of the Communications Act sought to introduce to the world of media. The elimination of barriers to critical information needs can spur entrepreneurship in the fields of telecommunications and information services. However, if the disadvantaged are unable to get the critical information they need to succeed, they are fated to suffer through a cycle of disadvantage. The power of communication can seemingly tear down walls, and, sometimes, it can help reinforce already existing barriers.

Notes

1. The eight categories of the CPRN were stated as: (1) emergencies and risk, both immediate and long term; (2) health and welfare, including specifically local health information as well as group specific health information where it exists;

(3) education, including the quality of local schools and choice available to parents; (4) transportation, including available alternatives, cost, and schedules; (5) economic opportunities, including job information, job training, and small business assistance; (6) the environment, including air and water quality and access to recreation; (7) civic information, including the availability of civic institutions and opportunities to associate with others; and (8) political information, including information about candidates at all relevant levels of local governance, and about relevant public initiatives affecting communities and neighborhoods.
2. See Senate Report on Telecommunications Competition and Deregulation Act of 1995, S. REP. 104–23 at 9, released March 30, 1995, where the United States Senate Committee on Commerce, Science, and Transportation submitted the original telecommunications bill for full Senate consideration; in the report, the Senate Committee provided reasons for the implementation of the bill, one of those reasons was to increase diversity of media.
3. In *Comcast v. FCC*, 600 F.3d at 659, at 659–60, (2010), the United States Federal Court of Appeals for the District of Columbia held that the FCC may enter the newsroom for specific purposes to accumulate data in preparation for reports to Congress. The Court of Appeals ruled the FCC could impose disclosure requirements in order to satisfy its triennial reporting requirement through use of its ancillary authority under Section 257.
4. In *Verizon v. FCC*, 740 F.3d 623, at 668, (2014), the District of Columbia Court of Appeals again noted that the FCC maintains the authority to require disclosure of management practices as an ancillary duty of its Section 257 goals.

References

Austin, C. (2011). Overwhelmed by big consolidation: Bringing back regulation to increase diversity in programming that serves minority audiences. *Federal Communications Law Journal*, 63(3), 733–764.

Bell, D. (1976). Serving two masters: Integrations ideals and client interests in school desegregation litigation. *Yale Law Review*, 85(4), 470–516.

Bradford, W. (2000). *Discrimination in capital markets, broadcast/wireless spectrum service providers and auction outcomes*. Federal Communications Commission. Retrieved from https://transition.fcc.gov/opportunity/meb_study/capital_market_study.pdf.

Clinton, W. J. (1996). *Statement on signing the Telecommunications Act of 1996*. Retrieved from http://www.presidency.ucsb.edu/ws/?pid=52289.

Cook, A.E. (1990). Beyond critical legal studies: The reconstructive theology of Dr. Martin Luther King Jr. *Harvard Law Review*, 103(5), 985–1044.

Federal Communications Commission (FCC). (2013). *Office of Communications Business Opportunities announces the release of critical information needs research design*. FCC Docket No., 12–30. Retrieved from https://apps.fcc.gov/edocs_public/attachmatch/DA-13-1214A1.pdf.

Friedland, L. (2013). Civic communication in a networked society: Seattle's emergent ecology. In J. Girouard & C. Sirianni (Eds.), *Varieties of civic innovation: Deliberative, collaborative, network, and narrative approaches* (pp. 92–126). Nashville, TN: Vanderbilt University Press.

Friedland, L., Napoli, P., Ognyanova, K., Weil, C., & Wilson, E. J. (2012). *Review of the literature regarding critical information needs of the American public*. Retrieved from http://transition.fcc.gov/bureaus/ocbo/Final_Literature_Review.pdf.

Kim, D. H. (2011). *The triangle of minority ownership, employment and content: A review of studies of minority ownership and diversity*. Unpublished manuscript. University of Michigan.

Kim, Y. C., Jung, J. Y., & Ball-Rokeach, S. J. (2006). Geo-ethnicity and neighborhood engagement: A communication infrastructure perspective. *Political Communication*, 23(4), 421–441.

Knight Commission on the Information Needs of Communities in a Democracy. (2009). *Informing communities: Sustaining democracy in the digital age*. Washington, DC: The Aspen Institute.

Lloyd, M. (2006). *Prologue to a farce: Communication and democracy in America*. Chicago, IL: University of Illinois Press.

Sandoval, C. J. K. (2011). Minority commercial radio ownership: Assessing FCC licensing and consolidation policies. In P. M. Napoli & M. Aslama (Eds.), *Communications research in action: Scholar-activist collaborations for a democratic public sphere* (pp. 88–113). New York, NY: Fordham University Press.

Smith, L. (2009). Consolidation and news content: How broadcast ownership policy impacts local television news and the public interest. *Journalism & Communication Monographs*, 10(4), 387–453.

Social Solutions International. (2013). *Research design for the multi-market study of critical information needs: Final research design for the Federal Communications Commission*. Silver Spring, MD. Retrieved from https://apps.fcc.gov/edocs_public/attachmatch/DA-13-1214A2.pdf.

Strate, L. (2006). *Echoes and reflections: On media ecology as a field of study*. Cresskill, NJ: Hampton Press.

Subervi, F. (2010). *An Achilles heel in emergency communications: The deplorable policies and practices pertaining to non-English speaking populations*. Unpublished manuscript. Center for the Study of Latino Media and Markets, School of Journalism and Mass Communication, Texas State University-San Marcos.

Turner, S. D. (2013). Cease to resist: How the FCC's failure to enforce its rules created a new wave of media consolidation. *Free Press*. Retrieved from https://www.freepress.net/sites/default/files/resources/Cease_to_Resist_Oct._2013_0.pdf.

U.S. Census Bureau (2015). *Detailed languages spoken at home and ability to speak English for the population 5 years and over for United States: 2009–2013*. Retrieved from http://www.census.gov/data/tables/2013/demo/2009-2013-lang-tables.html.

Upton, F., Walden, G., Barton, J. Blackburn, M., Shimkus, J., Terry, L., ... Ellmers, R. (2013). *Letter to chairman Wheeler from representatives of the house energy and commerce committee*. Retrieved from http://energycommerce.house.gov/sites/republicans.energycommerce.house.gov/files/letters/20131210FCC.pdf.

Viswanath, K., & Kreuter, M. W. (2007). Health disparities, communication inequalities, and e-health: A commentary. *American Journal of Preventative Medicine*, 32(5 Suppl.), S131–S133.

2 Courting Minority Commodity Audiences
Bounce TV in the Age of Media Conglomeration

Leah P. Hunter and Jennifer M. Proffitt

In April 2011, notable African American men including Martin Luther King III and former Atlanta Mayer Andrew Young formed Bounce TV, the first television broadcast network targeting African American viewers. Within months of the announcement, numerous proposals for urban-focused cable and satellite networks emerged. What distinguishes Bounce TV, however, is its broadcast status. Taking advantage of the broader digital spectrum, Bounce TV is offered to consumers for free, without the need for cable or satellite.

In the Radio Act of 1927 and the subsequent Communications Act of 1934, the government gave broadcasters licensing rights with the condition that those broadcasters serve in the public interest (McChesney, 2004). The public interest is traditionally defined as localism, diversity, and competition (Napoli, 2001). This mandate is primarily self-regulated, so there are few repercussions if broadcasters do not comply (McChesney, 2004). Typically, when broadcasters address fair representation, it is due to the opportunity to increase revenues rather than to serve the public interest.

While it appears that Bounce TV's programming choices serve an underserved audience, offering a broadcast network aimed at African American audiences is also smart business. In 2013, 13.8% of total U.S. TV households were African American (Nielsen, 2013). These numbers increase to more than 50% in some Southern urban cities (Nielsen, 2011; Steadman, 2005). African American households, on average, watch two more hours of television per day than other groups (Nielsen, 2011) and view ad-supported cable and network affiliates at a higher rate than the rest of the United States (Steadman, 2005). More ad viewership means that networks have a stronger bargaining tool when negotiating with advertisers. This recognition of the African American audience as a potential draw for advertisers has been building over decades as media producers slowly convinced advertisers of the value of minority viewership.

Using a critical historical approach, this chapter examines whether a niche broadcast network such as Bounce TV can survive in today's political economy. We first explain the economic interests that affect advertisers and broadcasters, examine the history of African American programming, and then determine whether the network satisfies the issues of diversity as defined by the Federal Communications Commission (FCC) and other governmental regulations. We also explain why ethnic media such as Bounce TV are important to the overall diversification of media and the challenges the network faces in today's political economy.

Commodity Audience, Conglomerates, and Advertising Incentives

In analyzing the goals of corporate media and the products they create, Smythe (1981/2001) argued that the only commodity media sell and advertisers purchase are audiences.[1] Advertisers use generalizations gathered from the audience to market their products back to the audience, allowing advertisers and networks to set the price that particular audiences are worth based on a combination of current demand and historical value (Smythe, 1981/2011). Not only are audiences a commodity sold by programmers, but also television trains viewers to choose the particular brands they use. For the sake of profit in a capitalist market, producers cater to the larger majority of the population, even if it means that they supply more programming than the majority desires (Gandy, 2000).

The media's relationship with advertisers is far more significant than the relationship with their audience (Jhally, 1989; McChesney, 2004; Meehan, 2005). The influence advertisers have on media corporations is often subtle, with advertisers discouraging media companies from placing their ads into programming that is too controversial, edgy, or reflects badly on the company (Croteau & Hoynes, 2006). Advertisers expect their products to reach the largest audience possible to get the most "bang for their buck" (McChesney, 2004). Broadcast television programs must attract large numbers of people, attract the right type of audience, and deliver the audience in the right state of mind for the advertiser's product (Jhally, 1989). In general, the "right" commodity audience is comprised of White males age 18 to 34 (Meehan, 2005). As such, according to Bettig and Hall (2012), "the capitalist marketplace, in which the advertising industry plays so central a part, *cannot* deliver diversity" (p. 171; emphasis in original). At best, there can be fragmentation of the audience that mimics diversity.

As fragmentation results in programming that falls along racial lines, both the broadcaster and the audience suffer. According to Gandy (2000), with advertisers placing less importance on capturing minority viewers, companies that create content with minority audiences in mind are penalized. Upscale advertisers practice "No urban/No Spanish" dictates; that is, advertisers shy away from urban stations, believing that no amount of advertising will convince these audiences to purchase their products (Reed-Huff, 2010). The resulting smaller revenues then affect the network's ability to create quality programming.

When researchers target minority audiences, race is typically considered along with demographics such as gender, age, and income. Broadcasters who cater to undervalued populations such as minority audiences typically struggle financially (Gandy, 2000). However, there are examples in television history in which programming that seemed to focus on African American audiences have thrived, bringing in larger audiences and helping to establish new networks. The type of programming these networks used is called narrowcasting; that is, programming created for a specific segment of viewers on one network that is direct counter-programming against shows on other networks (Zook, 1999). Successfully implemented by News Corporation's network channel FOX in the 1980s, for example, African American audiences became a commodity worthy of broadcasters' attention. While FOX's narrowcasting was notable in its establishment of the network, the premise of focusing on minority audiences to attract the majority is one that has been successfully utilized since the comedies of Norman Lear in the 1970s.

From Minority Programming for a Majority Audience to Narrowcasting

The tradition of the American family as the focus of television programs, especially in situation comedies, dates back to the early days of television. However, what Norman Lear contributed to the genre in the 1970s is considered groundbreaking. While earlier television families depicted the family unit in an ideal light, Lear implemented elements of "fear, anxiety, and anger" into the homes and families of his series (Mayerle, 1987, p. 225). He showed characters that were flawed, but realistic (Stark, 1997). For example, Lear called Archie Bunker, the lead character of his hit program *All in the Family* (1971–1979), "a bigot motivated not by hate, but by fear—fear of change, fear of anything he doesn't understand" (Lear, 1971, para. 12).

With the success of *All in the Family*, Lear was able to push forward more programs that appeared controversial, but in actuality were familiar to the audience. With *Sanford and Son* (1972–1977), Lear and his partner Bud Yorkin adapted the British sitcom *Steptoe and Son* (1962–1974), replacing the original White main characters with African Americans (Bogle, 2001). Though wildly successful, the program received criticism for its lack of consciousness. According to H. Gray (1995), "the television programs involving blacks in the 1970s were largely representations of what White liberal middle-class television program makers assumed (or projected) were 'authentic' accounts of poor black urban ghetto experiences" (p. 77). Creating programming that depicts minority groups as identifiable to the White audience is one of the primary ways to get these shows on television. The idea of commodity audience argues that for this to occur, producers must accommodate the White audience, because not all audiences are equally valuable to advertisers (Gandy, 2000).

Good Times (1974–1979) pushed its White audience farther than *Sanford and Son*. One big difference from *Sanford and Son* was that African American writers—Eric Monte and Mike Evans—created *Good Times*

(Bogle, 2001). "The mere presence" of these African American "producers, directors, and writers ... helped to bring different, often more complex, stories, themes, characters, and representations of blackness to commercial network television" (H. Gray, 1995, p. 73). Initially, critics praised *Good Times* for its depiction of a two-parent household and for its political acumen. It became clear, however, that instead of representing the experiences of African Americans in urban cities, the focus of the comedy would be on J.J. Evans, the outlandish eldest son of the family. Monte shared the message he consistently received in writers' meetings: "'Get rid of the father, a strong black man in a sitcom won't work. All the White writers on the show wanted to do stereotypes and I refused, so we'd argue and fight'" (Izrael, 2005, para. 7).

In *The Jeffersons* (1975–1985), another spin-off of *All in the Family*, Lear continued the assimilation of African Americans into mainstream media. In contrast to *Good Times*, George and Louise Jefferson had already "made it." George runs a successful dry-cleaning business, enabling the couple to live in an Upper East Side high-rise apartment (Bogle, 2001). *The Jeffersons* was a successful show that was notably popular with African Americans because though George focused on gaining wealth and materialism, he never gave the impression that he wanted to be White (Bogle, 2001).

In the 1980s, *The Cosby Show* (1984–1992) was groundbreaking in that it not only reinvigorated the situation comedy genre, but it did so with an African American cast (Bogle, 2001). It was rated number one in four of the eight seasons it aired, making it one of the all-time most popular programs (Stark, 1997). *The Cosby Show* serves as an example of what is possible when a person of color who is an established commodity within broadcasting has an opportunity to develop and produce a show without pressure from network executives to include stereotypes typically associated with minority programs. Cosby shepherded the show and its images as direct counter-programming for earlier stereotypical images of African Americans.

However, it should be noted that the show was highly marketed and earned increased advertising rates (Havens, 2000; Tolman, 1992). Additionally, Cosby was already a familiar face in successful television shows such as *I Spy*. Even then, the success of *The Cosby Show* surprised many industry experts (O'Connor, 1990). It, along with other successful series with African American casts, such as *A Different World* (1987–1993) and *The Fresh Prince of Bel Air* (1990–1996), resurrected NBC to the top of the ratings and provided a template for the FOX network and its urban lineup (Zook, 1999).

FOX was established in the mid-1980s, as its owner, Rupert Murdoch, gained political favor and American citizenship to circumvent U.S. broadcast laws (Bagdikian, 2004). With Murdoch's global conglomerate established, FOX's daring programming choices were balanced by the many other holdings in Murdoch's media corporation. This gave FOX executives the freedom to target programming without the worry of having to produce immediate results.

One of FOX's first uses of narrowcasting was a variety show—*In Living Color* (1990–1994), created by Keenan Ivory Wayans as a direct response to *The Cosby Show*. *In Living Color* was not only street smart and irreverent, but the show also went out of its way to mock both White culture and African American icons (O'Connor, 1990). Critics charged *In Living Color* with exaggerating stereotypes instead of fighting against them, and some suggested that this humor would not be permitted if it did not come from African Americans. Notably, despite Wayans being the executive producer, writer, and one of the stars of the program, the majority of the program's writers were White (Bogle, 2001).

The popularity of *In Living Color* led the fledgling network to produce additional shows catering to the urban audience. The casts on the shows that followed, including *Roc* (1991–1994), *Martin* (1992–1997), *The Sinbad Show* (1993–1994), *New York Undercover* (1994–1998), and *Living Single* (1993–1998), represented a majority of minorities, not just African Americans, who appeared on television (Zook, 1999). Eventually, FOX's narrowcasting efforts helped it compete with the "big three" networks. After it brokered a deal with the NFL to carry its games, FOX's priorities changed. Some insiders say that FOX wanted to re-establish its "legitimacy" with the White audience (Zook, 1999), while others suggest that FOX decided to "age-up" its programming and pursue a mainstream audience (Abbott, 1995). Whatever the reason, FOX's discarded programming strategy was later used by both UPN and The WB.

Established in 1995, Viacom/Paramount and Chris-Craft's UPN seemed to pick up where FOX left off. Beginning with the success of *Moesha* (1996–2001), UPN increased programming of African American situation comedies, primarily in its Monday night lineup (Carter, 1996), in a narrowcasting effort. The networks added programs including *Everybody Hates Chris* (2005–2009), *Girlfriends* (2000–2008), *The Parkers* (1999–2004), *Malcolm and Eddie* (1996–2000), and *In the House* (1995–1999) to boost its fledgling ratings.

Meanwhile, Time Warner's The WB established programs such as *The Wayans Brothers* (1995–1999), *The Parent 'Hood* (1995–1999), and *The Jamie Foxx Show* (1996–2001). The network picked up *The Steve Harvey Show* (1996–2002) and *Sister, Sister* (1994–1999) after they were canceled on ABC (Zook, 1999). In 1997, FOX, UPN and The WB had 16 of the 20 television programs featuring African Americans in primetime (H. S. Gray, 2005). However, by 1999, The WB already moved toward courting White teen audiences, leaving African American audiences behind.

The Emergence of a Minority-Based Cable Network

While the instances of narrowcasting by new broadcast networks provide a framework with which to determine Bounce TV's viability, a more direct correlation can be made between Bounce TV's potential success and the prior success of Black Entertainment Television (BET). Robert L. Johnson founded BET in 1980, after quitting the National Cable Television Association and persuading his boss to provide him with a consulting contract worth $15,000. Johnson used that money to obtain a loan to launch BET (Greene, 1985). Early on, Johnson stated, "I want to provide a showcase for black enterprise that would be attractive to blacks and whites" (Hall, 1980, p. D1).

Johnson's goal was to turn the network into a media conglomerate, complete with film and radio divisions. However, in 1981, BET found the component that changed the network's direction: music videos (Fry, 1991). For BET, music videos were a source of free programming and an easy way to attract the core teenage audience. Music videos provide the same benefits as regular programming: They sell audiences to advertisers and the music industry (Bettig & Hall, 2012).

Though there were efforts at original programming, Johnson did not follow through on his promise of providing uplifting programming. Johnson argued that the cable network could not afford to create original programming because advertisers and cable operators did not pay the bigger rates needed (Roberts, 1996). While "No urban/No Spanish" dictates are a real issue for minority-owned media companies, BET, and Johnson in particular, amassed great wealth from programming choices (Perl, 1997).

Johnson also attempted to create barriers to entry for competitors. His vision was to create a platform of channels for jazz (BET on Jazz), movies (BET Movies/Starz!), and pay-per-view (BET Action) that would cover the needs of any cable or satellite company (Perl, 1997). Additionally, evidence suggests he had no desire of using his network as a platform to help other African Americans. Johnson said, "What are my responsibilities to black people at large? If I help my family get over ... then I have achieved that one goal that is my responsibility to society at large" (Perl, 1997, p. W08). Johnson's goal for BET was not diversity or fair representation but rather making a profit. A BET producer said, "You can criticize BET all you want, but it's about money ... You put all these high-minded, socially conscious programs on and your profits dip, you're right out of there" (Wiltz, 2008, p. M01).

For BET, profit came at the expense of programming. Johnson chose syndicated programs and free music videos to give his network an opportunity in this media market. Now a subsidiary of Viacom, BET has the financial backing to take more risks in programming. His successor, Debra Lee, supported the creation of original programming on the channel. Encouraged by online fans, BET acquired CW's *The Game* (2006–2015) in 2011. Within the first few episodes, ratings for the show quadrupled from 1.9 million on the CW to 9.9 million (Stelter, 2011). Since then, BET continued to expand its original programming, including the hit drama *Being Mary Jane* (2013–).

Unlike Bounce TV, BET has the luxury of being financed by Viacom, a media conglomerate that can afford to finance the cable channel's original programming without major risk. With the increase in competition, it was not clear if there would also be an increase in advertising dollars.

The executive vice president at ID Media stated that, "Just because more supply is added doesn't mean advertisers will increase their budget, but if these new networks substantially grow ratings [advertisers] might put in more money" (Poggi, 2012, para. 4).

The Future: Bounce TV as an Example of a New Era of Narrowcasting

After the principals of Bounce TV announced the formation of the network, a number of other cable networks with the same intended audience were announced. Though there is more competition for the African American audience online and on cable, Bounce TV is at a distinct advantage by being a broadcast network.

Thomas and Litman (1991) note several benefits to owning a broadcast (rather than a cable) network. First, there is a level of esteem associated with owning a broadcast network. Broadcast networks also receive premium spaces on local television lineups. As such, broadcast networks have greater potential in terms of audience reach. Cable does not have the audience that a broadcast network has because the number of households that have access to broadcast television is larger, and cable networks fragment audiences. Initially, Bounce TV was at a disadvantage because of its distribution. It debuted September 26, 2011, in only 32% of the country. As of April 2014, it aired in 88 markets, including all of the top African American markets. More important to its bottom line, Bounce TV became the second highest rated African American targeted network, only behind BET (Bounce TV, 2014). In the first quarter of 2015, the network made double-digit gains of 15% in African American households (Bibel, 2015).

In his discussion of segmentation, Gandy (2000) argues that the scarcity of bandwidth has typically been the justification given by the networks to control the level of access afforded to those willing to bring diversity to network programming. With the advent of the digital switch, multiple channels can now be broadcast within the bandwidth of what used to be only one channel (Allan, 2007). As such, it can be argued that Bounce TV should be only the first in a line of broadcast networks that can cater to minorities and other specialized segments of the population. The advent of multicast channels has, for example, brought about multiple Spanish-language digital TV networks such as Azteca America, Estrella TV, and Telefutura (Nielson, 2012).

Bounce TV's political connections have been instrumental in its establishment as a competitive network. As noted earlier, Bounce TV has the benefit of having dignitaries such as Martin Luther King III and former U.N. Ambassador and Atlanta Mayor Andrew Young among its founders. Evidence of their importance to Bounce TV can be seen in its interactions with other media organizations. Young, in particular, often represents Bounce TV publically, including within the Future of TV Coalition (Wharton, 2011). The National Association of Broadcasters, a powerful trade organization, facilitates the coalition. The coalition's mission statement states that members "work together to advance public policy initiatives that allow broadcasters to continue to rigorously innovate and invest to better serve consumers" (Wharton, 2011, para. 2). Formed in part to promote diversity within digital broadcasting, the group argues that digital multicast channels are a way for broadcasters to serve minority populations (Eggerton, 2014).

A digital multicast channel system allows networks like Bounce TV to appear as a side channel for prominent television groups. Being a multicast digital channel has allowed Bounce TV to increase its reach, including a deal with Univision Communications in which Bounce TV will be multicast through its television groups in seven major markets including New York, Los Angeles, and Dallas (Elliot, 2013). While increasing its level of outreach is an important goal for Bounce TV within the current political economy, its existence is important when considering diversity within the marketplace.

Diversity is one of the central principles of the marketplace of ideas and a primary goal of agencies that regulate the media (Gandy, 1998; Napoli, 2001). Historically, media outlets have been evaluated based on their ability to show diversity in all areas, including source, workforce, and ownership diversity. Diversity is one of the components of a democracy that works to create an efficient marketplace of ideas. Within the marketplace, diversity aids in encouraging "goals such as informed decision making, cultural pluralism, citizen welfare, and a well-functioning democracy" (Napoli, 2001, p. 127). Despite the importance of diversity within media, it has been difficult for policy makers, media professionals, and media scholars to agree on a clear definition for the principle and how it can be most effectively reflected within media.

There are those critics who question the need for forced diversity, especially in terms of the mandated diversification of media. A diverse workforce is important primarily because it offers multiple perspectives. People of color, women, seniors, and people with disabilities need to not only be employed by media outlets, but also they should be present at all levels of management because they can offer multiple viewpoints about issues involving their communities (Brooks, Daniels, & Hollifield, 2003).

In addition, diversity, competition, and localism are major tenants within broadcasters' mandate to serve in the public interest. To ensure that broadcasters serve in the public interest, the FCC has emphasized the importance of the diversification of viewpoints within both programming and programming decisions. The Commission determined that one way that the public interest is fulfilled is by recruiting and employing a satisfactory number of minorities and women (The Media Bureau, 2008). While the public interest can be applied to all media outlets, the government mandates that broadcast media in particular serve in the public interest because they have free access with which to broadcast their programming (Bettig & Hall, 2012; Byerly, 2011; McChesney, 2004). Issues of diversity go beyond that of affirmative action and equal employment opportunities, but these topics are important to creating a workforce that is representative of all people. Through equal employment opportunity regulations, the FCC shows its commitment to fair representation through ownership and workforce diversity (Brooks et al., 2003).

In terms of ownership diversity, Bounce TV fulfills the FCC's standard. Through earlier methods such as tax certificates and distress sales, the FCC attempted to increase the number of minority-owned stations, believing that "there is substantial likelihood that diversity of programming will be increased" (Honig, 1984, p. 869). As noted, prominent African American men such as Martin Luther King III, Andrew Young, Andrew Young III, and Ryan Glover started the network. Both of the Youngs, as well as African American filmmakers Rob Hardy and Will Packer, were listed as part of the ownership team (Nordyke, 2011).

This level of diverse representation in ownership is important because of the overall dismal numbers of African American television station owners. In response to these numbers, FCC Chairman Tom Wheeler and Commissioner Mignon Clyburn have pushed Joint Sales Agreements (JSAs), which would allow larger TV stations to sell advertising for a weaker station, as an option to increase minority media ownership (Clyburn & Wheeler, 2014). After the FCC worked toward closing loopholes that allowed for "sidecar" models to circumvent ownership rules, this policy seems to have made a slight difference, because after falling to zero at the end of 2013, there are now seven African American-owned stations out of the nearly 1,400 TV stations in the U.S. (Vogt, 2015).

In addition to its ownership diversity, Bounce TV satisfies the FCC's issues of workforce diversity. In the implementation of the public interest, the FCC sees the importance in establishing a diversification of viewpoints in both programming and programming decisions. The recruitment and employment of minorities and women are important ways to fulfill the public interest mandate, according to the FCC (The Media Bureau, 2008). While information about the makeup of Bounce TV's staff is not readily available, a majority of the network's top executives are African American. With so many African Americans in positions of authority, Bounce TV could offer future researchers a direct link between workplace diversity and the presence of diverse, quality programming.

Bounce TV is at a disadvantage in terms of advertising potential, though. Media conglomerates can work with advertisers to create deals across outlets, including advertising, promotions, and product placement (McChesney, 2004). As such, media companies merge for the purpose of attracting more advertising dollars (Bettig & Hall, 2012). Bounce TV is not owned by a conglomerate and thus cannot offer advertisers the same deals. Without the benefit of multiple outlets that can balance a struggling network, Bounce TV's programming would need to be established quickly.

It seems as if the network is prepared to answer these questions. Once its viewership began to be measured by Nielsen, it responded by hiring a New York-based advertising executive. The network tripled its number of advertisers and now sells commercials to blue chip organizations such as General Motors, McDonald's, and Wal-Mart (Elliot, 2013). Despite this, syndicated programming remains an attractive option for the network. The slow release of original programming by Bounce TV is more comparable to cable channels than to the other broadcast networks, whose prime-time line-ups are almost exclusively original programming. In relying on a schedule filled with classic films and TV programs, Bounce TV executives state that it is setting a tone with a more mature audience. Molloy (2011b) suggests that this ploy will help the network avoid spending millions of dollars like Oprah Winfrey's OWN did when it released too many originals too quickly.

Bounce TV is in an enviable position compared to its direct competition, though. GlobalHue Executive Vice President Detavio Samuels stated, "There are a few other solid African-American networks, but I love that Bounce TV is not on cable, because the opportunity to get more eyeballs to the network is great" (Elliot, 2013, para. 12). Airing its programming on a local digital channel will give an option to those viewers who feel as if they have been underserved by the major broadcast networks as well as those viewers who do not have access to cable channels such as BET. On the other hand, Bounce will not be able to collect licensing fees that BET and other cable networks get per subscriber (Molloy, 2011a).

Bounce TV executive Will Packer's interview in *Black Enterprise* made it clear that the network would be nothing like BET (Anderson, 2011). However, its programming choices, at least in the beginning, are strikingly similar to BET's initial programming. Despite the level of diversity in ownership and staffing at Bounce TV, the resulting programming has been sparse. Since it began airing programming in 2011, the network debuted four original series: situation comedies *Family Time* (2012–) and *Mann and Wife* (2015–), and stand-up comedies *Uptown Comic* (2012–) and *Off the Chain* (2014–) (Albiniak, 2014; Ho, 2012). The network will premiere its first drama, *Saints and Sinners* in the 2015–2016 season (Bounce TV, 2015). Elverage Allen, executive vice president of Advertising Sales, stated, "We continue to expand our original programming line-up to offer marketing partners fresh and engaging new programming ... to make the network a must-buy for brands seeking to reach the African American consumer" (Bounce TV, 2015, para. 6). With limited programming, however, it still remains to be seen if the network can thrive in the current political economy. The primary programming for Bounce TV has been old movies, syndicated programs, and African American sporting events (Anderson, 2011). While it may be intentional, this may not be enough to compete against the major networks and their programming, especially as they begin to create more diverse, original programming. In addition, the acknowledgment of African Americans as viable consumers has resulted in multiple cable networks that target the audience, including Centric, TV One, and Magic Johnson's Aspire.

While this is a promising start, history suggests that Bounce TV has additional challenges in regard to programming. Earlier cable channels that produced programming targeting African American audiences could take risks because they were a part of conglomerates, and as such, the channels were only one small part of the company's vast holdings. These conglomerates also have the benefit of cross-promotion between their companies that Bounce TV does not have (McChesney, 2004). History shows that Bounce TV will not have the luxury of time the other broadcast networks had without that same synergistic backing. Even its future connection with Univision will not give it the audience necessary to compete with other broadcast networks.

Conclusion

Though the African American audience has proven itself a worthy commodity audience as evidenced historically by Norman Lear, Bill Cosby, FOX, The WB, and UPN, none of these examples were tested long-term. Repeatedly, the networks chose to move away from successful African American programming, returning instead to their primary commodity target: White audiences. Until the arrival of Bounce TV, BET was the best example of African American-targeted programming that succeeded financially, but it has been plagued with criticism about its programming choices. Also, it is questionable whether the cable network would have been as successful if it had direct competition for the African American audience in its early stages.

Media scholars such as Bagdikian (2004), McChesney (2004), and Meehan (2005) argue that media programming is not created for the audience, but for the advertisers. Advertisers determine the success of any network based on the audience the programming will attract. With "No urban/No Spanish" dictates being challenged by the FCC, there is potentially an opportunity for a network aimed at minority audiences to compete with mainstream networks (Reed-Huff, 2010). Bounce TV is already at a disadvantage, as the major broadcast networks have an established oligopoly that controls the market. Further, advertisers tend to discourage programming that would result in a potential loss in revenue (Croteau & Hoynes, 2006).

Though ethnic media are a critical component for a diverse media system, primarily in the service of minority populations, we cannot forget that, like BET, Bounce TV is a profit-driven network. It is likely that the focus will be on entertainment rather than public affairs programming. Because of the importance of the commodity audience and the commercial nature of broadcast, Bounce TV must make sure that it serves all parts of the African American community, not just the wealthy.

Although Bounce TV is an important addition to the television spectrum, adding a single broadcast network does not address the lack of diversity in the overall number of choices audiences have. To address this, there would need to be more channels that are minority-owned and offer minority-based content. Further, the continued viability of the network may be a hard sell if long-term, increased profit margins are the main objective. Perhaps as the number of original programs on the network grows, it will not only be able to compete with other broadcast networks, but will also substantiate the viability of programming featuring not only African American programming but also all underrepresented groups.

Note

1. As Meehan (2002) explains, Smythe's argument critiqued Western Marxism's focus on the "consciousness industry" approach—analyzing the ideologies maintained by corporate media—leading to what is known as the Blindspot Debate. We use commodity audience to refer to the idea that, based on the construction of ratings, advertisers buy access to desired audiences, and programmers attempt to provide programming to attract that coveted audience.

References

Abbott, R. (1995). Television and children: Issues in black and white. *Sacred Heart University Review*, 15(1), Article 8. Retrieved from http://digitalcommons.sacredheart.edu/cgi/viewcontent.cgi?article=1039&context=shureview&sei-redir=1#search=%22television%20children%3A%20issues%20black%20white%22.

Albiniak, P. (2014). Bounce TV to launch two new sitcoms. *Broadcasting & Cable*. Retrieved from http://www.broadcastingcable.com/news/syndication-and-distribution/bounce-tv-launch-two-new-sitcoms/130901.

Allan, M. D. (2007). Are you ready for the switch?; If you don't already own a digital TV or converter, all you see is static on Feb. 17, 2009, because of a government mandate requiring stations to broadcast in digital. *Washington Post*, p. Y05.

Anderson, T. (2011). Film executive Will Packer wants to be clear: Bounce TV will be nothing like BET. *Black Enterprise*. Retrieved from http://www.blackenterprise.com/2011/05/09/film-executive-will-packer-wants-to-be-clear-bounce-tv-will-be-nothing-like-bet/.

Bagdikian, B. H. (2004). *The new media monopoly*. Boston, MA: Beacon Press.

Bettig, R. V., & Hall, J. L. (2012). *Big media, big money: Cultural texts and political economics*. Lanham, MD: Rowman & Littlefield.

Bibel, S. (2015). Bounce TV posts strongest quarter in history. *Zap2it.com*. Retrieved from http://tvbythenumbers.zap2it.com/2015/04/02/bounce-tv-posts-strongest-quarter-in-its-history/383723/.

Bogle, D. (2001). *Prime time blues: African Americans on network television*. New York: Farrar, Straus and Giroux.

Bounce TV. (2014). *Bounce TV posts fifth consecutive quarter of growth, grows viewership by 50% in prime*. Retrieved from http://www.bouncetv.com/news/.

Bounce TV. (2015). *Bounce TV unveils 2015–16 upfront programming slate*. Retrieved from http://www.bouncetv.com/bounce-tv-unveils-2015-16-upfront-programming-slate.

Brooks, D. E., Daniels, G. L., & Hollifield, C. A. (2003). Television in living color: Racial diversity in the local commercial television industry. *Howard Journal of Communications*, 14(3), 123–146.

Byerly, C. M. (2011). Behind the scenes of women's broadcast ownership. *The Howard Journal of Communications*, 22(1), 24–42.

Carter, B. (1996, May 17). UPN is adding comedies with black casts. *New York Times*, p. B19.
Clyburn, M., & Wheeler, T. (2014). *Making good on the promise of independent minority ownership of television stations*. Retrieved from https://www.fcc.gov/blog/making-good-promise-independent-minority-ownership-television-stations.
Croteau, D., & Hoynes, W. (2006). *The business of media: Corporate media and the public interest*. Thousand Oaks, CA: Pine Forge Press.
Eggerton, J. (2014). Bounce TV criticizes retrans reforms. *Broadcasting & Cable*. Retrieved from http://www.broadcastingcable.com/news/washington/bounce-tvcriticizes-retrans-reforms/133969.
Elliot, S. (2013). A channel reflects the reshaping of TV demographics. *New York Times*. Retrieved from http://www.nytimes.com/2013/02/27/business/media/a-channel-reflects-the-reshaping-of-tv-demographics.html?_r=0.
Fry, D. (1991, April 1). A new form of networking. *St. Petersburg Times*, p. 1D.
Gandy Jr., O.H. (1998). *Communication and race: A structural perspective*. London: Arnold.
Gandy Jr., O. H. (2000). *Audience construction: Race, ethnicity and segmentation in popular media*. Retrieved from http://www.asc.upenn.edu/usr/ogandy/targeting.pdf.
Gray, H. (1995). *Watching race: Television and the struggle for blackness*. Minneapolis, MN: University of Minnesota Press.
Gray, H. S. (2005). *Cultural moves: African Americans and the politics of representation*. Berkeley, CA: University of California Press.
Greene, M. S. (1985, August 5). The district's cable kingpin: In a jam, Bob Johnson turns once again to his friends. *Washington Post*, p. C1.
Hall, C. (1980, January 25). Celebrating the birth of a network: Salesmen and stars at a kickoff for BET. *Washington Post*, p. D1.
Havens, T. (2000). "The biggest show in the world": Race and the global popularity of The Cosby Show. *Media, Culture and Society*, 22(4), 371–391.
Ho, R. (2012). Atlanta's Bounce TV introduces first new series "Family Time," "Uptown Comic." *Access Atlanta*. Retrieved from http://blogs.ajc.com/radio-tv-talk/2012/06/18/atlantas-bounce-tv-introduces-first-new-series-family-time-uptown-comic/.
Honig, D. (1984). The FCC and its fluctuating commitment to minority ownership of broadcast facilities. *Howard Law Journal*, 27, 859–877.
Izrael, J. (2005). Q&A: TV writer Eric Monte; the creator of TV classics *The Jeffersons* and *Good Times*. *The Jacksonville Free Press*, p. 13.
Jhally, S. (1989). The political economy of culture. In I. Augus & S. Jhally (Eds.), *Cultural politics in contemporary America* (pp. 65–81). New York, NY: Routledge.
Lear, N. (1971, October 10). As I read how Laura saw Archie .... *New York Times*, p. D17.
Mayerle, J. (1987). A dream deferred: The failed fantasy of Norman Lear's *a.k.a. Pablo*. *Communication Studies*, 38(3), 223–239.
McChesney, R. W. (2004). *The problem of the media: U.S. communication politics in the 21st century*. New York, NY: Monthly Review Press.
The Media Bureau. (2008). *The public and broadcasting*. Retrieved from http://webcache.googleusercontent.com/search?q=cache:bXJZ45CwrJ8J:www.fcc.gov/guides/public-and-broadcasting-july-2008+&cd=2&hl=en&ct=clnk&gl=us.
Meehan, E. R. (2002). Gendering the commodity audience: Critical media research, feminism, and political economy. In E. R. Meehan & E. Riordan (Eds.),

Sex & money: Feminism and political economy in the media (pp. 209–222). Thousand Oaks, CA: Sage.

Meehan, E. R. (2005). *Why TV is not our fault: Television programming, viewers, and who's really in control.* Lanham, MD: Rowman & Littlefield.

Molloy, T. (2011a). BET gets new competition for "desperately underserved" black audiences. Retrieved from http://www.thewrap.com/bet-gets-more-competition-finally-26529/.

Molloy, T. (2011b). *Black-oriented Bounce TV begins, betting on classic movies.* Retrieved from http://www.thewrap.com/tv/article/bounce-begins-network-looks-qualitymovies-search-african-american-audiences-31274/.

Napoli, P. M. (2001). *Foundations of communications policy: Principles and process in the regulation of electronic media.* Cresskill, NJ: Hampton Press.

Nielsen. (2011). *State of the media: US TV trends by ethnicity.* Retrieved from http://www.nielsen.com/us/en/insights/reports/2011/tv-trends-by-ethnicity.html.

Nielsen. (2013, March). *Free to move between screens: The cross-platform report.* Retrieved from http://www.nielsen.com/content/dam/corporate/us/en/reports-downloads/2013%20Reports/Nielsen-March-2013-Cross-Platform-Report.pdf.

Nielson, J. (2012). *TV stations multiplatform analysis '12 update: New digital networks, mobile TV channels expand content options.* Retrieved from http://www.nab.org/documents/newsRoom/pdfs/020312_SNL_Kagan_multicasting.pdf.

Nordyke, K. (2011). Martin Luther King III, Andrew Young launching network aimed at African-Americans. *The Hollywood Reporter.* Retrieved from http://www.hollywoodreporter.com.

O'Connor, J. J. (1990, April 29). On TV, less separate, more equal. *New York Times*, p. H1, 35.

Perl, P. (1997, December 14). His way; Bob Johnson wants to turn his Washington-based Black Entertainment Television into an African American Disney—but he doesn't want to be anyone's role model. How should his achievements be measured? *Washington Post*, p. W08.

Poggi, J. (2012). BET is winning back advertisers, but competition will soon abound. *Advertising Age.* Retrieved from http://adage.com/article/media/bet-winning-back-advertisers-black-cable-tv-flourishes/234132/.

Reed-Huff, L. N. (2010). Statement of Lavonda N. Reed-Huff, Associate Professor of Law, Syracuse University College of Law. *FCC Media Ownership Workshop.* Retrieved from http://transition.fcc.gov/ownership/workshop-012710/reed-huff.pdf.

Roberts, J. L. (1996, April 1). Trials of a black mogul. *Newsweek*, p. 71.

Smythe, D. W. (1981/2001). On the audience commodity and its work. In M. G. Durham & D. M. Kellner (Eds.), *Media and cultural studies keyworks* (pp. 253–279). Malden, MA: Blackwell.

Stark, S. (1997). *Glued to the set: The 60 television shows and events that made us who we are today.* New York, NY: The Free Press.

Steadman, J. (2005). *TV audience special study: African-American audience.* Retrieved from http://www.nielsenmedia.com/E-letters/African-AmericanTVA-final.pdf.

Stelter, B. (2011). "The Game" is a winner, helped by BET loyalists. *New York Times.* Retrieved from http://www.nytimes.com/2011/01/17/business/media/17bet.html?ref=media.

Thomas, L., & Litman, B. R. (1991). Fox broadcasting company, why now? An economic study of the rise of the fourth broadcast "network." *Journal of Broadcasting & Electronic Media, 35*(2), 139–157.

Tolman, L. (1992, April 30). Researching Cosby show educates local professor. *Telegram & Gazette*, p. 1.

Vogt, N. (2015). *African-American media: Fact sheet*. Pew Research Center. Retrieved from http://www.journalism.org/2015/04/29/african-american-media-fact-sheet/#fn49255-2.

Wharton, D. (2011). *The future of TV coalition launches to support preservation of free and local television*. Retrieved from http://www.nab.org/documents/newsroom/pressRelease.asp?id=2637.

Wiltz, T. (2008, May 4). Channel changer. *Washington Post*, p. M01.

Zook, K. B. (1999). *Color by Fox: The Fox network and the revolution in black television*. New York, NY: Oxford University Press.

3 New Media and New Possibilities
The Online Engagement of Young Black Activists

Nathan Jamel Riemer

On July 14, 2013, the day after George Zimmerman was exonerated from the murder of Trayvon Martin, a group of young Black activists, who now constitute the Black Youth Project 100 (BYP100),[1] video recorded a collectively written response and began circulating it via their social media accounts. The fact that the immediate reaction of these activists was to independently produce a piece of media is telling. It not only tells of the changes in the media landscape brought on by the emergence of new media[2] (that made it possible for the BYP100 to input their collective voice into a public conversation that traditional mass media would likely not have invited them to participate), but it also speaks to these activists' understanding of the use of new media as a method of political engagement. The high speed, ease, and low cost at which individuals and organizations are now able to independently produce and circulate media are affordances that are unique to the rise of new media. This is quite different from the production and circulation processes of traditional mass media. Consequently, the long-standing dependent relationship between activists, who wish to interject alternative framings into mainstream conversations, and traditional mass media, has been altered. Activists no longer require traditional mass media coverage in order to fulfill vital goals of social movement work (e.g., mobilization, scope enlargement, and validation), and activists that do not gain traditional mass media coverage no longer necessarily go unknown to the broader public.

The value of traditional mass media to activists and social movements, both past and present, is undeniable. However, the level of dependence marginal voices had on traditional mass media outlets has been reduced by the exponential increase in media channels brought on by the emergence of new media and social media platforms. New media and their attendant technologies have made it possible for any activist or network of activists who have Internet access via phone, computer, or tablet, and a basic level of computer literacy to engage, organize, and mobilize. The ability to produce and circulate media is now widely shared; traditional mass media are no longer the only means of communicating to the public.

Many people, both laymen and scholars alike, may not believe that these digitally enabled acts constitute meaningful political engagement. They may disregard such behavior by pejoratively labeling it as "slacktivism" and, therefore, largely or completely ineffectual. However, some have a broader understanding of political engagement and see such online activity as a new norm in activist engagement and a form of participatory politics. Broadly defined, participatory politics are "ways young people seek to exert voice and influence on issues of public concern by taking advantages of new opportunities available through the use of new media" (Rogowski & Cohen, 2015, p. 49). Using data from a case study of the BYP100, this chapter highlights the centrality of new media in the activism and development of the BYP100 by focusing on two digitally enabled acts of participatory politics, each drawing attention to the marginalization of young Black Americans.

In what follows, I first highlight scholarship that has addressed the historic relationship between activist movements and the mass media. This scholarship makes clear the longstanding importance of traditional mass media to social movement work. New media scholarship, however, points to a number of affordances brought on by the expanding media landscape that have complicated this relationship and brought about new possibilities for engagement: participatory politics. I will then return to the work of the BYP100 to exemplify ways in which young Black people are making use of new media to publicly voice their grievances on their terms.

A Changing Media Landscape

Traditional Mass Media, New Media, and New Possibilities

Whereas protest actions were once each bounded by a unique place and time, with activists airing their grievances directly to local power holders as bystanders watched, the rise of traditional mass media exploded the boundaries of protest activities allowing the number of people to be exposed to the communicated grievances to be nearly limitless. Consequently, media portrayals have become the primary point of contact between those who choose to contest the distribution and functioning of power, the broader public, and power holders. As Koopmans claimed, "it is no longer the co-present public that counts most, but the mass audience that sits at home and watches or reads the media coverage of the demonstration" (2004, p. 368). For this reason, activists and social movements have historically been dependent on traditional mass media in order to gain the attention of the mass public (Gamson & Wolfsfeld, 1993; Snow, Rochford, Worden, & Benford, 1986). This dependence has frequently led activists to structure their activities and messages in particular ways in efforts to gain traditional media coverage (Cottle, 2008; Lunceford, 2012; Wolfsfeld, 1984).

Referring to traditional mass media, political scientist Joachim Raschke stated, "A movement that does not make it into the media is non-existent" (as quoted in Rucht, 2004, p. 29). While this statement may no longer hold true due to the affordances new media have brought to the media landscape, scholars continue to highlight the significance of traditional mass media for social movement causes (Cottle, 2008; Graeff, Stempeck, & Zuckerman,

2014). For example, traditional mass media outlets across the country, and at points across the world, aired the protest actions that took place in Oakland, Miami, Detroit, Ferguson, and New York City of those who contested the murders of Oscar Grant, Trayvon Martin, Renisha McBride, Michael Brown, and Eric Garner. Although the role of new media in the coverage and spread of these activist actions is undeniable, the televised airing of these protests amplified their reach allowing the actions and the grievances of the protesters who took to the streets to be visible to a larger audience than they would have reached otherwise. This mass media amplification contributed to eliciting not only local responses but also national and sometimes international responses to these events and their causes. It is important to keep in mind that the emergence of new media did not create a parallel media landscape that operates exclusively from traditional mass media. There is constant and complex interaction between traditional mass media and new media (Asur, Huberman, Szabo, & Wang, 2011: Graeff et al., 2014).

Graeff, Stempeck, and Zuckerman (2014) nicely tease out this interaction by looking at the development of traditional mass media and new media coverage of the murder of Trayvon Martin. They found that local news outlets initially covered the murder of Trayvon Martin; it then received coverage by two national news outlets (Reuters and CBS This Morning). This national coverage was followed by the further spread of the story through new media outlets (e.g., Change.org and Twitter). The authors stated,

> We believe the national attention brought to the story through broadcast media allowed groups like the Black Youth Project to amplify stories to their online communities, and informed actors like [Kevin] Cunningham[3] who launched campaigns like the Change.org petition. Without the initial coverage on newswires and television, it is unclear that online communities would have known about the Trayvon Martin case and been able to mobilize around it ... The power of social media in the context of stories like Trayvon Martin's, where a local tragedy sparked a national debate, may be less about bringing these stories to light than about shaping their arc.
> (Graeff et al., 2014, pp. 21–22)

Although the story of Trayvon Martin broke on traditional media, new media played a significant agenda-setting function. Activists organized protest actions such as the Million Hoodies March that kept Martin's story in the public eye. Additionally, online communities like the Black Youth Project utilized social media to insist that Martin's death be understood as a function of a race-based society. The large amount of online support for this alternative framing resulted in it being indelibly wed to the story of Martin's murder in ongoing public discourse across all forms of media. The impact of new media activity on the unfolding of Trayvon Martin's story provides an example of new media–traditional mass media interaction. It also shows the vulnerabilities of traditional media's gatekeeping and agenda setting to new media influences (Cottle, 2008; Rosen, 2009).

Traditional mass media gatekeepers can be bypassed as online new media platforms are used as alternative media (Postmes & Brunsting, 2002). Through these platforms, potentially, millions of people can be reached without the aid of traditional mass media outlets (Friedland & Rogerson, 2009). Activists can now independently produce media, circulate it via their social network accounts or websites, and, thereby, input counternarratives and new voices into public conversations (Bimber, Flanagin, & Stohl, 2005; Cottle, 2008; Graeff et al., 2014). The multiple sources of information and the multiple means by which information can now be produced, shared, and accessed have weakened the gatekeeping ability of traditional mass media elites (Bimber, 2003; Williams & Delli Carpini, 2000). New media have reshaped the relationship between social movements and activists and mass media (Bimber et al., 2005; Friedland & Rogerson, 2009).

Scholars who challenge starry-eyed views of new media insist that new media has its own set of gatekeepers that affect the level of visibility of particular messages. "Even in the seemingly non-hierarchical internet, providers, internet browsers, and search engines pre-structure access to information on the web in such a way that certain sites are more easily and more frequently accessed than they would have been in the absence of such gatekeeping" (Koopmans, 2004, pp. 372–373). New media is not a level and open playing field. While almost anyone has the opportunity to speak, everyone is not equally positioned to be heard (Hindman, 2008). Others worry that the communicative affordances of new media allow for the ease of false information to be vastly spread (Newman, 2011). Still others are concerned that the increased sources for media content and the increased ability to select from them will lead people to filter the information they consume in a manner that simply reinforces their opinions and neglects alternative viewpoints (Sunstein, 2009).

Slacktivism, Participatory Politics, and the BYP100

The addition of new media to the media landscape has certainly altered the relationships among traditional mass media, activists, and the broader public, and facilitated new means and modes of political engagement, organization, and mobilization. The affordances of new media can be leveraged to support offline protest actions, create online versions of traditional forms of engagement, or produce novel forms of participation that occur entirely online (Christensen, 2011; Earl & Kimport, 2011; Jordan & Taylor, 2004). Some criticize these new forms of online activism and pejoratively label them as "slacktivism." Rather than understanding the ease of engagement as a boon for political participation, they question whether online activism is a meaningful and impactful way to achieve real political outcomes (Hindman, 2009; Morozov, 2009; Shulman, 2009).

Critics also claim that online activism may reduce participation in offline forms of engagement, which they believe to be more efficacious efforts (Gladwell, 2010; Lee & Hsieh, 2013; Morozov, 2009). The worry is that people may see online and offline forms of participation as equivalent and, therefore, when deciding how to become politically engaged they will opt for online forms of engagement because they are easier and more convenient than offline participation. When people can forward a link, change their profile pictures, post videos, or tweet in order to express their political viewpoints, attempt to leverage power holders, or expose others to civic and political matters, they will do that rather than stage a sit-in, stand in line to vote, walk in a march, or gather signatures for an offline petition (Morozov, 2009). After engaging in these low-effort online actions, individuals will feel content with their level of participation and feel no need to take part in offline efforts (Lee & Hsieh, 2013). Consequently, Morozov (2009) claims that slacktivism is "the ideal type of activism for a lazy generation."

Scholars of the MacArthur Research Network on Youth and Participatory Politics (YPP), however, have a broader understanding of political engagement: "Our conceptualization of politics extends beyond the electoral focus that often dominates literature about political participation and includes a broad array of activities undertaken by individuals and groups to influence how the public sets agendas and addresses issues of public concern" (Kahn, Middaugh, & Allen, 2014, p. 6). Scholars of the YPP network would call the BYP100's video response an example of participatory politics.

> Young people engage in participatory politics by collecting and consuming information distributed through non-traditional sources, commenting on or providing feedback on political issues through digital means, circulating information and opinions, producing original online content and mobilizing their communities and members of their digital networks.
> (Rogowski & Cohen, 2015, p. 49)

Traditionally, voting rates have been the main, and often sole, measure of political engagement. This measure has never captured the diversity of ways in which people engage in efforts to impact the distribution of power and challenge policy; and has particularly neglected the political lives of young people who have historically had low voter turnout rates or are ineligible to vote due to age. This problem of measurement has fueled public discourse regarding the political apathy of young people. However, when specifically assessing the political engagement of young people, researchers have found that "41 percent of young people engage in at least one act of participatory politics, which is roughly equal to the 44 percent who engage in other acts of politics. This suggests that participatory politics make up a substantive part of youth political activity" (Kahn et al., 2014, p. 18). Interestingly, engagement in participatory politics is nearly equal across racial groups; this is in stark contrast to voting rates across race (Cohen, Kahn, Bowyer, Middaugh, & Rogowski, 2012). The growing accessibility of new media is facilitating increased opportunities for activists, in groups or as individuals, to engage in various forms of participatory politics. In doing so, those who do not fall within "conventional elite groups" are finding new modes of exerting agency and influence in the political realm (Kahn et al., 2014).

Data and Methods

The collection of the data that are presented throughout this chapter began at the Beyond November Movement Convening (BNMC), which was hosted by the Black Youth Project (BYP) in Itasca, Illinois, during the July 12–14, 2013, weekend. The BYP launched in 2005 as a national research project led by Cathy Cohen of the University of Chicago. It "examined the attitudes, resources, and culture of African American youth ages 15 to 25, exploring how these factors and others influence the decision-making, norms, and behavior of Black youth" (www.Blackyouthproject.com/about/). In an effort to make data from the BYP available to a larger public Cathy Cohen took it online and created Blackyouthproject.com. The BYP website hosts survey data and corresponding reports, a database of youth organizations across the nation, a database of rap lyrics compiled from 20 years of releases, and a blog populated by an array of Black youth contributors, among a number of other resources for youth, educators, activists, and scholars. The work of the BYP has three guiding concepts:

> KNOWLEDGE: We are committed to producing research about the ideas, attitudes, decision making, and lived experiences of Black youth, especially as it relates to their political and civic engagement.
>
> VOICE: Unlike any other organization, we amplify the perspectives of young Black people daily without censorship or control. We have built a space on the Internet where Black youth can speak for themselves about the issues that concern them.
>
> ACTION: Informed with culturally-specific knowledge, we will work to mobilize Black youth and their allies to make positive change and build the world within which they want to live. (http://research.Black youthproject.com/about-us/)

It was in the spirit of the third guiding concept that the BYP came to organize the BNMC, which brought together young Black activists from across the nation.

I was in attendance as a note taker tasked with documenting the event for the BYP. I participated in the majority of convening activities; conversing while also documenting the event with field notes. I also attended a portion of a BYP100 convening in Washington, DC. Immediately following the BNMC, I began sitting in on many of the BYP100's conference calls. My permission to attend these calls came from the cochairs of the BYP100. In addition to my notes from the field and on the phone I conducted 32 semistructured interviews with members of the BYP100 and those who organized the BNMC. Last, I also gathered data for this project by following the BYP100's Twitter profile and YouTube channel.

The Zimmerman Verdict: A Racial Crisis

As the second day of the BNMC was coming to a close, the jury for the George Zimmerman trial reached a verdict. A stream of the trial coverage was projected on the conference room's overhead screen. The room filled with nerve-wracking anticipation and near silence as everyone present stood hand-in-hand in solidarity and awaited the verdict. As the not guilty verdict was read participants yelled in agony and anger. Many broke down in tears. Few remained silent.

It was "a national disaster for the Black community, it may not have been a hurricane or a tornado, but for all intents and purposes, the Zimmerman verdict and that whole process really was a natural disaster for our community just in the way that it affected each of us so deeply," stated one member of the BYP100. The fact that George Zimmerman was not held accountable for Trayvon Martin's death was not just traumatic for his family and friends. For many young Black people beyond Trayvon Martin's immediate social circles "it basically was a statement from the state and all these people saying 'Black life doesn't matter,'" stated one BYP100 member. This moment was one that heightened these activists' sense of their racial position in this country.

#BYP100 Responds

The next morning the members of the BYP100 squeezed in close in order to fit within the scope of a video camera. As everyone stood in silence, two members of the BYP100 seated at center, one female and the other male, took turns reading portions of the following statement from an iPad.

> To the Family of Brother Trayvon Martin and to the Black Community:
>
> May this statement find us in the spirit of peace and solidarity.
>
> We know that justice for Black life is justice for humanity.
>
> Our hope and community was shaken through a system that is supposed to be built on freedom and justice for all. We are your sons and daughters. We are the marginalized and disenfranchised. We are one hundred next generation leaders. We are the Black Youth Project 100 (BYP100).

We see the hopelessness of a generation that has been broken trying to find its place in this world. We understand that we need to turn anger into action and pain into power.

As we waited to hear the verdict, in the spirit of unity, we formed a circle and locked hands. When we heard "not guilty," our hearts broke collectively. In that moment, it was clear that Black life had no value. Emotions poured out—emotions that are real, natural and normal, as we grieved for Trayvon and his stolen humanity. Black people, WE LOVE AND SEE YOU. We mourn, but there's hope as long as love endures.

Trayvon was manifested from ancestral excellence. The salt water falling from our eyes now, is not different from the salt water we were trafficked on then. If the soil of the United States could speak, before saying a word it would cough up our blood. Choking frantically, crust-curdling with the gore of a oppressed peoples it has been force-fed. White supremacy has water-boarded it with the remnants of its genocide of us.

This moment reminds us that we can't look to others to see our value but we have to recognize our own value. In spite of what was said in court, what verdict has been reached, or how hopeless we feel, Trayvon did NOT die in vain. A mother should never have to bury her son. However, his death will serve as the catalyst of a new movement where the struggle for justice will prevail.

Instead of a moment of silence, we raise our voices together. As Audre Lorde said, "our silence will NOT PROTECT US." We are young leaders standing on the shoulders of our ancestors, carrying the historical trauma embedded in a legal system that will NOT PROTECT US. We are the legacy of Black resilience that compels us to fight for our lives.

We continue to call out Black Love, Black Power and Black is Beautiful in the face of continued devaluation of Black life. We affirm a love of ALL Black life, no matter if we are in hoodies or business suits, incarcerated or in boardrooms, on welfare or in the WNBA, on the corner or in the White House. We declare the fundamental value, beauty and power of ALL Black people. The poet Claude McKay once said, "Though far outnumbered, let us show us brave ... we'll face the murderous, cowardly pack. Pressed to the wall, dying, but fighting back!"

JUSTICE FOR TRAYVON.

Within two days of the video being produced and posted to the BYP website and the social media sites of the BYP100 members, it was reposted and further circulated online by such noted websites as HuffingtonPost.com, Ebony.com, and AlJazeera.com. The amount of coverage that the BYP100 video received by corporate digital media sites caught the attention of many and helped the video garner 23,000 views within the first few days.

On account of the video's release, the BYP100 gained a significant online media presence long before it had established a formal organizational structure. The online media attention created an air of organizational development that was not yet present. For example, shortly after the video's release, theRoot.com expressed interest in doing feature stories on the "leaders" of the organization. However, while the BYP100 left the BNMC with plans and fervor, "the only structural thing at the time was a semblance of a commitment to a coordinating council," noted one member of the BYP100. Additionally, just a few weeks after the BNMC, five members of the BYP100 went to Florida to attend an event organized by the Dream Defenders and Power U, founded in 2012 and 1998, respectively. The event was a rally in support of the Take Over Florida campaign in which members of the Dream Defenders occupied the Florida governor's office in Tallahassee. When the attending BYP100 members reported back to the larger group regarding their participation, one of them exclaimed, "BYP100 was an organization in everyone's eyes! It was a real thing. A representative of Black youth action in the country." This was prior to the BYP100 formally implementing an organizational structure or engaging in any public collective action or campaigning beyond the release of their video response to the Zimmerman verdict.

BYP100: Black Youth, Black Police, and Transformative Justice

On March 12, 2014, the BYP100 released another video. It was recorded during a BYP100 convening that was hosted by Princeton University's Center for African American Studies. The video was posted to the BYP100's YouTube account. It captured footage of a dialogue between a Black police officer and some members of the BYP100 on March 8, 2014. The officer pulled over a car carrying a number of BYP100 members as they were leaving the Princeton University campus after attending a small party for the organization and heading back to their hotel. The officer cited a broken taillight as the reason for the stop. The taillight, however, was found to be in working condition once the car was stopped and further inspected. Before letting the BYP100 members go, the police officer reportedly asked where they were heading and said that he would beat them there. When they arrived, he was sitting in his patrol car in front of their hotel. A conversation ensued and was videotaped by a member of the BYP100.

The conversation dealt with issues of the criminalization of Black youth. Members of the BYP100 approached the police officer as he sat in his vehicle and attempted to explain to him how they, as young Black people, felt criminalized by police through racial profiling. One member of the BYP100 explained to the officer,

> You guys have a responsibility to protect and serve and we just really want you guys to protect and serve. As youth—as Black youth we don't feel like we get that level of protection. We don't get that benefit of the doubt that like white students running around Princeton campus get.

The police officer tried to convey that profiling and criminalizing members of the BYP100 was not his intention when he stopped their car. One BYP100 member recounted the interaction with the police officer in a blog post.

> After our party, a group of us were pulled over by a Black police officer. The tension was high, Black youth at a white university, all of whom have an inherent distrust of the police, and a system that has an inherent distrust of Black youth. Although we were doing nothing wrong we know all too well the realities of the Trayvon Martins of the world and that we are often "guilty until proven innocent." The misunderstanding was able to evolve into a teachable moment for both parties where race issues and the lack of safety Black youth feel was discussed. We are on our way to creating policies that address stop & frisk and the shoot first law, but our first accomplishment I think, is sparking those conversations the world is afraid to have. Conversations that build bridges.
> (Tiara, 2014)

The Princeton video, like the video response to the Zimmerman verdict, quickly gained the attention of traditional mass media outlets. It was first picked up by theRoot.com and reposted in a short article on March 18, 2014. It was then reposted on BET.com, and picked up by other noted websites such as Bossip.com and UrbanCusp.com. Members of the BYP100 did not pitch this video to media outlets, yet it received nearly 130,000 views.

The affordances of new media made it possible for the BYP100 to share this experience with a large audience. Most likely, this police encounter would never have come to the attention of anyone other than the participants otherwise. The drama and sensationalism that often draws the attention of traditional mass media news coverage was absent. Because the BYP100 both produced and distributed this piece of media on their own, they had sole control of its original framing. The BYP100 framed this police encounter as an example of transformative justice rather than simply highlighting the negative aspects of the interaction. Fresco Steez, a member of the BYP100, provided the following definition of transformative justice: "A means to transforming the systems, institutions, and environments that we interact with on a daily basis. So they are no longer systemically violent" (BYP100, 2014). This framing created a counternarrative to most publicized interactions between police and young Black people. Consequently, when readers came across theRoot.com's headline, "Black Youths Attending Princeton Conference Pulled Over by Police, Then This Happened …," or UrbanCusp.com's headline, "Watch: Youth Activist Group BYP100 Members Pulled Over by Princeton Police," many were likely surprised to see a peaceful conversation between a police officer and members of the BYP100. Additionally, readers on Bossip.com were likely made equally curious by the counternarrative when seeing the headline "A Lil Positivity: Black Youths At Princeton Have 'Healthy Dialogue' With Cop Who Racially Profiled Them [Video]."

Discussion and Conclusion

The BYP100's claims of marginalization, questioning of a justice system supposedly "built on freedom and justice for all," and feelings of the criminalization of Black youth (#CriminalizedLives) that were expressed in the videos discussed in this chapter are not sentiments unique to the BYP100. Rather, these claims reflect a widespread sense of marginalization and political alienation among many young Black Americans (Cohen, 2010; Rogowski & Cohen, 2015). Cohen's work notes that over 60% of young Black Americans reported that they agreed with the statement "it is hard for young Black people to get ahead because they face so much discrimination" (2010, p. 121). Young Black Americans also expressed "the belief that they are relatively powerless to influence government (Rogowski & Cohen, 2015, p. 55). And, unfortunately, only 11% of young Black Americans claimed that racism would very likely be eliminated in their lifetime. Even after the 2012 presidential election of Barack Obama, 69% of young Black Americans reported, "Racism remains a major problem" (Cohen, 2010, p. 222).

Although these sentiments loom large for young Black Americans, and extant scholarship demonstrates a particular racial experience wherein Black Americans are at a structural deficit (e.g., Alexander, 2012; Pager, 2007; Massey & Denton, 1993), declarations of racial inequality are consistently delegitimized by an American ideology of colorblindness. Colorblindness vehemently restricts claims of racism as a source of racial disparity and instead "explains contemporary racial inequality as the outcome of nonracial dynamics" (Bonilla-Silva, 2010, p. 2). Those who adhere to colorblind ideology paint traumatic events such as the murder of Trayvon Martin,[4] the unpunished beating of Rodney King, and Hurricane Katrina and her aftermath as unfortunate incidents, tough justice, isolated events, or an unprecedented natural disaster. The ideology of colorblindness refuses to concede that such events exemplify the "marginalization and disenfranchisement" the BYP100 assert. But these are not novel atrocities. The ubiquity of new media and its attendant technologies have created a context wherein firsthand footage captured and circulated across the Internet by amateurs demonstrates that although months and miles may sometimes separate the most popularized incidents of race-based brutality, each is a point in a pattern. This pattern demonstrates a social structure in which race matters. The lived experience of young Black Americans is in direct contrast to colorblind ideology. Consequently, mainstream racial discourse is reluctant to Black youth voicing their grievances; and mainstream media, which has long been charged with supporting the status quo and the interests of the elite (Herman & Chomsky, 1988; McLeod & Detenber, 1999), is most often not a viable outlet.

New media, on the other hand, provide ample opportunities for grievances regarding racial inequality to be publicly voiced and racial inequality publicly challenged. This is clear to activists such as the BYP100 and others who feel that their voices are unwelcomed or unheard in traditional mass media. "It's power," stated one member of the BYP100 describing new media:

> We've seen lots of movements whether we want to talk about Occupy the Hood or we want to talk about the movement with Trayvon Martin and the movement with Marissa Alexander. All of these movements should be waged on and offline and most of these movements are being led by young people of color and so I think social media is very critical and I think social media presents an opportunity to folks who didn't necessarily have the financial means or didn't necessarily have the resources that other people with traditional power used to have, but I think that social media gives people especially people who have traditionally been marginalized the power to make a footprint.

Other BYP100 members referred to new media as "a platform to the masses"; and explained that it allows you to post "your message in your terms" and "have a voice in some incredible way." Even so, BYP100 members were sure to express that traditional offline organizing and activism is still vital to social movement work. It is imperative to have an "online–offline connection."

By providing individuals and organizations the ability to relatively easily produce and distribute their own media, the emergence of new media has made it possible for the voices of activists, such as the BYP100, to effectively engage in media framing and agenda-setting processes. The traditional media landscape did not lend itself well to the inclusion of marginalized voices and alternative viewpoints. The relatively small number of media outlets created an intensity of gatekeeping pressures, as media producers aimed, and continue to aim, to gain the biggest percentage of the mainstream audience. The addition of new media to the media landscape now provide increased opportunity for marginalized voices to actively influence the variety of media, frames, and social issues that contribute to public discourse by taking an active part in independently producing and circulating digital content. In general, Black youth have higher rates of online political activity than their White and Latino peers (Rogowski & Cohen, 2015). The BYP100's videos addressed herein exemplify this type of digitally enabled participatory politics.

Notes

1. The BYP100 is a national social movement organization of young Black activists. See BYP100.org.
2. While definitions of "new media" are many, in this chapter the term will refer to digital media that are created with and accessed through the use of computing technologies. Such media are generally characterized by their low barriers to production and distribution and allow for interactive, two-way communication.

3. Kevin Cunningham is the Howard University alum that began a Change.org petition on March 8, 2012, after viewing the Reuters piece on Trayvon Martin's murder. The petition received more than a million signatures.
4. Due to space, I use Trayvon Martin's name to call attention to his own untimely death and also to represent the numerous other unarmed Black people that have been killed by armed police officers and vigilantes.

References

Alexander, M. (2012). *The new Jim Crow: Mass incarceration in the age of colorblindness*. New York, NY: The New Press.

Asur, S., Huberman, B., Szabo, G., & Wang, C. (2011). *Trends in social media: Persistence and decay*. Retrieved from http://www.hpl.hp.com/research/scl/papers/trends/trends_web.pdf.

Bimber, B. (2003). *Information and American democracy: Technology in the evolution of political power*. Cambridge, UK: Cambridge University Press.

Bimber, B., Flanagin, A. J., & Stohl, C. (2005). Reconceptualizing collective action in the contemporary media environment. *Communication Theory, 15*, 365–388.

Black Youth Project 100 (BYP100). (2014, March 26). BYP100 methods of social change hangout [Video file]. Retrieved from https://www.youtube.com/watch?v=XIHEyba1vzw&feature=youtu.be.

Bonilla-Silva, E. (2010). *Racism without racists: Color-blind racism and the persistence of racial inequality in the United States*. Lanham, MD: Rowman & Littlefield.

Christensen, H. S. (2011). Political activities on the Internet: Slacktivism or political participation by other means? *First Monday, 16*, 2–7.

Cohen, C. J. (2010). *Democracy remixed: Black youth and the future of American politics*. Oxford, UK: Oxford University Press.

Cohen, C. J., Kahne, J., Bowyer, B., Middaugh, E., & Rogowski, J. (2012). *Participatory politics: New media and youth political action*. Retrieved from http://ypp.dmlcentral.net/sites/all/files/publications/YPP_Survey_Report_FULL.pdf.

Cottle, S. (2008). Reporting demonstrations: The changing media politics of dissent. *Media Culture Society, 30*(6), 853–872.

Earl, J., & Kimport, K. (2011). *Digitally enables social change: Activism in the Internet age*. Cambridge, MA: MIT Press.

Friedland, J., & Rogerson, K. (2009). *How political and social movements form on the Internet and how they change over time*. Institute for Homeland Security Solutions.

Gamson, W. A., & Wolfsfeld, G. (1993). Movements and media as interacting systems. *Annals of the American Academy of Political and Social Science, 528*, 114–125.

Gladwell, M. (2010, October 4). Small change: Why the revolution will not be tweeted. *The New Yorker*. Retrieved from http://www.newyorker.com/reporting/2010/10/04/101004fa_fact_gladwell.

Graeff, E., Stempeck, M., & Zuckerman, E. (2014). The battle for "Trayvon Martin": Mapping a media controversy online and off-line. *First Monday, 19*(2–3). Retrieved from http://firstmonday.org/ojs/index.php/fm/article/view/4947.

Herman, E. S., & Chomsky, N. (1988). *Manufacturing consent: The political economy of the mass media*. New York, NY: Pantheon Books.

Hindman, M. (2008). *The myth of digital democracy*. Princeton, NJ: Princeton University Press.

Jordan, T., & Taylor, P. (2004). *Hacktivism and cyberwars: Rebels with a cause*. London, UK: Routledge.

Kahn, J., Middaugh, E., & Allen, D. (2014). *Youth, new media, and the rise of participatory politics*. Oakland, CA: Youth and Participatory Politics Research Network.

Koopmans, R. (2004). Movements and media: Selection processes and evolutionary dynamics in the public sphere. *Theory and Society, 33*(3–4), 367–391.

Lee, Y.-H., & Hsieh, G. (2013). Does slacktivism hurt activism?: The effects of moral balancing and consistency in online activism. *CHI'13 Proceedings of the SIGCHI Conference on Human Factors in Computing Systems* (pp. 811–820). New York, NY: ACM.

Lunceford, B. (2012). *Naked politics: Nudity, political action, and the rhetoric of the body*. Lanham, MD: Lexington.

Massey, D., & Denton, N. (1993). *American apartheid: Segregation and the making of the underclass*. Cambridge, MA: Harvard University Press.

McLeod, D. M., & Detenber, B. H. (1999). Framing effects of television news coverage of social protest. *Journal of Communication, 49*(3), 3–23.

Morozov, E. (2009). Foreign policy: The brave new world of slacktivism. *National Public Radio*. Retrieved from http://www.npr.org/templates/story/story.php?storyId=104302141.

Newman, N. (2011). *Mainstream media and the distribution of news in the age of social discovery*. Reuters Institute for the Study of Journalism. Retrieved from http://reutersinstitute.politics.ox.ac.uk/sites/default/files/Mainstream%20media%20and%20the%20distribution%20of%20news%20in%20the%20age%20of%20social%20discovery_0.pdf.

Pager, D. (2007). *Marked: Race, crime, and finding work in an era of mass incarceration*. Chicago, IL: University of Chicago Press.

Postmes, T., & Brunsting, S. (2002). Collective action in the age of the Internet: Mass communication and online mobilization. *Social Science Computer Review, 20*(3), 290–301.

Rogowski, J., & Cohen, C. (2015). *Black Millennials in America: Documenting the experiences, voices and political future of young Black Americans*. blackyouthproject.com. Retrieved from http://blackyouthproject.com/wp-content/uploads/2015/11/BYP-millenials-report-10-27-15-FINAL.pdf.

Rosen, J. (2009). *Audience atomization overcome: Why the Internet weakens the authority of the press*. PressThink. Retrieved from http://archive.pressthink.org/2009/01/12/atomization.html.

Rucht, D. (2004). The quadruple "A": Media strategies of protest movements since the 1960s. In W. Van De Donk, B. D. Loader, P. G. Nixon, & D. Rucht, *Cyberprotest: New media, citizens and social movements* (pp. 25–48). London, UK: Routledge.

Shulman, S. (2009). The case against mass e-mails: Perverse incentives and low quality public participation in U.S. federal rulemaking. *Policy and Internet, 1*(1), 23–53.

Snow, D. A., Rochford, J. E., Worden, S. K., & Benford, R. D. (1986). Frame alignment processes, micromobilization, and movement participation. *American Sociological Review, 51*(4), 464–481.

Sunstein, C. (2009). *Republic.com 2.0*. Princeton, NJ: Princeton University Press.
Tiara, D. (2014, March 22). The Princeton Xperience [Web log post]. Retrieved from http://darlingtiara.blogspot.com/search?q=princeton.
Williams, B. A., & Delli Carpini, M. X. (2000). Unchained reaction: The collapse of media gatekeeping and the Clinton-Lewinsky scandal. *Journalism, 1*(1), 61–85.
Wolfsfeld, G. (1984). Collective political action and media strategy: The case of Yamit. *Journal of Conflict Resolution, 28*(3), 363–381.

Part II
Navigating Contention Behind the Scenes

4 Black, Asian, and Latino Directors in Hollywood

Maryann Erigha

> You're in L.A., you've got to try not to hire Mexicans.
> —Chris Rock

In his December 2014 essay in *The Hollywood Reporter*, Chris Rock noted the irony of the dearth of Latinos working in Hollywood. As Rock (2014) pointed out, "you've got to try" to have a racially homogeneous workforce in an area that boasts residents from an array of racial and ethnic backgrounds. The greater metropolitan area of Los Angeles, unlike the Hollywood industry within it, is sprawling with diversity. According to United States Census figures, in 2013 Los Angeles County recorded a population of 9.2% Black, 14.6% Asian, 27.2% White, and 48.3% Latino (U.S. Census Bureau, 2015). With such a diverse population, one might naturally expect the city of Los Angeles and its greater metropolitan area to reflect diversity in all areas of social life, including its cultural institutions. It seems rather counterintuitive that Latinos would reside in such large numbers in the greater Los Angeles area where the film industry is headquartered, but then not comprise some sizeable portion, or at least a noticeable slice, of Hollywood workers. A cursory glance at the racial/ethnic demographics of Hollywood workers is all one needs to suggest that the film industry does, in fact, try exceedingly hard to be racially exclusive.

Despite a diverse population of Los Angeles residents, major Hollywood studios have yet to embrace the diversity of their surrounding locale. Although nearly 50% of the population in Los Angeles is Latino and 72% are members of racial minority groups, neither of these groups have a palpable presence in Hollywood. In his essay, Chris Rock lambasted Hollywood studios and mostly White studio executives for their failure to hire Black, Asian, and Latino workers on all aspects of film projects, from roles that require little to no education and formal training to roles that wield ultimate decision-making power. Regarding the latter upper-management positions, Rock expressed little optimism that people of color would ever occupy them. Though headquartered in the Los Angeles area, the Hollywood industry still remains racially homogeneous in all areas of behind-the-scenes and on-screen employment, with Whites monopolizing the production of popular culture, while groups constituting the racial majority in Los Angeles remain on the fringes.

Scholars have previously described Hollywood as a racialized industry wherein workers are sorted into unequal and hierarchical strata, in positions of advantage and disadvantage, based on race (Bonilla-Silva, 1997; Thakore, 2014). For decades, U.S. racial/ethnic minorities have struggled to gain increased representation behind the scenes of mainstream media organizations and to integrate into key positions—namely, acting, producing, and directing—within the film industry's core institutions. Despite their gradual yet wholly incomplete progress concerning struggles over representation, research has shown that people of color working in behind-the-scenes positions have historically faced difficulties accessing core institutions in the center of Hollywood production and more often gained representation at marginal organizations (Erigha, 2015a; Hunt, Ramon, & Price, 2014). Lacking representation in core institutions excludes them from benefits like greater reputation, resources, and strategic networks to help further their careers (Bielby & Bielby, 1999; Schatz, 2009). Further research has also shown that members of underrepresented racial groups are segregated into niche areas in cultural institutions, on few projects about race, and in limited genres (Smith & Choueiti, 2011; Yuen, 2004, 2010). In this present moment of post-racial discourses, what racial dynamics of representation exist behind the scenes of contemporary media structures wherein cinematic images are constructed?

In this chapter, I examine the racial dynamics of representation for Black, Asian, and Latino directors behind the scenes of Hollywood filmmaking. Specifically, I delve into the social locations of Hollywood directors behind the scenes of contemporary films in the post-2000 era to consider: how present are Black, Asian, and Latino directors behind the scenes; in which studios and genres do they find work; and in which areas are they underrepresented? I also investigate where women of color stand in the fight to gain representation behind the scenes as film directors, in particular, how intersectionality combines racial inequality with gender inequality to forge deeper representational obstacles. Drawing on over 1700 Hollywood films distributed by Hollywood studios and theatrically released to U.S. cinemas between 2000 and 2011, the results show that Hollywood still remains a racialized place in 21st century media.[1] In the film industry, directors' opportunities and outcomes—including allocation of production budgets, placement in genres, and representation in studios—are largely structured based upon racial group membership.

Racial/Ethnic Diversity in Hollywood

Film directors play a vital and important role on film projects, overseeing the production process from start to finish and interacting with nearly every role on the film set. However Black, Asian, and Latino directors are vastly underrepresented in Hollywood filmmaking. During the first decade of the 21st century, between 2000 and 2011, they collectively directed less than

13% of Hollywood films released to theaters. Of these racial groups, Black directors were the most present, directing 7.5% of Hollywood films theatrically released between 2000 and 2011. Three percent of directors were Asian, while less than 2% were Latino.

In Hollywood, there are marked differences in whether directors of different races are American-born or foreign-born. In general, Hollywood far more often draws on narratives from foreign-born Latino and Asian directors than from Latinos and Asians born in the U.S. Meanwhile, the industry disseminates more stories told by African Americans born in the U.S. and fewer stories of Africans abroad in the diaspora. Although the overwhelming majority of Black directors in Hollywood are American-born, a few were born on the African continent: Sunu Gonera, director of *Pride* (2007), was born in Zimbabwe; Sanaa Hamri, director of *Just Wright* (2010), *Something New* (2006), and *The Sisterhood of the Traveling Pants 2* (2008), was born in Morocco; and Cheryl Dunye, director of *My Baby's Daddy* (2004), was born in Liberia. Besides American- or African-born directors, some hailed from other regions of the world: Robert Adetuyi, director of *Turn It Up* (2000), is from Canada; *Soul Plane* (2004) director Jessy Terrero was born in the Dominican Republic; and Sylvain White, director of *Stomp the Yard* (2007) and *The Losers* (2010), was born in France.

In contrast, most of the Latino and Asian directors are born outside of the United States, suggesting that Hollywood rarely draws from its American-born populations of Latinos and Asians to hire directors. Latinas Carmen Marron, director of *Go For It* (2011), and Linda Mendoza, director of *Chasing Papi* (2003), were both born in the United States. Miguel Arteta, director of *Cedar Rapids* (2011) and *The Good Girl* (2002), hails from the U.S. territory of Puerto Rico. But numerous popular Latino directors who have films distributed by Hollywood studios were born outside of the U.S. For instance, Alejandro Gonzalez Inarritu, director of *21 Grams* (2003), *Babel* (2006), and *The Others* (2001), was born in Chile. Mexican-born Guillermo del Toro directed *Blade II* (2002), *Hellboy* (2004), and *Hellboy II: The Golden Army* (2008). For Asians, Jon Chu, director of *Step Up* (2010); Kevin Tancharoen, director of *Fame* (2009); and Joseph Kahn, director of *Torque* (2004), are all U.S.-born. However, the majority of Asian directors had birthplaces outside of the U.S.—in China, Japan, and Hong Kong, while a smaller contingent of directors were from Thailand, Taiwan, India, or various other countries. To some extent, one might conclude that African Americans are more able to contribute to the Hollywood cinematic narrative than are Latino or Asian Americans, though African Americans' participation in Hollywood and access to all aspects of production remains, nonetheless, limited.

Generally, there was a declining inclusion of Black, Asian, and Latino directors over the 12-year period between 2000 and 2011, as their share of directing opportunities decreased during the latter years, especially between 2009 and 2011. Understandably, during the years following the Great

Recession, the total number of directing opportunities for all races declined. Yet compared to Whites, Black, Asian, and Latino filmmakers absorbed the hardest hit and saw a smaller proportion of directing opportunities following the economic recession.

It is not in the least surprising that filmmakers from racially underrepresented backgrounds are the most disadvantaged behind the scenes as film directors at major Hollywood studios. In fact, fewer directed movies distributed by core studios compared to noncore studios. Despite comprising over 36% of the U.S. population, according to the 2010 U.S. Census, and representing 13% of directors of Hollywood films between 2000 and 2011, Black, Asian, and Latino filmmakers directed only 8% of films distributed by the six major studios—Sony, Paramount, 20th Century Fox, Universal, Warner Brothers, and Disney. Of these major studios, Warner Brothers had the smallest percentage behind the camera with only 6% of directors from these racial groups, while Paramount had the largest percentage with 12%. However, even Paramount's proportion of Black, Asian, and Latino directors was only one third of their percentage of the general population (36%), which means that the major studio that hired the most directors from underrepresented backgrounds would need to triple its representation in order to reach parity. On the other hand, Warner Brothers executives would need to hire 6 times the number of Black, Asian, and Latino filmmakers than they currently staff if their behind-the-scenes composition of directors were to truly reflect the nature of the U.S. population.

There were also racial differences in what proportion of directors from each racial group had their films distributed by a major studio. Only Asian directors had an equal proportion of films distributed by major studios as they did by studios outside of the Big 6. In contrast, the majority of films directed by African Americans and Latinos was distributed by studios outside of Hollywood's core. Only 32% of Latino-directed films was distributed by a major studio compared to 41% of Black-directed films and 50% of Asian-directed films.

Outside of major studios, other studios are generally more inclusive, although they, too, fall short of employing a percentage of Black, Asian, and Latino directors that would match or exceed the level at which they are represented in the general population. At Fox Searchlight, Black, Asian, and Latino filmmakers directed 26% of films. Sony Screen Gems, Metro Goldwyn Mayer (MGM), and Lions Gate each had 19%–20% of films with directors who were Black, Asian, or Latino. Industry records also indicate that African Americans, Asians, and Latinos experience greater inclusion at studios that are further from the central operations of the Hollywood film industry and are substantially less integrated into its inner core (Erigha, 2015a, pp. 82–83).

One disadvantage of not working with a major studio is distribution. In a 2003 interview with Lia Chang from AsianConnections, Asian American filmmaker Justin Lin discussed the disadvantages of his earlier films not having a major studio attached. Lin said:

That is the hypocrisy of distribution. The way the studios work. They know how to make mainstream films with big stars, put them in 3000 screens and the per screen average can be really low but they have 3000 screens. They can make millions of dollars in one weekend. It's a business of volume. They'll spend tens of millions on billboards and commercials and everything. For all independent films that are going through platform release, they are only going to put you into ten theaters to begin with. They are not going to put any money into prints and advertising but they expect you to do five times the business of a regular Hollywood film. If you can do that you prove to live another a week. Then they will expand.

(Chiang, 2003)

Lin described the hindrances directors face when major studios are unwilling to spend large amounts on marketing and promotion or widely exhibit their films across theaters nationwide.

Though few surmount the barriers and break into Hollywood filmmaking, some directors are successful at forging a relatively stable working relationship with big studios, directing several films that are distributed by the majors. Later in his career, Justin Lin directed a number of movies distributed by major Hollywood studios, including three from the internationally popular *Fast and Furious* franchise: *Fast Five* (2011, Universal), *Fast and the Furious* (2009, Universal), and *The Fast and the Furious: Tokyo Drift* (2006, Universal). Lin also directed films that were distributed outside of major studios. Comparable success is also characteristic of the careers of African American filmmakers, including Antoine Fuqua and Tim Story. With major studios, Fuqua directed *Training Day* (2001, Warner Brothers), *King Arthur* (2004, Buena Vista), *Shooter* (2007, Paramount), and *Bait* (2000, Warner Brothers). With 20th Century Fox, Tim Story directed *Fantastic Four* (2005), *Fantastic Four: Rise of the Silver Surfer* (2007), and *Taxi* (2004). Although filmmakers like Lin, Fuqua, and Story were able to navigate the racially exclusive Hollywood studios and direct multiple films, opportunities to have lucrative Hollywood careers remain the exception and not the norm for the majority of Black, Asian, and Latino directors.

Production Budgets and Genre

In addition to racialized representation at studios, average production budgets for films were stratified by the director's race. For Asian directors, the average film budget was $41 million. The average production budget for Latino directors was $34.5 million. Black directors registered the smallest average budgets at $28 million. In stark contrast, White directors had the largest average budgets at $46 million.

Between 2000 and 2011, four Asian-directed films at Hollywood companies were budgeted at or over $100 million: Ang Lee's *Hulk* (2003),

John Woo's *Mission Impossible II* (2000), and Justin Lin's *Fast Five* tapped out at $125 million. John Woo's *Windtalkers* (2002) was produced on a $115 million budget. Only three Black filmmakers directed Hollywood films with budgets at or over $100 million. The upper limit of production budgets for African Americans was $130 million, achieved by Tim Story for *Fantastic Four: Rise of the Silver Surfer* (2007, Fox). Antoine Fuqua's *King Arthur* (2004, Buena Vista) was made for $120 million, while Tim Story's *Fantastic Four* (2005, Fox) was made for $100 million. No Latino-directed film crossed the $100 million mark. The largest budget for a Latino-directed film was $85 million for Guillermo del Toro's *Hellboy II*.

Unlike Asian, Latino, and Black filmmakers, White directors received considerably larger production budgets with over 150 White-directed films having production budgets at or over $100 million and more than 20 with budgets above $200 million. The upper limit for White directors was $300 million for Gore Verbinski's *Pirates of the Caribbean: At World's End* (2007, Buena Vista), the third film in the *Pirates of the Caribbean* franchise. All of the top budgeted films for Black, White, and Asian directors were blockbuster franchises, suggesting that only White directors are hired to direct the most lucrative franchise films (Erigha, 2015b).

Clearly, Whites in Hollywood occupy the highest rungs of production budgets. They also direct the majority of films in the lucrative science fiction/fantasy genre, with the largest average budgets, theatrical releases, and box office grosses of any genre. Filmmaker Reginald Hudlin expressed his frustration with not being able to direct a science fiction (SF) film in Hollywood. Hudlin said:

> For me, I sort of looked at George Lucas' career. He did the teen comedy *American Graffiti* and went on to do *Star Wars*. I always wanted to do the same thing. I figured I'd do *House Party* and then do my version of *Star Wars*. I had a big sci-fi project, several of them, that I kept trying to get off the ground and wasn't successful at getting those off the ground. It hit this glass ceiling in Hollywood.
>
> (Morales, 2012)

Hudlin's SF project never took off, perhaps because this is a genre where few African Americans ever produce Hollywood films. Collectively, Black, Asian, and Latino directors experience great underrepresentation in the SF/fantasy genre. Not only are their voices notably absent from making conjectures about the future, they also miss out on projects that are lucrative for prosperous career trajectories.

In contemporary Hollywood cinema, racial groups are segregated into specific film genres and virtually excluded from others. For instance, Black directors are overrepresented behind the camera of music genre films, which have strong elements and themes of musicality, singing, hip-hop culture, rap, and dance. Part of Black directors' overrepresentation in the music genre stems from the number of African Americans who, prior to becoming film directors, had careers directing music videos. For example, DJ Pooh, F. Gary Gray, and Sanaa Hamri forged careers directing music videos for prominent artists before making the transition to feature filmmaking. Additionally, Black directors' overrepresentation in the music genre is a likely consequence of their tendency to be excluded from presumed intellectually minded SF genres and typecast within the entertainment and performance fields where they are assumed, stereotypically so, to have innate talents and abilities (Friedman, 2011; Rhines, 2003).

With regard to genre, Latino directors primarily direct dramas, though they also have a substantial presence in horror/thriller, romance, and comedy genres. Asians were most represented in the horror/thriller genre, directing popular horror films like Hideo Nakata's *The Ring Two* (2005), James Wan's *Saw* (2004) and *Dead Silence* (2007), James Wong's *Final Destination* (2000) and *Final Destination 3* (2006), and Takashi Shimizu's *The Grudge* (2004) and *The Grudge 2* (2006). Though this segmentation reflects the popularity of the horror genre in Asian popular culture, it is also indicative of Hollywood's propensity to concentrate the inclusion of Asian directors into a niche market.

Intersectionality

Hollywood film directing remains a male-dominated occupation, perhaps due to its location in technical fields, wherein women have been historically underrepresented and women of color have been virtually nonexistent. For each racial/ethnic group, men were the majority of directors, while women were in the minority. As the most established group in the directing occupation, White men directed 82% of films compared to 6% directed by White women. A gender gap also existed between the presence of Black male and female directors, albeit a much smaller gap than that between White men and women, since both Black men and women make up only a small percentage of the total population of Hollywood directors. Black men comprised of 6% of Hollywood directors, while Black women approached 1%. Even for Asians and Latinos, the gender gap in directing persisted. Asian men accounted for around 2% of directors, while Latino men accounted for 1% of directors. Together, Latinas and Asian women comprised of less than 1% of directors. Therefore, altogether women of color comprised of less than 2% of Hollywood directors of contemporary films, a dismal percentage that is in dire need of attention to increase women of color's presence in technical behind-the-scenes positions in the film industry.

Due to the double burden of race and gender inequality, it is no surprise that women of color are vastly underrepresented in Hollywood filmmaking (Collins, 2009). Few women of color are able to sustain careers directing multiple films. Some notable exceptions are Gina Prince-Bythewood, who directed *Love & Basketball* (2000) and *The Secret Life of Bees* (2008), and

Kasi Lemmons, the filmmaker behind the camera of *The Caveman's Valentine* (2001) and *Talk to Me* (2007). Kasi Lemmons discussed the challenges of being a female filmmaker of color in Hollywood.

> I don't wake up every day and say: I am a Black woman what do I do? You know it's only when I'm in a meeting with a bunch of directors or I look at statistics that I'm like: I got to hold it down from where I am. I don't dwell on it. The biggest challenges are always getting into the rooms that you need to get into and having people open to the types of stories that I want to tell. And I feel that just being a female director and doing that is a big deal in this country. On my third movie, I worked with a French DP [director of photography]. I asked him has he ever worked with a woman director before? He said in France a third of directors are women; so you can't avoid them. So I realized that the US is behind.
>
> (Dowell, 2013)

Lemmons suggested that Hollywood studio executives are not always open to the types of stories that she, as a Black woman, would like to tell. Another striking remark was that gender inequality was not as stark in France compared to the U.S. She noted "the U.S. is behind" with its failure to incorporate racial and gender diversity in its national agenda. Culture industries like Hollywood need only to look across the Atlantic Ocean to France, or also to Nigeria's Nollywood industry, to see noteworthy examples of film industries that include rather than exclude myriad ethnic and gender groups from their populations.

Unlike films helmed by male directors, female-directed films are not as likely to be distributed by major studios, but rather distributed by studios outside of Hollywood's core. For example, each of Asian filmmaker Gurinder Chadha's three films was distributed by studios outside of Hollywood's core: *Bend It Like Beckham* (2003, Fox Searchlight), *Bride and Prejudice* (2005, Miramax), and *What's Cooking* (2000, Lionsgate). Furthermore, Latinas, Black women, and Asian women are also concentrated into few genres, primarily directing comedies, dramas, and romance films, and largely excluded from more financially lucrative action and SF/fantasy genres. With women of color vastly underrepresented in Hollywood and relegated to few movies, their sole method of effectively producing popular culture remains on the independent track, though this path has limitations for reaching mainstream audiences.

Conclusion

Behind-the-scenes representation of Black, Asian, and Latino directors in Hollywood remains limited and problematic. Their persistent inability to construct images and characters that appear in mainstream media raises questions about the extent of their influence over media images. Furthermore, their placement in restricted genres raises the issue of which roles they are able to penetrate behind the scenes and which roles still remain elusive for them to occupy. With Black, Asian, and Latino directors having little representation in mainstream studios and facing near exclusion in lucrative genres, contemporary racial ideologies in cinema will likely continue to reaffirm the status quo of a White power structure, rather than offer nuanced characters derived from a diverse set of cultural creators. Likely, more filmmakers from diverse racial/ethnic groups working on cultural products in a variety of genres will move us closer to ensuring that on-screen images more appropriately reflect the desires and worldviews of diverse audiences. What remains most surprising is the fact that racial minorities in the U.S. are actually the collective racial majority in Los Angeles, with Latinos being the majority group. Yet, these demographic increases appear to have no bearing on the racial/ethnic composition of Hollywood studios, which still remain inflexible to changes in the surrounding social milieu.

However, it is ever vital that diverse racial groups participate in the production of mainstream culture for many reasons. Movies, in particular, have an expansive reach in American and global culture. Thus, exclusion from being a vibrant faction in the construction and manufacturing of mainstream culture prevents underrepresented groups from exerting their influence on what is at present a monolithic representation of America. Being underrepresented in the film industry also constitutes a denial of citizenship rights, including the right to produce and be recognized in the nation's dominant cultural myths, narratives, and images (Tillet, 2012). Moreover, the film industry is yet another area where high unemployment disproportionately plagues underrepresented racial/ethnic groups in America. Alternatively, media and cultural industries should be places where people can strive for and potentially achieve access to greater employment opportunities, from highly visible positions like actors, producers, and directors, to positions with considerably less visibility like costume designers, sound engineers, and colorists. Gaining work in film directing reaps benefits for employment in a high-paying and lucrative occupation. Employment of Black, Asian, and Latino filmmakers in directing also holds importance for increasing their presence in other behind-the-scenes and on-screen positions. In positions of influence on film sets, African American, Asian, and Latino filmmakers are able to advocate for and address diversity in other positions, which leads to breaking down color barriers on "lily-white" film crews (Reid, 2005). Hence, their employment as directors has pronounced benefits that extend beyond any single individual.

While Black, Asian, and Latino representation as Hollywood film directors lags well behind their proportion of the U.S. population, ironically, their support for Hollywood productions actually surpasses their share of the population. As audiences, they are overrepresented, comprising 44% of frequent moviegoers (MPAA, 2015, p. 12). Because of this disproportionate representation at the box office, one might say that these groups actually *overpay* as moviegoers. To their misfortune, their overexcitement to spend hard-earned dollars supporting the film industry does not readily translate into more support behind the scenes of Hollywood. Since their percentage of behind-the-scenes employment does not meet their percentage of the general population, much less exceed it to meet their share of box office receipts, it is fair to suggest that Black, Latino, and Asian audiences are being shortchanged—paying more proportionally for movies, but not receiving their comparable piece of the pie in exchange in the back end. At this contemporary moment, members of underrepresented racial groups still have a long way to go to make their mark on an industry that creates and disseminates mainstream culture, presumably on behalf of all Americans. Rather than trying not to hire Mexicans, a disservice that Chris Rock intimated studios regularly commit, Hollywood studios must make the effort to prioritize diversity if its films are to ever reflect the rich, multifaceted character of the American populace.

Note

1. I compiled data on films, directors, actors, film organizations, and box office receipts on films using three online databases as primary sources: Box Office Mojo (www.boxofficemojo.com), the Internet Movie Database (www.imdb.com), and The Numbers (www.the-numbers.com). A number of scholars have used these databases in previous research (e.g., Banjo, 2013; Hughey, 2009; King, 2008; Lincoln & Allen, 2004; Ndounou, 2014; Zuckerman, Kim, Ukanwa, & von Rittmann 2003).

References

Banjo, O. O. (2013). For us only? Examining the effect of viewing context on Black audiences' perceived influence of Black entertainment. *Race and Social Problems*, 5, 309–322.

Bonilla-Silva, E. (1997). Rethinking racism: Toward a structural interpretation. *American Sociological Review*, 62(3), 465–480.

Bielby, W., & Bielby, D. (1999). Organizational mediation of project-based labor markets: Talent agencies and the careers of screenwriters. *American Sociological Review*, 64, 64–85.

Chiang, L. (2003). *Better Luck Tomorrow*, today: An interview with director Justin Lin. *AsianConnections*. Retrieved from http://v1.asianconnections.com/entertainment/interviews/2003/04/17/justin.lin/.

Collins, P. H. (2009). *Black feminist thought: Knowledge, consciousness, and the politics of empowerment*. Boston, MA: Unwin Hyman.

Dowell, M. (2013). Interview: Kasi Lemmons & Raphael Saadiq talk "Black Nativity"—Casting, soundtrack & more. *Indiewire*. Retrieved from http://blogs.indiewire.com/shadowandact/interview-kasi-lemmons-raphael-saadiq-talk-black-nativity-casting-soundtrack-more.

Erigha, M. (2015a). Race, gender, Hollywood: Representation in cultural production and digital media's potential for change. *Sociology Compass*, 9(1), 78–89.

Erigha, M. (2015b). *Black directors, science fiction film, and race bound practices in contemporary Hollywood.* Unpublished manuscript.

Friedman, R. J. (2011). *Hollywood's African American films: The transition to sound.* New Brunswick, NJ: Rutgers University Press.

Hughey, M. W. (2009). Cinethetic racism: White redemption and Black stereotypes in "magical Negro" films. *Social Problems, 56*(3), 543–577.

Hunt, D., Ramon, A. C., & Price, Z. (2014). 2014 *Hollywood diversity report: Making sense of the disconnect.* Los Angeles, CA: Ralph J. Bunche Center for African American Studies at UCLA.

King, N. (2008). Generic womanhood: Gendered depictions in cop action cinema. *Gender & Society, 22*(2), 238–260.

Lincoln, A. E., & Allen, M. P. (2004). Double jeopardy in Hollywood: Age and gender in the careers of film actors, 1926–1999. *Sociological Forum, 19*(4), 611–631.

Morales, W. (2012, July 1). Exclusive: Director Reginald Hudlin talks *Boomerang* 20 years later, *Black Panther*, and producing *Django Unchained*. *Black Film.* Retrieved from http://www.blackfilm.com/read/2012/07/director-reginald-hudlin-talks-boomerang-20-years-later-black-panther-django-unchained/.

MPAA. (2015). Theatrical market statistics 2014. *Motion Picture Association of America.* Retrieved from www.mpaa.org/wp-content/uploads/2015/03/MPAA-Theatrical-Market-Statistics-2014.pdf.

Ndounou, M. W. (2014). *Shaping the future of African American film: Color-coded economics and the story behind the numbers.* New Brunswick, NJ: Rutgers University Press.

Reid, M. (2005). *Black lenses, black voices: African American film now.* Lanham, MD: Rowman & Littlefield.

Rhines, J. A. (2003). Black film/Black future. *The Black Scholar, 33*(1), 47–53.

Rock, C. (2014). Chris Rock pens blistering essay on Hollywood's race problem: It's a white industry. *The Hollywood Reporter.* Retrieved from http://www.hollywoodreporter.com/news/top-five-filmmaker-chris-rock-753223.

Schatz, T. (2009). *Film theory and contemporary Hollywood movies.* New York, NY: Routledge.

Smith, S. L., & Choueiti, M. (2011). *Black characters in popular film: Is the key to diversifying cinematic content held in the hand of the Black director?* Los Angeles, CA: Annenberg School for Communication and Journalism.

Thakore, B. (2014). Must-see TV: South Asian characterizations in American popular media. *Sociology Compass, 8*(2), 149–156.

Tillet, S. (2012). *Sites of slavery: Citizenship and racial democracy in the post-civil rights imagination.* Durham, NC: Duke University Press.

U.S. Census Bureau. (2015). *State and county quick facts.* Retrieved from http://quickfacts.census.gov/qfd/states/.

Yuen, N. W. (2004). Performing race, negotiating identity: Asian American professional actors in Hollywood. In J. Lee & M. Zhou (Eds.), *Asian American youth culture, identity, and ethnicity* (pp. 251–262). New York, NY: Routledge.

Yuen, N. W. (2010). Playing "ghetto": Black actors, stereotypes, and authenticity. In D. Hunt & A. C. Ramon (Eds.), *Black Los Angeles: American dreams and racial realities* (pp. 232–242). New York, NY: New York University Press.

Zuckerman, E. W., Kim, T. Y., Ukanwa, K., & von Rittmann, J. (2003). Robust identities or nonentities? *American Journal of Sociology, 108*, 1018–1074.

5 Is Carlos Mencia A White Wetback?
*Media*ting the (E)Racing of U.S. Central Americans in the Latino Imaginary

Maritza Cárdenas

Buried within the files of YouTube is a video that illuminates the location U.S. Central Americans occupy within the U.S./Latino imaginary.[1] In the video, an Anglo-American man confronts a Honduran-born immigrant over his identity. One of the accusations was that said man had created a fake identity in order to perform and keep his job. To authenticate himself to his Anglo-American accuser, the Honduran man pulls out his "green card" to verify not his citizenship, but his ethnoracial ancestry. Watching the video, one witnesses an odd inversion taking place, since generally individuals who have phenotypical brown and dark features are automatically located as racialized subjects. However, in this video it is clear that the Honduran—and by extension the Central American—body is read *outside* Latino and U.S. American imaginaries. That U.S. Central Americans are omitted from the larger Anglo-American imaginary is not a new revelation, as it has been repeatedly asserted within Latino scholarship that ethnoracial subjects like Latinos are perpetually perceived as "foreign" both civically and culturally to the U.S. American body politic (Flores & Benmayor, 1997; Habell-Pallán & Romero, 2002; Lima, 2007). What is particularly noteworthy then, and what this chapter aims to highlight, is the way U.S. Central American bodies are not as legible as other Latino subgroups due to dominant media representations of *Latinidad*. Although the category "Latino" is a complex signifier used to refer to a strategic positioning within identity politics (Oboler, 1995; Padilla, 1985), a form of cultural citizenship for national groups from Latin America (Flores & Benmayor, 1997), a type of larger panethnicity (Flores, 2000), or a marketing ploy (Dávila, 2001), a general definition of the term sees it as one which is applied to "any citizen or resident with Latin American heritage" (Allatson, 2007, p. 140). Within all these varied definitions, U.S. Central Americans should be viewed as a part of this larger panethnicity and yet, they are routinely displaced from the Latino imaginary.

In the context of the aforementioned video, this Central American marginal body politic is different, perhaps even peculiar, because the individual is none other than Honduran-born comedian Carlos Mencia, one of the most visible faces in U.S. popular culture, and the YouTube video is the notorious "Joe Rogan Vs Carlos Mencia" (2007)—a text for which its "virality" is continually indexed in media spaces as the source for Mencia's decline into obscurity.[2] In February 2007, Mencia was enjoying a type of cultural visibility rarely given to Latino performers, his comedic hybrid show comprised of sketches, skits, and standup, titled *The Mind of Mencia* (2005–2008) on Comedy Central was averaging 2.1 million viewers, making it the highest rated show in cable television for its time slot. Earlier that month Bud Light had chosen him as its spokesperson when he starred in its Super Bowl commercial, and later that year he would be featured in a minor role in a major motion picture film *The Heartbreak Kid* (2007). In all of these media spaces Mencia is (self-)portrayed as an ethnoracial subject, leading one to ask, what made Mencia's hypervisible racialized brown body and ethnic cultural features so unintelligible in that confrontation with Rogan for him to be required to prove that he was "ethnic" by using his green card?

This chapter argues that the ethnoracial erasure present in the crisis over Mencia's identity is an effect of media representations of Latinidad, which have made this term synonymous with particular racial, national, and cultural markers that inadvertently exclude other collectivities like U.S. Central Americans. In it, I read Carlos Mencia as a text whose physical and discursive body operates as the site where relations of power are enacted upon, due to the structuring effects of dominant media narratives, which make the signifiers "Honduran" and "Central American" unintelligible. Using examples from Internet blogs, YouTube videos, film, television and print, this chapter highlights the impact media constructions of Latinidad have in coding certain social bodies and groups as "Latino" and excluding others by analyzing the discourse surrounding the accusation that Carlos Mencia is not "ethnic" but a "White" man passing as "Mexican."

Methods

Drawing on discourse analysis, this chapter uses the Mencia controversy as a case study to examine the effects of media representations and ideologies about Latino ethnoracial identity. According to Fiske (1996), a discursive analysis "focuses on what statements are made rather than *how* they are made" and calls attention to the processes "by which discourses work to repress, marginalize, and invalidate others" (p. 305). As Avila-Saavedra (2011) and Valdivia (2010) have noted, discourse analysis illuminates "how media language legitimates or defies social relations and cultural perceptions" (Avila-Saavedra, 2011, p. 277). Therefore, a detailed interrogation of the socio-cultural factors that generated the Mencia controversy, as well as the language deployed within it, is critical since it serves to reveal how power and the parameters of Latinidad become enforced in media spaces and everyday practices that regulate and govern bodies, institutionalize certain discourses, and produce subjects.

To accomplish this task, the texts and citations from online forums were chosen for this analysis as representative of common thematic concerns about Mencia and his ethnoracial illegibility. Using major online search engines, I produced 737,000 preliminary results using "Mencia" as a keyword. These results were narrowed to 188,000 using the search heading "Carlos Mencia not Hispanic," and further edited down to 82,600 using the search title "Carlos Mencia not Mexican." Interestingly, despite the popular perception that the Mencia controversy was about plagiarism, there were only 17,100 results for the search "Carlos Mencia joke thief." Once narrowed, I took sample citations from forums with postings during the height of the controversy years (2005–2007), as well as from different online spaces related to Mencia such as Carlos Mencia's own official website, reviews of Mencia's work on popular online merchants like Amazon.com, and websites devoted entirely to the craft of comedy like Chucklemonkey.com (now defunct). Noteworthy is that despite the fact that none of these forums were directly about ethnoracial topics and all catered to particular subject positions ("fan," "consumer," or fellow "comedian"), they all shared an interest in deciphering Mencia's ethnoracial status.

Constructing a Latino "Grid of Intelligibility"

Post-structuralist theorists have asserted that our epistemological understandings are formed by "grid(s) of intelligibility," which operate as conceptual frameworks for the way we come to understand subjects or recognize modes of selfhood (Butler, 1990; Foucault, 1978, 2003). As McWhorter (2004) explained, such "grids" are more than just "a network of knowledge" since they function as "the routine exercise of social and political power. It is a network of power/knowledge" (p. 153). Butler (1990) revealed that for gender and sexual identities, a heterosexual matrix renders some bodies as intelligible, while those that do not conform "appear only as developmental failures or logical impossibilities" (p. 17). For Butler, dominant modes of understanding limit the kinds of bodies we see and place within a particular type of social order. Those that "fail" or are unintelligible are those that fall outside the matrix of heterosexual desire. However, it is these "developmental failures or logical impossibilities" that can lead us to interrogate these regulatory modes of legibility (Butler, 1990, p. 17).

Like Butler, I seek to expose visible dominant modes of cultural understanding by arguing that the Carlos Mencia controversy is a result of how Honduran experiences, and by extension U.S. Central American experiences, fall outside of hegemonic articulations of Latinidad circulated in the media. Indeed, media texts are critical institutional sites for producing their own matrix of intelligibility and ordering among social bodies. Kellner (1995) has claimed that media culture is "both constituted by and constitutive of larger social and political dynamics" (p. 5) and as such becomes an organizing principle for societies as dominant media forms "shape everyday life, influencing how people think and behave, how they see themselves and other people" (p. 2). Similarly, Beltrán (2009) has suggested that media representations of Latinoness "provide images to non-Latinos of who and what Latina/os might be" (p. 2), and arguably prevent the broader culture from viewing certain subjects as Latino. In what follows I outline how the media has been a vital component in the racialization of Latinos, often rendering the term legible of only certain national experiences.

The Racialization of Latinos in the Media

Several institutions, including census categories, state policies, and the media have been pivotal in delineating what it means to be Latino (Dávila, 2001; Omi & Winant, 2014). According to the U.S. Census Bureau, Hispanic/Latinos are not a racial group but an ethnic group. Those who classify themselves as Hispanic/Latino ethnicity can mark themselves as being any race including White. Yet, within representational practices, particularly in mass media forms such as films, television, major magazines, and newspaper print, "Latino" is viewed as both an ethnic and racial category. Media scholars have repeatedly demonstrated how the media has been instrumental in the process of racialization for Latinos (Berg, 2002; Dávila 2001; Noriega & López, 1996; Rodriguez, 1997; Valdivia, 2010). Racialization, as described by Miles (1989), "refers to the process of categorization, a representational process of defining an Other (usually, but not exclusively) somatically" (p. 75). In the case of Latinos, Oboler (1995) has argued that 19th century popular print forms like journalistic and travel writing narratives served to solidify racist ideologies like Manifest Destiny and Social Darwinism that positioned people of "Mexican, and later Latin American descent" not only as inherently "foreign Others" (p. 42) but also inherently inferior to Anglo-Americans (p. 34). Early films continued circulating these racial ideologies, where Mexican characters were often visually portrayed not only as racially different in phenotype, but also depicted as dishonest, irrational, violent, and dirty (Berg 2002, p. 113). This one-dimensional characterization was not limited to just Mexicans; as Perez (1997) has revealed, anti-Puerto Rican stereotypes that had dominated print media were also re-created cinematically (p. 147). According to Berg (2002), cinematic representations of Latinidad can be categorized into six stereotypes—the Bandito, the Half-Breed Harlot, the Male Buffoon, the Female Clown, the Latin Lover, and the Dark Lady—all of which not only mark Latinos as racial subjects but radically different to Anglo-American characterizations.

Latinos have also been ascribed with particular phenotypical and ethnic characteristics. Rodriguez (1997) has contended that a dominant phenotypic face of Latinidad can be seen in the media, one embodied by a person who is "slightly tan, with dark hair and eyes" (p. 1). Likewise, Dávila (2001) has noted that a generic pan-Hispanic look has been fostered in the media by advertisers who link Hispanic "with features such as darker/olive complected skin and brown-black hair" (p. 111). These racialized and classed visual images, which Rodriguez and Dávila refer to as "Latin Looks," have influenced how many U.S. Americans come to understand and categorize who falls within and outside a term like "Latino."

If the media has served to ferment the notion of Latinos as a particular ethnoracial subject, it has also linked this construct with particular national experiences.[3] As mentioned, throughout the 20th century, film, television, and print often linked certain national signifiers such as Puerto Rican and Mexican as inherently outside of the Anglo-American imaginary by perpetually representing these groups with negative qualities and characteristics (e.g., Mexicans as "greasers" or *bandidos* in Western films and Puerto Ricans as gang members in *West Side Story*). However, as problematic as these representations were for positioning these populations as inherently racially and culturally inferior, these constructions nonetheless rendered them legible for audiences. That is, although clearly construed as "Latin" Others, and a threat to Anglo-American civility, the hypervisibility of these negative stereotypes enabled legibility because being framed as second-class citizens still posited these groups within that broader national imaginary (albeit negatively). These early negative media representations of "Mexicans" and "Puerto Ricans," therefore, enabled the conditions to conceive of a panethnic category like Latino; their constant positioning as racial, linguistic, and cultural outsiders allowed these various groups to collectively see themselves as a broader social problem and facilitate a mode of belonging (Padilla, 1985). These media-based codifying practices, inadvertently sustain a Latino grid of intelligibility by allowing audiences and society to view certain bodies, geopolitical spaces, and nationalities as Latino, while those not represented become rendered as "logical impossibilities." As such, the Mencia controversy can be seen as an effect of these processes of legibility that render Honduranness unintelligible within dominant mediated understandings of Latinidad.

The Mind of Mencia

On July 6, 2005, the cable network Comedy Central premiered a new television show titled *The Mind of Mencia*. The show was created and hosted by Ned Arnel Mencia, also known by his stage persona of Carlos Mencia. Mencia, who was born in San Pedro Sula, Honduras, immigrated to the United States as a young child to live with extended family in Los Angeles. It seems odd that a subject with this immigrant background and whose career firmly entrenched him as an "ethnic" comedian, would one day have to prove himself a racialized Non-White subject. From the outset of his career, media producers labeled Mencia as a "Latino" comic. His participation and hosting of "Latino" marketed shows such as *Comedy Compadres* (1993), *Loco Slam* (1994), *Funny is Funny* (1998), and the comedy tour *The Three Amigos* (2002), furthered the notion that Mencia was the new up-and-coming Latino comedian. Not surprisingly, in 2005 when *The Mind of Mencia* debuted, journalists viewed the show and its creator as decisively ethnic. The *New York Post* confidently defined Mencia as a "Latino comic" (Kaplan, 2005); *Variety* described the show in ethnoracial tropes labeling it "salsa-flavored" and "racially tinged comedy" (Lowry, 2005); while the *New York Times* referred to Mencia's style of comedy as "ethnic barbs," one emerging from a "very specific [Hispanic] point of view" (Ogunnaike, 2005).

The show itself also promoted this notion of Mencia as an ethnoracial Latino subject. The opening sequence for the pilot episode, for example, contained a Mariachi band playing in the background. While Mariachi musical sound and the aesthetics that contribute to that style of performance are of Mexican origin, they are considered icons of Latino culture both within Anglo-American and Latino imaginaries (Beebee, 2014, p. 458). In using the images and sounds of Mariachi for the debut episode, the show and its creator were appealing to established culturally sanctioned norms of Latinoness. In addition to infusing the show with such authenticating measures, Mencia would also commonly refer to himself as a "beaner"—a derogatory term usually ascribed to "a person of Hispanic background." Indeed, one of the show's segments was called "Out the Beaner" where Mencia showcased celebrities who despite not being viewed as Latino by popular media outlets could be considered part of that group. In one segment Mencia focused on the athlete Reggie Jackson, telling the audience that he is "actually a Puerto Rican" and concluding with "Sorry Black people, he's one of ours" (Mencia, 2005). In claiming Jackson as "one of ours" Mencia not only exposes how media depictions of Latinidad frame it outside of Blackness, but also squarely positions himself as Latino via his iteration and identification with a collective " us/ours." Though at times segments in Mencia's show cast light on the fact that Latinos could be of any racial group, other moments stressed the notion that beaner was a Non-White category. Many of Mencia's stand-up jokes involved using the second and distant pronoun "you" to refer to White people. One joke titled "White People Camping" begins by Mencia saying, "White people you do things I just don't understand," adding, "I'm sure you look at what some of the beaners do and say, 'what the hell are you doing?'" (Mencia, 2007). In structuring his joke in this manner Mencia creates an "us/them" racial binary that posits White people as outside of the category of beaner—a term he uses as a mode of self-identification.

Outside of his show, Mencia would use moments of authorized speaking in media spaces like television interviews to highlight the way dominant representations of Latinidad limit the kind of subjects and signifiers deemed recognizable as Latino. One of his more poignant comedic performances emerged in a television interview with Conan O'Brien (2006), where Mencia narrated how his nationality as a Honduran at times makes him unintelligible among audiences:

> I grew up in East LA, where like everybody's Mexican ... I was known as the "White wetback" because of my name, "Ned." And then they would call me the "wetter wetback" because I was born in Honduras ... They didn't even know where Honduras was. My friends would come

up to me and say, "Ned, tell them where you were born." I was born in Honduras. "See, I told you he's Cambodian!" [...] Then when I started to do comedy, the owner of the Comedy Store [Mitzi Gaynor] would tell me, "You can't be an angry Mexican named Ned." First of all, I'm not Mexican, "everybody thinks your Mexican. You're in LA!" So that's kind of weird because everybody thinks I'm Mexican when I'm in LA. And then I come here [New York], and everyone's like "Puerto Rican," no Honduran. And then when I go to Miami they're like "Cuban."

Mencia's performance directly addresses the way audiences, peers, and the culture writ large has rendered his Honduranness undefinable. His statements also highlight how racial ideologies and national/cultural identities like Mexican and Latino become defined and regulated in seemingly inconsequential cultural exchanges, often at the exclusion of U.S. Central Americans. For example, the pejorative and dehumanizing "White wetback" designation hurled at Mencia is strange—in a rich, troubling, and complicated way. As a racialized term often associated with illegal immigration, "wetbacks" have been seen as "those people" falling outside the U.S. national imaginary.[4] Since the term invariably connotes Non-Whiteness, to be a "White wetback," then, seems like an oxymoron, an irony that casts light on the racialization process of Latinos who can simultaneously be White and Non-White. And yet, Mencia is not only the White wetback but also the "wetter wetback," a double alien, an illegible wetback deviating from standard East LA Mexican/Mexican-Americanness and recognizable Latin/Americanness. Again, the moniker of wetter wetback reads paradoxical for how can some Latino immigrants be more illegal or wetter than others when the state views all undocumented and arguably all Latino immigrants, as alien and foreign? More than the standard alien in the United States, Mencia is a derivative unrecognizable one, further orientalized geographically and phonetically through an unknown region where Honduran is not distinguished from Cambodian. The term "Honduran" in this anecdote is an empty signifier; it means nothing, it is simply read as "foreign" and not "Mexican." Honduran here is translated into a "Third World" Otherness, whereby a country like Honduras can be substituted for a Non-Latin American/Spanish speaking country like Cambodia. Via this narration, Mencia elucidates how U.S. Central American experiences become expunged, as Honduranness is decisively viewed as Other, but not exactly a Non-White Latino Other.

Mencia's televised performance also emphasizes the powerful role the media landscape occupies in conceiving Latinidad by disclosing how the term has become synonymous with localized national identities in Los Angeles, New York, and Miami. His observation that whenever he performs in these metropolises people readily assume that he is Mexican, Puerto Rican, or Cuban, despite his insistence that he is Honduran, suggests that audiences can only understand or read his body via dominant representations of Latinidad. This homogenizing reading of Mencia's identity is further exemplified in his recollection of how his stage persona came to existence. According to Mencia, "Carlos" was born because the Comedy Store owner Mitzi Gaynor told him "he can't be an angry Mexican named Ned." Valdivia (2010) has asserted that the power to name is an "intensely political act"; it is a demonstration and an exercise of power since historically it was colonized peoples that were usually named by the colonizers (p. 9). Being able to name oneself is an assertion of autonomy, yet this act is denied to Mencia for when he insists that he is not Mexican, Gaynor tells him, "everyone thinks you're Mexican, you're in LA."

While Gaynor's declaration is an oversimplification, it nonetheless exemplifies the prominent visibility Mexican/Mexican-American cultural experiences occupy within media representations of Latinidad in Los Angeles and the Greater Southwest. For instance, films such as *La Bamba* (1987), *Stand and Deliver* (1987), and *Born in East LA* (1987), which are viewed as ushering in the epoch of the "Hispanic Hollywood Boom," or the "Latino Boom," did not showcase panethnic/national experiences (as the titles suggest), but focused on Mexican-American experiences in the Southwest. This trend would continue as other commercially successful films about "Latino" culture would make this term equivalent with Mexican-American culture, such as *American Me* (1992), *Mi Familia/My Family* (1995), and the hugely successful *Selena* (1997). With the exception of *I Love Lucy* and, more recently, *Ugly Betty* (2006–2010), the small screen would further solidify this association as most television shows with a lead Latino character have taken place in California and have been focused on Mexican-American culture.[5] Popular shows like *Chico and the Man* (1974–1978), *The George Lopez Show* (2002–2007), and not as commercially successful but critically acclaimed dramas like *American Family* (2002–2004) and *Resurrection Blvd* (2000–2002) all had Mexican-American lead characters and all of them utilized Southern California as their setting.

Thus, when Mencia claims that Gaynor tells him, "everyone thinks you're Mexican, you're in LA" he is bringing to bear the way media discourse taxonomizes Latino bodies in the Southwest. Mencia's narration elucidates the ways in which U.S. society enforces homogenization and inscribes racialized bodies by insisting that his brown body is easily legible as a Latino if it is also labeled Mexican. His admission to Gaynor of being Honduran, by contrast, bears no signification since it falls outside current media articulations of Latinoness. Consequently, the persona of "Carlos Mencia," as the public now recognizes him, needs to be read as an effect of mediated discourses of Latinidad, which try to discipline Mencia into becoming a proper intelligible Latino subject. His existence is produced from the idea that one cannot have an angry Honduran named Ned perform Latino comedy. Mediated notions of Latinoness necessitate, instead, an angry Mexican named Carlos to legitimize the position of serving as a Latino commentator.

78 *Maritza Cárdenas*

(E)Racing Mencia: the Controversy

Gaynor would not be the only one to find Mencia's Honduranness illegible. Despite Mencia's self-declaration of being a beaner, and media outlets labeling him as a Latino comic, in 2005 fellow comedian Joe Rogan and others began to publicly accuse Mencia of being a joke plagiarist and an ethnic imposter. One source of contention was Mencia's name change. While many actors and comedians adopt stage names for their public careers, this seemingly routine practice was read with a deeper sense of mistrust. Rather than seeing the imposition of the name "Carlos" onto the individual Ned as an effect of power—whereby Mencia's body lacks the autonomy to be interpreted as anything other than Mexican—his name change fueled a controversy surrounding Mencia's talent and ethnicity. Comedians Joe Rogan and George Lopez in particular, used his name change as evidence of how Mencia was an overall fraud:

> The latest, and most disgusting joke thief of all is a guy named "Carlos Mencia." The REALLY crazy thing is that's not even his real name. He sells himself as being Mexican, but the reality is his real name is Ned Holness, and he's actually half German and half Honduran. The Mexican hook is something he did to ingratiate himself with the local Mexican population of L.A.
>
> (Rogan, 2005)

> I'd check his lineage too ... The guy was pretty liberal with some of my [George Lopez's] material ... the guy is like Honduran-German ... Why would you pretend to be [Mexican]? Why not go for Basque or Sweden ... I think he had that intention from the beginning that he was going to play a Mexican.
>
> (Lopez & Stern, 2005)

Ironically, these accusations about Mencia being an ethnic imposter rely on essentialized notions of Latinoness and Mexican/Mexican-Americanness—ones circulated in stereotypical depictions of Latinos in the media. Why, for instance, is "Carlos" associated as an authentically Mexican/Latino name more so than "Ned"? What enables Lopez and Rogan to interpret Mencia's stand-up performance and public character as an enactment of Mexican/Mexican-Americanness? Does engaging in Latino humor automatically suggest that the speaker has to be Mexican/Mexican-American, lest they be accused of "playing Mexican"? Furthermore, the notion that some individuals are "performing" or "playing Mexican" implies that there are certain static characteristics that constitute Mexicanness. In addition to relying on a static notion of Mexican identity, these statements automatically assume that certain cultural markers are invariably fixed as Mexican/Mexican-American, thereby denying the possibility for other Latino groups to employ similar types of cultural codes. They also problematically think of Mexican/Mexican-American and by extension Latino as being synonymous with particular racial groups and limited to a particular Spanish colonial history. The idea that Mencia has German heritage and this negates his ability to perform Latino comedy endorses the media characterization that Latinos are Non-White, Non-European subjects.

Their comments, however, also simultaneously challenge uncritical notions of an inter-Latino essence whereby national groups are assumed to inherently understand each other's socio-political location due to their marginalization from the broader U.S. American culture. For instance, although Rogan's assumption that Mencia can only ingratiate himself into the Mexican/Mexican-American community is problematic because he minimizes the city's Central American presence, he is still cognizant of the ways Mexican-American experiences have obtained a type of cultural dominance within the Los Angeles landscape. Conversely, Lopez, who is Mexican-American, seems oblivious to the hegemonic location Mexican-American culture occupies within the Los Angeles Latino imaginary with the inquiry, "why would anyone pretend to be Mexican?"

Indeed, as narrated in Mexican-American produced films like *El Norte* (1983) and *Born in East LA* (1987), as well as the cultural expressions of U.S. Central Americans, the notion of passing is often less of a choice and more of an economic or social necessity.[6] The fact that both Central American and other Latino groups are aware of this cultural practice of passing and display it in cinematic representations reveals the disciplinary power of the Latino matrix of intelligibility. If Mencia, like so many other U.S. Central Americans, is opting to pass, then how can we explain the need of a Honduran—a supposed member of Latinidad—to adopt a Mexican/Mexican-American identity in order to be seen as a "legitimate" commentator on Latino culture?

Rogan's and Lopez's public charges generated a discursive explosion concerning Mencia's talent and ethnicity. Audiences, especially within cyberspace, became more obsessed with trying to decipher Mencia's ethnoracial status rather than the accusations of him being an unoriginal comic. Mencia was defamed in various Internet websites not so much for his "joke thievery," but for having an uncertain national identity, and specifically a Non-Mexican identity. In fact, these two states of alleged inauthenticity dialogue with one another as they both reduce Mencia to a copy, a mere mimic of someone else's intellectual and cultural property. His nationality became the central focus for most social media spaces where online users exhibited a desire to concretely situate him into one Latino national subgroup. Ironically, these attempts at deciphering his "true" ethnoracial national identity inadvertently ended up creating more ambiguity. Note these web blog postings about Mencia:

> Last I heard he's all Honduran, but being from LA he has a lot of the Mexicanisms. Saying he's part Mexican throughout his acts would, of course, give him more credibility.
>
> (Anonymous 1, 2006)

80 *Maritza Cárdenas*

> Carlos Mencia, a bad human being, a joke thief, and, even, a fake Mexican. He's half Guatemalan and half German, and all unoriginal comic. His name is only "Carlos Mencia" because his real name, Ned Holz [*sic*], didn't sound Mexican enough.
>
> (Anonymous 2, 2005)

> OMFG! Are you all idiots................Mencia is El Salvadorean [*sic*] he's said so himself look up his bio yes that's his birth name too MENCIA check that too.
>
> (Anonymous 3, 2005)

> Do you think the powers of PC would allow a white guy to get away with having a show like *Mind of Mencia*? Nein mein herr! Why am I speaking German? Because Carlos aka Ned Holness is actually half German and half Central American, not Mexican.
>
> (Anonymous 4, 2005)

Although one is tempted to read these comments by bloggers and online content users as an example of what Jenkins (2006) has labeled as "rogue readers"—audiences that are not passive consumers of media codes but instead resignify those codes—in this context they seem to illuminate the reverse. That is, while some of these statements resist the dominant framing of Mencia as Latino by viewing him as White, it is also clear that these readings are predicated upon a media-constructed grid of intelligibility about Latinidad. Even those statements that are trying to defend Mencia demonstrate how the signifier of Honduran functions as a "logical impossibility" within current understandings of Latinoness. Since the term lacks any dominant visual and media representations associated with it, in these Internet comments Honduran yet again occupies a space of empty signification. It is so forgettable and amorphous that it can easily be substituted for any other Central American "Third World" terrain. For these online users, Honduran does not conjure any distinct cultural references as it becomes easily substituted by other national categories like Guatemalan and Salvadoran (which appear here to be equally nebulous). Even more troubling is the implication that being Honduran is somehow less of a Latino experience than being Mexican-American. This lack of association between Honduran and Latino is best exemplified in the last comment cited, where the cyberuser refers to Mencia as a "White guy," presumably because of his half-German heritage. By seeing Mencia as only White, this facile reading erases tinges of his *othered* racial cultural formations, re-enacting the same form of exclusionary politics—and odd rhetoric of "White wetbackness"—that Mencia claims he faced as a child.

Though a limited sample, these blog discussions reveal how some media readers view Honduran as incommensurate with being Mexican-American. A Honduran American/ U.S. Central American identity in these discussions does not provide Mencia the same "credibility" that a Mexican-American experience does. The accusation that Mencia needed to pretend to be Mexican to obtain credibility, as stated by Rogan, Lopez, and Internet commentator Anonymous 1, at best implies that to be Honduran is to not have the same type of insight into Latino cultures as a Mexican-American experience provides, and at worse, does not read him as being Latino at all. The controversy here does not emerge exclusively because of Mencia's Honduranness but is produced from the fact that Mencia might be a Non-Mexican-American performing Latino comedy, a point emphasized by the fact that most online searches regarding Mencia's ethnoracial and national identity are presented in a negative manner (e.g., Is Carlos Mencia *not* Mexican?). The notion that some Latino subgroups are more authentic than others abounds in media culture. For example, newspaper reviews about *The Mind of Mencia,* even those that viewed him as Latino, often made it a point to note that Mencia was not Mexican (Obukenne, 2005; Booth, 2005). Via constant depictions of certain racialized bodies and national experiences in popular media forms, an internal hierarchy—if not expectation—emerges that allows audiences to assume which national constituencies are more representative of Latinidad than others. As such, the Mencia controversy needs to be read as the effect of media-circulated representations and ideologies regarding the ethnoracial and national status of Latinos. Far from innocuous, the controversy over Mencia's identity reveals the way media structures epistemology and, in the process, displaces Central Americans in Latino/U.S. American imaginaries.

Conclusion

Habell-Pallán and Romero (2002) remind us that "as emergent signifiers 'Latina' and 'Latino' have no fixed definition; historical and social location create shifting fields of meaning. The power to define these terms is political and economic and plays out symbolically in the imaginative products of the popular culture machine" (p. 2). As a component of that "popular culture machine," the controversy about Mencia's status as an ethnoracial subject highlights how the Latino matrix of intelligibility becomes enforced in every day practices and media spaces that maintain and create the parameters of what is included and excluded within Latino/U.S. American imaginaries. Within Mencia's own performances and statements made about him in online social media, his body as text becomes the site of disciplinary power where he is subjected to dominant modes of reading about who "he is" or "should be" by others. In doing so, the discourse surrounding this controversy reveals that while the category of Latino is not static, there are some problematic limitations that are deployed in certain cultural domains. It also illuminates the critical role media sites occupy for producing their own grid of intelligibility and ordering among social bodies. Additionally, it demonstrates the ways in which the media constitutes modes of legibility, positioning national identities and signifiers, such as Honduran and Central American, as incommensurate to other signifiers like Mexican-American and Latino. Although no longer a popular figure in the broader U.S. American imaginary, the Mencia controversy still proves to be a rich text as it exposes the limits of regulatory discourse within the media landscape.

Notes

1. By U.S. Central American I am referring to individuals of Central American descent that have been born and/or raised in the United States.
2. A year after "Joe Rogan Vs Carlos Mencia" went viral, Mencia's cable television show was canceled and according to Mencia the backlash from the public and comedy community "forced him to step away and reevaluate himself" (Gomez, 2013).
3. This is in large part due to the U.S. involvement in colonial and imperial practices, such as the U.S. Mexican War (1846–1848) and the Spanish-American War (1898), which would lead to the colonial/imperial connections between these geopolitical spaces and the United States.
4. In 1954 the Eisenhower administration labeled its large-scale clampdown of illegal immigration "Operation Wetback."
5. October 2014 marked the debut of two more Latino shows, *Jane the Virgin* and *Cristela*. The setting for *Jane the Virgin* is Miami, Florida, and the setting for *Cristela*, whose lead character is Mexican American, is Dallas, Texas.
6. Literary works by (U.S.) Central American writers like the novel *Odyssey to the North* by Mario Benacastro and the memoir essay *Always Say You're Mexican* by Marlon Morales highlight this cultural practice of interethnic passing.

References

Allatson, P. (2007). *Key terms in Latino/a cultural and literary studies*. Malden, MA: Oxford.

Anonymous 1. (2006). Carlos Mencia is a thief [Web log comment; no longer available]. Retrieved from http://www.carlosmencia.com/forums/ index.php?s=4d29521fa7614b45677e4022f8760ba7&act=Print&client=printer&f=2&t=95.html.

Anonymous 2. (2005). Re: Carlos Mencia sucks [Web log comment; no longer available]. Retrieved from http://www.chucklemonkey.com/forums/printthread.php?t=26.html.

Anonymous 3. (2005). Re: Carlos Mencia [Web log comment]. Retrieved from http://hedonistica.com/2005/09/carlos_mencia_i_locked_my_keys.php.

Anonymous 4. (2005). Ned Holness sucks something fierce [Web log comment]. Retrieved from http://www.amazon.com/review/R3I2CY5EYA52ZX.

Avila-Saavedra, G. (2011). Ethnic otherness versus cultural assimilation: U.S. Latino comedians and the politics of identity. *Mass Communication and Society, 14*(3), 271–291.

Beebee, T. (2014). Mariachi. In I. Stavans (Ed.), *Latin music: Musicians, genres and themes* (pp. 459–468). Santa Barbara, CA: Greenwood Press.

Beltrán, M. (2009). *Latina/o stars in U.S. eyes: The making and meanings of film and TV stardom*. Urbana, IL: University of Illinois Press.

Berg, C. R. (2002). *Latino images in film: Stereotypes, subversion, resistance.* Austin, TX: University of Texas Press.

Booth, W. (2005, September 28). The mouth of Mencia. *Washington Post.* Retrieved from http://www.washingtonpost.com/wp-dyn/content/article/2005/09/27/AR2005092701875.html.

Butler, J. (1990). *Gender trouble: Feminism and the subversion of identity.* New York, NY: Routledge.

Dávila, A. (2001). *Latinos, Inc: The marketing and making of a people.* Berkeley, CA: University of California Press.

Fiske, J. (1996). *Media matters: Race and gender in U.S. politics.* Minneapolis, MN: University of Minnesota Press.

Flores, J. (2000). *From bomba to hip-hop: Puerto Rican culture and Latino identity.* New York, NY: Columbia University Press.

Flores, W. V., & Benmayor, R. (1997). *Latino cultural citizenship: Claiming identity, space, and rights.* Boston, MA: Beacon Press.

Foucault, M. (1978). *The history of sexuality volume 1: An introduction.* New York, NY: Pantheon Books.

Foucault, M. (2003). *Society must be defended: Lectures at the Collège de France, 1975–76.* New York, NY: Picador.

Gomez, L. (2013, January 1). Interview: Comedian Carlos Mencia swears he has changed for better. *The Chicago Tribune.* Retrieved from http://articles.chicagotribune.com/2013–01–01/entertainment/ct-ott-0104-luis-20130101_1_carlos-mencia-comics-joke.

Habell-Pallán, M., & Romero, M. (2002). *Latino/a popular culture.* New York, NY: New York University Press.

Jenkins, H. (2006). *Fans, bloggers, and gamers: Exploring participatory culture.* New York, NY: New York University Press.

Kaplan, D. (2005, August 21). Mind of Mencia-Latino comic rips racial stereotypes on Comedy Central. *New York Daily Post.* Retrieved from http://nypost.com/2005/08/21/mind-of-mencia-latino-comic-rips-racial-stereotypes-on-comedy-central/.

Kellner, D. (1995). *Media culture: Cultural studies, identity, and politics between the modern and the postmodern.* New York, NY: Routledge.

Lima, L. (2007). *The Latino body: Crisis identities in American literary and cultural memory.* New York, NY: New York University Press.

Lopez, G. (Interviewee), & Stern, H. (Interviewer). (2005). *The Howard Stern Show* [Radio broadcast]. United States: CBS Broadcasting.

Lowry, B. (2005, July 5). Review: Mind of Mencia. *Variety.* Retrieved from http://variety.com/2005/film/awards/mind-of-mencia-1200524715/.

Marin, C. (Director). (1988). *Born in East L.A.* [Motion picture]. United States: Universal Pictures.

Mencia, C. (Writer & Producer). (2005). *The Mind of Mencia* [Television series]. Los Angeles, CA: Comedy Central.

Mencia, C. (Writer & Producer). (2007). *The Mind of Mencia* [Television series]. Los Angeles, CA: Comedy Central.

Mencia, C. (Interviewee), & O'Brien, C. (Interviewer). (2006). *Late Night with Conan O'Brien* [Television broadcast]. United States: NBC studios.

McWhorter, L. (2004). Practicing practicing. In D. Taylor & K. Vintges (Eds.), *Feminism and the final Foucault* (pp. 143–162). Urbana, IL: University of Illinois Press.

Miles, R. (1989). *Racism*. New York, NY: Routledge.
Nava, G. (Director). (1984). *El Norte* [Motion picture]. United States: Cinecom International Films.
Noriega, C. A., & López, A. M. (1996). *The ethnic eye: Latino media arts*. Minneapolis, MN: University of Minnesota Press.
Oboler, S. (1995). *Ethnic labels, Latino lives: Identity and the politics of (re)presentation in the United States*. Minneapolis, MN: University of Minnesota Press.
Ogunnaike, L. (2005, July 6). Sharpening ethnic barbs and hoping for a hit. *New York Times*. Retrieved from http://www.nytimes.com/2005/07/06/arts/television/sharpening-ethnic-barbs-and-hoping-for-a-hit.html?_r=0.
Omi, M., & Winant, H. (2014). *Racial formation in the United States*. New York, NY: Routledge.
Padilla, F. (1985). *Latino ethnic consciousness: The case of Mexican Americans and Puerto Ricans in Chicago*. Notre Dame, IN: University of Notre Dame Press.
Perez, R. (1997). From assimilation to annihilation: Puerto Rican images in U.S. films. In C. Rodriguez (Ed.), *Latin looks: Images of Latinas and Latinos in the U.S. media*. Boulder, CO: Westview Press.
Rodriguez, C. (1997). *Latin looks: Images of Latinas and Latinos in the U.S. media*. Boulder, CO: Westview Press.
Rogan, J. (2005). Carlos Mencia is a weak minded joke thief [Web log post]. Retrieved from http://joerogan.net/blog/carlos-mencia-is-a-weak-minded-joke-thief.
Valdivia, A. N. (2010). *Latina/os and the media*. Malden, MA: Polity Press.

6 Sofía Vergara

On Media Representations of *Latinidad*

Salvador Vidal-Ortiz[1]

By now, everyone has heard of Sofía Vergara: comedian, actress, model, producer,[2] and singer, best known for her role of Colombian wife to a middle-aged Anglo American man in the TV series *Modern Family* (2009–present). From the coastal region of Barranquilla, Colombia, Sofía Margarita Vergara Vergara may be placed, if we use basic phenotypical markers of dark or light skin, somewhere between Rosario Dawson and Cameron Díaz, although she does not really resemble either of them. Vergara's image is suspended along the lines of that of one too many Latina actresses: a voluptuous woman with a stereotypical accent and often, silly comments surrounding her body, beauty tips, and her foreign origins.[3] While erotically charged, and stereotypically feminine, Vergara is also racialized by virtue of her accent (Lippi-Green, 1997), her origins, and her presentation of self, which is most squarely situated outside of a representation of Whiteness. Sofía Vergara also acts as a reminder to "USAmericans" that Latinas come from more than the three historically (or most commonly) known ethno-racial nationalities (Mexican, Puerto Rican, and Cuban), complicating the "USAmerican" imaginary of *Latinidad*. In this context, Valdivia's (2015) definition of *Latinidad* as "the process of being, becoming, and/or performing a Latina/o subjectivity" (p. 579) is precisely what situates the present chapter.

Vergara has acted in the United States for over a decade, in a range of movies including *Big Trouble* (2002), *Chasing Papi* (2003), *Meet the Browns* (2008), *Madea Goes to Jail* (2009), *Gigolo* (2013), *Machete Kills* (2013), and, most recently, *Hot Pursuit* (2015). In 2012 and 2013, Forbes announced Vergara to be the highest paid TV actress; with ads for Pepsi and Kmart, and other appearances, Vergara continues to work her way up in an ethno-racial and gender ladder. But just how high could Vergara go? Even if she reaches the top—like renowned actresses Julia Roberts, Drew Barrymore, or Sandra Bullock—will she ever be recognized as a great female actress or will she remain a (racialized) Latina actress?

Vergara is not Black, and certainly too racially marked to be White—in media representations, she is not portrayed as either. Because she has been the highest paid actress in U.S. television, we can no longer ignore her presence. She is certainly unique to Latina/o portrayals in Hollywood, particularly because of the ways she distances herself from other Latinas by claiming her *Colombianidad*. At the same time, Vergara carries with her the echo of a social memory of dozens of Latina bombshell actresses before her, and, in general, of media's representation of Latinas/os in its market. Both individualized and yet part of a stereotyped gendered/sexualized/racial portrayal, Vergara sits comfortably as a figure that reenacts what USAmerican media successfully produces *as* Latinas—or what we consume as female *Latinidad*.

This chapter explores the slippery readings of Sofía Vergara produced by the media lens, since the media serves as a very powerful institution that structures our views on certain groups. While the chapter focuses on her racial readings, gender and sexuality can hardly be separated from her public image, and are explored as well. I utilize Vergara's representations, media appearances, and public interviews in order to depict her cementing as an always already Colombian (read: foreign) actress in the U.S. terrain. At the same time, the production of these elements cannot be solely attributed to her and to her decision-making; rather, those are produced and reproduced, and flow, from media expectations of an ethno-racial social order.

This chapter is, and it is not, about Sofía Vergara.[4] It is, in that I focus on the actress as a public persona with a personal narrative that is shared in interviews and popular interventions; it isn't, in that the chapter depends on public representations of her life—how others view her. But Vergara is not responsible of representing *Colombianidad* or *Latinidad*, nor is she responsible for defying racial, gender, or sexual stereotypes, or dismantling a media enterprise. In both being about her and not about her, this chapter implicitly invites a set of questions for future work about Latina women in the U.S.— not just Latina actresses. I aim to explore answers to the following questions: What is the USAmerican imaginary of *Latinidad*, and gendered *Latinidad*, in the media? How do those circulating images and representations of Latinas clash with the multiplicity of Latinas' ethnic, classed, sexual, racial, and gendered experiences? How are representations of Vergara looping back into stereotypes of previous actresses in the late 20th and early 21st century such as Rosie Perez or Jennifer Lopez? Does Vergara—the latest of countless Latina actresses—disrupt anything in the U.S., except for a neutral English accent? In order to explore these questions, I seek to interpret her public portrayal by looking back to the past experiences of other Latina actresses and the ways they were gendered in particularly racialized ways, but I am fully aware that her public portrayal is co-produced (she may be an avid participant, though certainly not the creator). It is important to consider the relationship between being ethnicized, being racialized, and the concept of *Latinidad* in the U.S. in general, and in media and Hollywood in particular.

Racialization, Latinas, and Hollywood

Racialization—the markings of people previously unmarked (Omi & Winant, 2014)—was a socio-historical concept developed in order to better explain U.S. racial formation, which was based on the colonization and exploitation of the land, human power, and distribution of the goods based on such exploitation (roughly, this process was engrained in the U.S. between the 16th and 18th centuries). The racial formation so basic to the USAmerican psyche, structured on racial binaries, was also structuring of other elements such as gender, sexuality, and class (Holland, 2012; see also Ferguson, 2004). Some groups we now consider Latinos gained recognition, albeit as they were racialized (sometimes back and forth) in their early contact with the U.S. efforts toward *manifest destiny*. By the time Puerto Ricans and Mexicans entered into a spatial negotiation with U.S. land (19th century), the racial formation system evolved to attempt to consume such groups into Whiteness or Blackness (Nobles, 2000)—until today (Dzidzienyo & Oboler, 2005; Guinier & Torres, 2002; see also Hernández, 2003). Racial processes began to evolve from skin color and hypo descent to complicating ethno-racial markers through other physical traits, country of origin, English dominance (or more precisely, lack thereof), and citizenship (symbolic and literal).

All of these elements come together in the increasing incorporation of the racialization of Latinas/os in the U.S., who are harder to categorize in terms of "race"—note that Latinas/os can be of any and all races, according to the U.S. Census (and are the only ones to have such a flexibility—a "fact" that is never explained in census analysis, thus naturalizing "ethnicity" and "race" as distinctive). Instead, in this mainstream imaginary, Latinas/os are ethnicized. To be sure, racialized and ethnicized carry different connotations. To be ethnicized is to have a culturalized reading of one self (or one's food, clothing, accent, gendered being) devoid of any political, social, or economic value; ethnic use of clothing or language (as in Spanish folk songs) is seen as ethnicized, because, among other things, it is rendered innocent (Urciuoli, 1996). But being Latino is both an ethnic and racial experience, in ways that may actually illustrate how Latinos are indeed a racial identity (see Alcoff, 2000).[5]

It is here where the concept of *Latinidad* takes more hold of us. Originally referencing U.S. Latinas/os in early ethnographic work on Mexicans and Puerto Ricans (Padilla, 1985), the term is invested in local configurations of Latina/o communities—and thus, it changes based on the specificity of the group or region discussed. In the U.S., Latin American and U.S. Latina/o people are homogenized; most people would not be able to tell the difference between a Southern Cone Latin American and a U.S. third-generation Mexican American. The USAmerican imaginary collapses any geopolitical, geocultural, and citizenship distinctions. But *Latinidad* is also a state of being; a way of engaging the world in what José Muñoz (2000) once noted as a "feeling brown" that moves beyond pan-ethnic terms. While *Latinidad* embraces a pan-ethnic (a pan-Latino) identification—welcome or not by those who presumably fall within it—it also comes with an external set of readings or preconceived notions; these are evident in Hollywood (Rodríguez, 2004) as well as Broadway (Román & Sandoval 1995). There is a logic here, one that Aparicio and Chávez-Silverman (1997) call *hegemonic tropicalization*, to bridge generic understandings of *Latinidad* of U.S. born Latinas/os and Latin Americans, to media representations. During the first half of the 20th century, Ibero American actors such as Carmen Miranda and Desi Arnaz (from Portugal and Cuba, respectively) arrived to the U.S. in what Román and Sandoval denoted as a "good neighbor" policy toward Latin America around World War II.[6] These images of Latin Americans who acted in/for U.S. audiences were originally conceived as the sexy young woman and the Latino Lover, respectively (Román & Sandoval, 1995), and notably, for purposes of our discussion on racialization, were not of Mexican or Puerto Rican origin. Shortly after that period emerged the troublemaker gang member, and the (by then) U.S. Latina/o troubled representation, with *West Side Story* being a primary stereotype (Negrón Muntaner, 2000).[7] *Latinidad* is not just an ethnic portrayal (in this case, of a sexy man, or a proper feminine woman), but a racial one, one that presumes delinquent traits, such as through the recent literature on deportability (De Genova, 2002). Within this, Latina women enact a particular set of racial/gender/sexual readings between whitening representations, "decency" expectations in routinely gendered behavior, and judgments based on sexual restrain/lack of control. Hollywood and public representations are no different than any of these other social landscapes; indeed, television, the movies, and other media help reproduce and repeat—in sum, magnify—those aspects.

My take in this chapter is that Vergara's portrayals offer a chance to see a movement across the racialized and ethnicized narratives, challenging these imaginary separations between the "ethnic" and the "racial"—especially as race is not based solely on skin color but a range of elements, and in many ways, race, ethnicity, and culture have merged in sociocultural analyses in the last 50 years, making an inherent separation difficult at best. A separation between the ethnic and the racial does not fit within notions of *Latinidad* in contemporary media representations, nor in the USAmerican imaginary of Latinas/os.

Rarely are Latina actresses in Hollywood and TV associated to Blackness.[8] While White dominance in their self-representation is the norm, it is not the only cue to read Latina actresses. Racial ambiguity is often a trademark for many Latina actresses, including, most notably, Jennifer López. *Latinidad* in this sense is used as a buffer between Black/White notions of race, while serving as a third space of sorts, accumulating (sometimes) ambiguous racialized readings, but not for the sake of anything other than business (within that logic, the more ambiguous a character is, the more people it can potentially reach).

Hollywood and U.S. television have produced a generic type of Latina actresses: from Carmen Miranda and Rita Moreno in the mid-part of the 20th century, to Rosie Perez, Salma Hayek, Jennifer López, and Jessica Alba in more recent years. Sofía Vergara is the latest iteration of this Latina bombshell formula: incredible bodily skills, be it dancing, fighting, or sex; a voluptuous body; dark, confused for Mediterranean or mixed-raced but not confused for Black; or a series of representations that mark her as Non-White: foreign accent, "ghetto" talk, and a low-class fashion that reproduces female *Latinidad* as sexually easy (Ortiz Cofer, 1996). There are over a dozen women from a Latin American or Latino background who have made strides in breaking a glass ceiling in Hollywood. And about the same number of women have been quite visible on television. But, to be clear, there is a certain formula. Basler (2013) discusses the long-standing repetition of six formulaic stereotypes (paired as in forms of evolutionary growth) of Latina/o portrayals in film, which are the "Bandito/Greaser" versus the "Latin Lover"; the "Male Buffoons/Female Clowns" and "Spitfires"; and last, the "Half-Breed Harlot" versus the "Dark Lady." The Bandito/Greaser is an old portrayal of dirty, irrational/emotional and not-so-smart Latino so common in gang-like characters; the Latin Lover, which comes from an Italian artist Rudolph Valentino, a more romantic and passionate man than his juxtaposed USAmerican counter. The Buffoons/Clowns are often similarly portrayed (in terms of personality traits) as the Bandito/Greaser, for their supposedly slow thinking, or emotional responses, although the former resorts in the buffoon being the center of jokes, whereas the Spitfire is often assigned to the Latina actresses in roles of "hot tempered, explosive, overtly emotional, and enslaved by their passions" (Basler, 2013, p. 125). In the Half-Breed Harlot the greaser is turned female; she is portrayed as breaking social norms and morality, especially as she desires non-Latino men (Basler gives Sofía Vergara as an example in the 2003 movie *Chasing Papi*). And the Dark Lady is virginal, innocent—even aloof—and juxtaposed to White characters that are direct (and thus not hiding anything).

In discussing the Moral Bandit, a new iteration of the Bandito/Greaser gang member character so (boringly) repetitive in U.S. media, Basler notes how newer filmmakers resort to old stereotypes and posits the question as to whether they are making singular cinematic choices, or indeed, the formulaic sense of the stereotype provides with profitable excesses that ultimately there is no other choice (to survive in the industry) than to assume these stereotypes. I posit that something similar might be occurring, if we evaluate the limited choices of the Latina actresses in question: their real lives and lives on the screen are fused, so much as to expect them to fulfill the spitfire (airhead) persona in and out of the film screen and the TV.

Latina actresses generally cannot step outside of that script; the few activists who have shown some leftist or progressive views (i.e., Rosario Dawson on immigration; Rosie Perez on poverty issues; Salma Hayek on gender violence issues) have done so after their 15 minutes of fame. As an example of the opposite—a Latina crossing from progressive politics into conservative ones—we see the case of María Conchita Alonso, a Cuban-Venezuelan actress (still referenced as "best known for her starring role in 1984's *Moscow on the Hudson* with Robin Williams"). She recently stated—on Fox News, nonetheless—how she has been the target of attacks for supporting a Tea Party candidate for the governor of California race, and that as a result, she was forced out of her performance in *The Vagina Monologues*, a play she was hired to start in San Francisco's Latino neighborhood, the Mission (Llorente, 2014). Fox News showcased her for her anti-communist stands and for wanting this candidate to make the oil industry respond to California's economic challenges. Even these simple examples—the Cuban-Venezuelan well-to-do actress that escaped Castro's regime; and the Mexican and Puerto Rican women fighting against oppression, poverty, and for immigration rights—are examples that may dismantle any simplistic sense or definition of what a "Latina" is, or ought to be, using their countries of origin as the basis for a meaning to their relationship to the U.S.

Next to these actresses who have for the most part left the spotlight, Vergara appears to offer too simplistic of a portrayal for Latina actresses, and to a certain extent, Latina women; indeed, for some, her lack of winning an Emmy derives from not "acting" but simply being the empty-headed Latina bombshell stereotype herself. She follows many other actresses who have walked in that limited space given to them in Hollywood.[9] Yet her visibility and her *Colombianidad* are features that make her stand out from the rest. What I illustrate in the next section is how her traits—as a Colombian trying to maintain features that differentiate her somewhat from the previous actresses, along with her intent to maintain a relaxed, public persona—benefit her greatly (especially since Colombia is a country that presently enjoys a good relationship with the U.S. government).

Media's Coverage of Vergara

Television consumes Vergara, but in particular ways. She gets close to formal (award) recognition, having been nominated several times for a Golden Globe for her work in *Modern Family*, but to date she has never won. Some people argue that she acts too closely to how/who she is, and that is not, for some, acting. Indeed, she portrays a Colombian wife of an Anglo man—a figure that may be perceived as dependent on him, his wealth, even citizenship; this was, until the time of this writing, parallel to her lived reality, given her dating "American" White men, and her outsiderness in terms of U.S. citizenship (she announced she became a U.S. citizen at the end of 2014). We see similar (even more stereotypical) portrayals in her 2015 movie *Hot Pursuit*, where she plays the widow of a Colombian drug dealer (not unlike the film *Chef*). The lines between her life outside of the screen and in it are so blurred that it impacts her chances of being seen as a multifaceted actress. Even her personal history is used to create a two-dimensional projection of her present self. For instance, at the 2013 Screen Actors Guild Awards, in a promotional video from the ceremony that included many U.S. actors (all of whom told a story about how they became actors or what they faced in earlier years), Vergara was portrayed as recalling a conversation with her dad. According to this very public, most certainly scripted narrative, her dad suggested she not be an actor, because she would look like a hooker, to what she responded, "with these big boobs [that I inherited from your mom] … I already look like a hooker" (Nudd, 2013). Her *Colombianidad* is used, unlike the script for the other actresses and actors, to speak to both her racialized and sexual public persona—and to sustain her outsiderness through racialized and sexualized ways. Is Vergara always already sexually racialized? What are the interarticulations of her body, her "ethnic" accent, her ever-present Colombian origin, and her success? And given these real/performed fusions, what exactly is her success, if she is to behave as she acts, and act as she behaves? These questions continue to evolve as we see Vergara in her various public performances.[10]

At the 2012 Emmy Awards, Vergara was seen in a stunning green dress. She was dubbed *La Sirenita* (The Little Mermaid), Latina style, by Joan Rivers in both her website and in her *Fashion Police* TV program (Merritt, 2012). Nominated 4 years in a row for her supporting role in *Modern Family*, Vergara is often portrayed as gorgeous and sensual, the envy of women and the object of desire for men, but her acting is rarely discussed. As a case in point, at the 2014 Emmys, Vergara was asked to pose and turn on a pedestal—literally—to celebrate how "our shows have had a meaningful impact around the world;" as the CEO and chairman of the Academy read a template promotion, words like "more diverse, both in front of, and behind, the camera," and "no matter the device or platform," would be enunciated just as her back (butt) was showing to the public (HollywoodBuzz, 2014). Of course the sketch was prepared for the show, but the play on her objectification is a focus on her body and beauty, not her capacity to act. No White or Black actress would have been portrayed in such a vulnerable and objectifying position, but someone in the fringe of USAmerican society serves many purposes such as this one.

For the critics, her portrayal, accent, and history are too close to her life outside the camera, deeming her acting negligible. While her commentary at those pre-award events is often read as inappropriate—she says, "with such a production, these dresses, make up, and hair, I look like a transvestite"— it is her looks, and not her contributions to the TV show, that is made evident. Little do TV stories, magazine interviews, or Internet coverage discuss her thyroid cancer, her brother's death in Colombia due to the structural violence there, and her life outside of the U.S. However, she does show resistance against that homogenizing narrative, in bringing up Colombia over and over—through coffee, candy, Colombian traditional foods, literature, and local places. In that, she remains one of the few Latin American actresses that somewhat resists this *Latinization* (through *Colombianidad*), and whose background is repeatedly reenacted for the public, as if saying "I may play this role on and off camera but I am not an empty brown canvas" in some ways, reclaiming specificity.

In her U.S. ads, she shows a sensual portrayal, either through Pepsi commercials or her Cover Girl ones. As well, she is portrayed as marketing her clothing line (sold at Kmart) in ways that foreground a "Latina embodiment." It is significant to recall a commercial where she draws on a mannequin, with an imaginary marker, a larger set of breasts and a bigger, rounder butt—all with a smile. She fought to become a Latina icon, and now that she has, she tends to maintain her hair lighter (she darkened her hair in the early seasons of *Modern Family* to fit the stereotype; see Valdivia, 2015), but her bodily features are foregrounded in significant ways. She produces and projects *Latinidad* in complex ways, perhaps profiting from it financially and, as important, symbolically. This contradiction of visibility through possible stereotyping is one of the elements that make the motivations behind her public persona so significant to study.

But what about what Vergara herself communicates? Like many other public figures, Sofía Vergara has her own webpage, as well as Facebook, Twitter, and Instagram accounts. She promotes her products, movies, and events where she appears (such as the Oscars or the Grammys), but she also posts snapshots and tips for better living, news, and general entertainment. Most centrally are her posts on *Modern Family*—it has, after all, brought her to stardom. There is a contrast between the commercial and non-commercial postings. In the commercial world, she plays with her sexuality quite often: in one recent promo (January 2015), Cindy Crawford and her share a Rooms to Go commercial where they seem to be talking about each other's curves and legs—only it turns out they are describing their love for each other's furniture, available of course through the company. Clearly alluding to a potential lesbian fantasy for the male gaze of heterosexual male viewers (Mulvey, 1975), the commercial once again capitalizes on her body, her sensuality, and her status as a sex symbol. But in terms of what seems to be the non-commercial, civic, or personal side, there are critical posts that merit attention for the transnational and gendered reach. In February 2015, for instance, she promoted "Stop Telling Women to Smile," addressing street sexual harassment. She continues to remind the public of her constant checkups after remission from cancer. Moreover, she is eager to highlight that she is not young and that she must produce a body and shape that will sustain her within the demands of the market where she is, thus inserting herself as a middle-aged woman in an industry that is certainly unfair to women (not men) her age.

The representation of her otherness extends from television and commercials to print and other forms of electronic media. In *Vanity Fair* (May 2015), Vergara is portrayed as so over-the-top sexual that the article fails to show anything about her life (Anolik, 2015). Writer Lili Anolik introduces her with envy and marking a shamelessly oppositional sense from USAmericans, without holding anything back:

> Sofía Vergara is hubba-hubba incarnate. She walks into a room, and all of a sudden, heads are on swivels, and jaws are on floors, tongues

unrolling from mouths like so many pink red carpets. There's something outrageous about her good looks. Something exaggerated, gaudy, blatant, preposterous. Something borderline indecent even. That luscious face—those kiss-puffed lips and velvety eyes, skin without a flaw, lustrous as a pearl—atop that bodacious bod—the softly swelling hips, the gently tapering waist, the oodles of breast and thigh and buttock—is too much. It's overkill. Not to mention in bad taste. I mean, shouldn't she be a little less explicit about her extraordinary physical assets? Wear them not quite so proudly? Act as if they're her burden rather than her glory? Or at least downplay them some? … Maybe because she's not an American by birth and therefore the crackpot notion that all men are created equal never even crossed her mind. Or maybe because she's a Catholic, convent-educated, and so understands that the need to worship isn't unseemly or evidence of weak character, that it's a perfectly natural human impulse, and is thus able to accept the rapture she inspires with a grace and an ease and an utter lack of neurosis. Small wonder that Sophia Loren (born in 1934) was her idol growing up. That's about how far back you have to go to find another un-ironic sex symbol.

While this is a representation of shameless beauty and sensuality, it also implies the lack of decorum (and placement of shame on her) for her hotness, somewhat rendering Vergara as vulgar for being so sexy. Also, Vergara is introduced to us almost as in a Sweet 16 ceremony. It isn't that she resists being a sex symbol—she clearly enjoys it all, even the reference to Sophia Loren; but being a woman who is not in her 20s, she does and undoes stereotyping by inserting herself within the sex market. But she does so carefully. As noted before, there are often mentions of her boyfriend, or her dad or her son—she is a partner, a daughter, and a mother—thus distancing from the very same sexual symbol space that makes her have access.

Oppositional readings of her as non-American are plenty; even her co-star Reese Witherspoon had a gentle, but still culturally different, framework to introduce Vergara in this Just Jared (2015) post:

> As soon as I met Sofia, I said, "I want to make a movie with you." I think she's the next Lucille Ball. She and I together are such a funny thing because we represent two completely different cultures and kinds of women, but we just love each other. We laughed so much. I couldn't understand what she was saying half the time. She couldn't understand what I was saying half the time. But we both love cake, clothes, kids and our families.

Now compared to Lucile Ball—in that unsurprisingly old way USAmericans always turn inward to understand the world—Witherspoon reduces Vergara's acting to comic relief. But she also clearly denotes completely different backgrounds between the two of them, in ways that reify an ethno-racial cultural representation of otherness with which Vergara is already familiar. This is not an innocent slippage, but the works of a cultural re-signification that separate the two (note that within a month, Vergara appears on the cover of *Vanity Fair*, while Witherspoon appears on the cover of *InStyle* magazine; with the former carrying more glamour than the often teenage-like emphasis of the latter).

This is what Vicky Woods, a *Vogue* reporter, said in her opening remarks after interviewing Sofía Vergara for an article. At the time (2013), Sofía discussed the possibility of postponing having a baby with her (then) boyfriend and freezing her eggs:

> Of course, when she first arrives, on heels as high as car jacks but sans any leopard print, I feel a small pang that she isn't Gloria Delgado-Pritchett, but luckily she talks like her (though she doesn't look as much like her as she used to). Vergara's hair is uncurled and natural and way blonder than it was; she has on a pretty embroidered blouse in soft white silk and light-blue jeans, and her heels are those suede Prada ones that look as though they'd had brass nails hammered into them. ("Surprisingly comfortable," she says.) But to return to freezing these eggs: She tells me it is a process she is starting around now and that "you have to put first some *peels,* and then after—"What kind of peels, pray?" "*Hormone* pills," she says, "and then after that it is hormone injections." Aww, does she have to have all those hormones tucked into her? She says yes; at her age, "they want to get as many eggs as they can because usually you produce them but they're not good. They have to be perfect, perfect, perfect ones. My boyfriend is 37, younger than me, never had kids. So."

The resemblance to the 2015 *Vanity Fair* portrayal is uncanny. Vergara is fighting against time, challenged by her accent, and sort of living the life of the role that made her famous. In that interview, recycled information from previous ones is shared—on her son, her accent, her acting, and her fashion needs. Never multidimensional, her portrayals are an extension of the other Latina women that have made it—temporarily—in Hollywood.

On May 7, 2015, Vergara was given a Hollywood star (#2551) on the Walk of Fame—the first Colombian ever to receive such an honor. She was introduced by her son, and her TV producers, and coworkers from *Modern Family*, and she shared a few words of thanks and motivational speech (Variety, 2015) for other "Latin[o]s":

> I don't have anything to say but thank you, and the first thanks I have to give is to *Modern Family* … if they had not invented Gloria Pritchett I would not be here … Thank you to all my new American fans, thank you so much, and to all my Latin fans, of 25 years, I love you, I would

not be here if I didn't have these amazing fans, the only thing that I could tell them is that I hope that they see me as an example and that working hard, and respecting yourself and respecting others, really pays off—don't stop dreaming and do what you have to do. ¿Ah en Español?

Here, after that request, she proceeds to say, not quite word by word, her sentiment in Spanish. Vergara conveys her American Dream narrative, common among Latinas (lest we forget Sonia Sotomayor?) in this celebration. While it is made clear that she is the first Colombian actress to receive a star, her speech signals the possibility of the American Dream to Latinas/os in the U.S. In doing so, Vergara oscillates between the national and the pan-ethnic, in order to sustain a larger fan base. As the news of her star was released, some claimed she has become the most powerful woman in the world (Oyola, 2015).

Conclusion

It is well established in both English and Spanish media that Vergara's portrayals stereotype Latinas; less has been said about the emergence of this representation. Sofía Vergara is part of a cadre of Latina/o actors whose public personas are coded in non-American terms, as excess, as Non-White, and sometimes, as deviant (suffice it to compare Vergara to John Leguizamo, counterpart both in terms of gender and of belonging to a Colombian diaspora and not really claiming *Colombianidad* like Vergara; see Alzate 2002). Because "cinematic representations of how 'foreigners' looked (Non-White), spoke (accented or 'broken' English), and behaved (usually threatening or amoral) helped reinforce notions of Latinos/as as not 'real' Americans" (Basler, 2013, p. 118), Sofía Vergara's work extends many stereotypical portrayals of Latinas in U.S. media. Vergara also signals an international background to herself, unlike previous actresses who are Mexican American, or Puerto Rican, or Cuban American. Yet unlike these other actresses, Vergara sustains that Colombian identity, establishing her *Colombianidad* in regular, even if temporal, ways, thus rupturing USAmerican portrayals of herself through mere pan-ethnic terms, while situating Colombia as an active aspect in a (now broader) registry of *Latinidad* in the USAmerican imaginary. Indeed, a productive comparison to singer Shakira may result in a critical, transnational sense of *Colombianidad* seldom discussed in Latino studies (for a discussion on Shakira, see Cepeda 2010). Furthermore, as more Colombian celebrities such as singer Juanes join Vergara in the U.S. spotlight, this may have direct implications on how Colombia turns its eye outward (imagine the impact: Colombian tourism advertisement featuring these celebrities to seek more U.S. tourism).

Vergara also allows for a focus on transnational work that deals with concepts of beauty "here" and "there"—from aspects as specifics as franchises that capitalize on Colombian women's objectification while adjusting for cultural attributes in commerce settings such as Hooters (Newton-Francis & Vidal-Ortiz, 2013), to thinking about the place of beauty within the arduously fought Colombian nationhood (Stanfield, 2013). In addition to corroborating the portrayals of Vergara with her own, further research should delve into complicating the role of media in the production of *Colombianidad* through Vergara's fame comparatively—that is, contrasting the media outlets' production of her success in the U.S. with the portrayals in Colombia and the rest of Latin America.

What remains to be seen, if and when Vergara's fame lessens, is the capacity in which Vergara will be able to produce and support, if so desired, work by other Latinas in ways that do not reify Latina stereotyping (Eva Longoria has already been accused of this for her production of *Devious Maids*). But as noted in the introduction, Latina actresses are not responsible for debunking stereotypes any more than women from other ethno-racial groups. Moreover, as Vergara remains in the U.S. as a citizen, it will be critical to see whether she continues to foreground *Colombianidad* or *Latinidad*, and to what extent she continues to inhabit an in-between, somewhere outside a Black and White racialized space, while rooting herself in Colombia.

For media, race, and gender studies, it is pivotal to see how a middle-aged woman gains so much popularity (perhaps a reason why she is celebrated too much by other women, not only her ethno-racial otherness but the fact that she can be a trendsetter) all while not being particularly political in her approach. Further research should incorporate more social media produced by Vergara, and interviews and more direct information collected from the actress herself. And like all other Latina actresses, it remains to be seen whether this portrayal is part and parcel of a Hollywood creation, or a breakaway from this mandated script in order to succeed in spite of the pressure to conform "in America." While these representations have an impact on Latina women and on the USAmerican imaginary of Latina women (and Latinos in general) in the U.S., they too impact the way "mainstream" USAmerica relates to Latinas/os.

Notes

1. I am thankful to the graduate students in my "Transnational Reach—Colombia" seminar for their insightful comments and criticisms to enhance and clarify elements from an earlier version of this chapter. Thank you Mackenzie Crowley, Kenya L. Goods, Shannon Hilsey, Hanna Dielman Koerner, Kaitlin Pericak, Diana Restrepo Arévalo, Nicolas Sforzini, and Christina Taylor. My gratitude extends to Bhoomi K. Thakore and Jason A. Smith for their support, patience, flexibility, and encouragement throughout the development of this chapter's ideas. Lastly, thanks to Cristina Khan - for many conversations on racialized sexualities, and to Lillian Jiménez, whose media smarts and critical views -behind and in front of the camera- are always an inspiration to me.
2. Vergara was a coproducer of a short-lived TV series based on an Argentinian drama, adapted for U.S. television. *Killer Women* was a new TV series that began January 7, 2014. It ran for six episodes (initially, ABC contracted for eight), ending on February 18, 2014.

3. Every rule has an exception, and among Latina actresses, women such as Alexis Bledel (known as the daughter character in the *Gilmore Girls*) serve as counter-evidence to this stereotype (which is, nonetheless, predominant). Actresses like Bledel may produce a Non-Latina or a predominantly-read-as-White actress portrayal, yet Bledel is the daughter of a Mexican-American and an Argentinian. Although important, it is beyond the scope of this chapter to evaluate the notably (and increasingly so) casting of light-skinned, blue-eyed actresses (in particular) in TV series as a potential form of homogenizing Latinos and U.S. Whites.
4. When I use terms like Vergara's image, I mean to connote public portrayals and readings; this is thus a representational analysis that does not and cannot take into account how Vergara sees it herself. Although an important project, interviewing Vergara is beyond the scope of the present work; moreover, Vergara, like other actresses such as Rosie Perez, cannot control media's construction of her and her public sense of *Latinidad* (for the latter, see Valdivia 1998).
5. A recent Pew Research report showed that about tow thirds of the Latino population identified being Latino as a race and ethnic, or just racial, categorization. The specific chapter discussing multiraciality can be found here: http://www.pewsocialtrends.org/2015/06/11/chapter-7-the-many-dimensions-of-hispanic-racial-identity/ (retrieved June 11, 2015).
6. Miranda was born in Portugal, but her parents moved with her to Brazil when she was very young. Miranda's transnational journey and entrance to the U.S. media through Brazil place her in an awkward position vis-à-vis Latina/o identity—which only often includes Brazilians, and generally does not include Portuguese and Spaniard people. For the sake of simplicity, and recognizing her early contributions to this lineage in U.S. media, I thus refer to her as Latina from hereon when mentioned in relation to other actors/actresses.
7. Mexican American and Puerto Rican portrayals have influenced not only media, but also policy and research, with Oscar Lewis' *The Children of Sanchez* and *La Vida* as a "culture of poverty" analysis that later influenced the USAmerican view of African Americans, as evidenced in Moynihan (1965).
8. In decades past, we saw the ambiguously Black, although certainly not White, Rosie Perez; we've seen Rosario Dawson and to a certain extent Jennifer López and Dania Ramírez play non-specific/ambiguous racial characters; most recently Zoe Saldaña is as an exception, playing Latina or characters of African descent.
9. For starters, it is important to mention close to a dozen Latina actresses and their films: Carmen Miranda (*Something for the Boys*, 1944; *Copacabana*, 1947), Sonia Braga (*Kiss of the Spider Woman*, 1985; *The Rookie*, 1990), Rosie Perez (*Do the Right Thing*, 1989; *Fearless*, 1993; *Perdita Durango*, 1997), Jennifer López (*Selena* and *Anaconda*, 1997; *Maid in Manhattan*, 2002; *Monster-in-Law*, 2005), María Conchita Alonso (*Colors*, 1988; *The House of the Spirits*, 1993), Salma Hayek (*Desperado*, 1995; *Fools Rush In*, 1997), Eva Mendes (*Training Day*, 2001; *2 Fast 2 Furious*, 2003), Jessica Alba (*Paranoid*, 2000; *Sin City*, 2005), and Rosario Dawson (*Kids*, 1995; *Down to You*, 2000; *Men in Black II*, 2002; *Rent*, 2005) to name but a few. Their limited portrayals in what seem most evidently stereotypical or marginal roles for women (maid, prostitute, vulnerable dependent, or wife) is the topic of another paper.
10. Marriage, as an extension of these public performances, is also important: Vergara married Joe Manganiello on November 22, 2015.

References

Alcoff, L. M. (2000). Is Latina/o identity a racial identity? In J. E. Gracia & P. De Greiff (Eds.), *Hispanic/Latinos in the U.S.: Ethnicity, race, and rights* (pp. 23–44). New York, NY: Routledge.

Alzate, G. A. (2002). When the subaltern is politically incorrect: A cultural analysis of the performance art of John Leguizamo. In L. A. Ramos-García (Ed.), *The state of Latino theater in the U.S.: Hybridity, transculturation, and identity* (pp. 131–151). New York, NY: Routledge.

Anolik, L. (2015, April 30). Sofía Vergara, Hollywood's hysterical, business-savvy, unapologetic sex symbol. *Vanity Fair*. Retrieved from http://www.vanityfair.com/hollywood/2015/04/sofia-vergara-hot-pursuit-may-2015-cover?mbid=social_twitter.

Aparicio F. R., & Chávez-Silverman, S. (Eds.). (1997). *Tropicalizations: Transcultural representations of Latinidad*. Hanover, NH: Dartmouth Press.

Basler, C. R. (2013). Latinos/as through the lens. In J. Sutherland & K. Feltey (Eds.), *Cinematic sociology: Social life in film*, 2nd ed. (pp. 116–129). Thousand Oaks, CA: Sage.

Cepeda, M. E. (2010). *Musical ImagiNation: U.S. Colombian identity and the Latin boom*. New York, NY: New York University Press.

De Genova, N. P. (2002). Migrant "illegality" and deportability in everyday life. *Annual Review of Anthropology*, 31, 419–447.

Dzidzienyo, A., & S. Oboler. (2005). *Neither enemies nor friends: Latinos, Blacks, Afro-Latinos*. New York, NY: Palgrave-MacMillan.

Ferguson, R. (2004). *Aberrations in Black: Toward a queer of color critique*. Minneapolis, MN: University of Minnesota Press.

Guinier, L., & Torres, G. (2002). *The miner's canary: Enlisting race, resisting power, transforming democracy*. Cambridge, MA: Harvard University Press.

Hernández, T. K. (2003). "Too Black to be Latino/a:" Blackness and Blacks as foreigners in Latino studies. *Latino Studies*, 1(1), 152–159.

Holland, S. P. (2012). *The erotic life of racism*. Durham, NC: Duke University Press.

HollywoodBuzz. (2014, August 25). Sofia Vergara gets put on a pedestal at Emmys 2014 [Video file]. Retrieved from https://www.youtube.com/watch?v=tZRkF2D9ipM.

Just Jared. (2015). Reese Witherspoon on Sofia Vergara: "She's the next Lucille Ball." Retrieved from http://www.justjared.com/2015/04/10/reese-witherspoon-on-sofia-vergara-shes-the-next-lucille-ball/.

Lewis, O. (1998/1963). The culture of poverty. *Society*, 35, 7–9.

Lippi-Green, R. (1997). *English with an accent: Language, ideology, and discrimination in the U.S.* New York, NY: Routledge.

Llorente, E. (2014, January 20). Backlash against actress Maria Conchita Alonso forces her to drop out of upcoming play. *Fox News Latino*. Retrieved from http://latino.foxnews.com/latino/politics/2014/01/20/actress-maria-conchita-alonso-drops-role-in-play-over-political-endorsement/.

Merritt, J. (Photographer). (2012). 2012 Emmys: Fashion Police [slideshow]. *E Entertainment Television*. Retrieved from http://www.eonline.com/photos/6184/2012-emmys-fashion-police/218516.

Moynihan, D. P. (1965). *The Negro family: The case for national action*. U.S. Department of Labor: Office of Policy Planning and Research.

Mulvey, L. (1975). Visual pleasure and narrative cinema. *Screen*, 16(3), 6–18.

Muñoz, J. E. (2000). Feeling brown: Ethnicity and affect in Ricardo Bracho's *The Sweetest Hangover (and Other STDs)*. *Theatre Journal*, 52(1), 67–79.

Negrón Muntaner, F. (2000). Feeling pretty: *West Side Story* and Puerto Rican identity discourses. *Social Text*, 63, 83–106.

Newton-Francis, M., & Vidal-Ortiz, S. (2013). ¡Más que un bocado! (More than a mouthful): Comparing Hooters in the U.S. and Colombia. In A. Jafar & E. Masi de Casanova (Eds.), *Global Beauty, Local Bodies* (pp. 59–81). New York, NY: Palgrave Macmillan.

Nobles, M. (2000). *Shades of citizenship: Race and the census in modern politics*. Stanford, CA: Stanford University Press.

Nudd, T. (2013). How SAG stars got their start: Sofia Vergara credits her "hooker looks." *People Magazine*. Retrieved from http://www.peoplestylewatch.com/people/stylewatch/package/article/0,,20658242_20668555,00.html.

Omi, M., & Winant, H. (2014). *Racial Formation in the U.S.* New York, NY: Routledge.

Ortiz Cofer, J. (1995). *The Latin deli: Telling the lives of barrio women*. New York, NY: WW Norton.

Oyola, M. (2015, May 7). Sofia Vergara, Hollywood Walk of Fame: 5 fast facts you need to know. *Heavy.com*. Retrieved from http://heavy.com/entertainment/2015/05/sofia-vergara-star-on-hollywood-walk-of-fame/.

Padilla, F. (1985). *Latino ethnic consciousness: The case of Mexican Americans and Puerto Ricans in Chicago*. Notre Dame, IN: University of Notre Dame Press.

Rodríguez, C. (2004). *Heroes, lovers, and others: The story of Latinos in Hollywood*. Oxford, UK: Oxford University Press.

Román, D., & Sandoval, A. (1995). Caught in the web: Latinidad, AIDS, and allegory in *Kiss of the Spider Woman, the Musical*. *American Literature*, 67(3), 553–585.

Stanfield, M. S. (2013). *Of beasts and beauty: Gender, race and identity in Colombia*. Austin, TX: University of Texas Press.

Urciuoli, B. (1996). *Exposing prejudice: Puerto Rican experiences of language, race, and class*. Boulder, CO: Westview Press.

Valdivia, A. N. (1998). Stereotype or transgression? Rosie Perez in Hollywood film. *The Sociological Quarterly*, 39(3), 393–408.

Valdivia, A. N. (2015) Latinas on television and film: Exploring the limits and possibilities of inclusion. In C. Carter, L. Steiner, & L. McLaughlin (Eds.), *The Routledge companion of media and gender* (pp. 578–588). Oxford, UK: Routledge.

Vargas, D. R. (2010). Representations of Latina/o sexuality in popular culture. In M. Asencio (Ed.), *Latina/o sexualities: Probing powers, passions, practices, and policies* (pp. 117–136). New Brunswick, NJ: Rutgers University Press.

Variety. (2015). Sofia Vergara Walk of Fame ceremony [Video file]. Retrieved from https://www.youtube.com/watch?v=EOzpQh6Vvmg.

Woods, V. (2013, March 13). Sofía Vergara: Dangerous curves. *Vogue*. Retrieved from http://www.vogue.com/865250/sofia-vergara-dangerous-curves/.

7 Color-Blind Racism in the Media
Mindy Kaling as an "Honorary White"

Sheena Sood

TAMRA: Hmm, White people problems.
MINDY: I'm obviously not White Tamra, come on.
BRENDAN: For the record, a person of color can have White people problems.

This dialogue excerpt is from an episode of the first season of the television sitcom *The Mindy Project* (Kaling, 2012–2015). In the episode "Take Me with You" (season 1, episode 24), protagonist Mindy Lahiri and her boyfriend Casey are hosting a farewell party as they prepare to embark on a year-long service trip to Haiti. In the scene, Lahiri expresses her apprehension about the pending move to Casey, who proceeds to walk out of the party upset. Tamra (Mindy's Black coworker) and Brendan (a White man and friend of Lahiri's) comment with the aforementioned remarks. I highlight this discourse of Lahiri—a neither White-nor-Black South Asian American doctor—as having "White people problems," because it frames the arguments I present in this chapter regarding the unique role and responsibility that Mindy Kaling and *The Mindy Project* bear in the world of mass media production and the depiction of racial minorities on television.

Mass media are an inseparable part of our social lives. Operating in the context of the surrounding political economy and social environment, television shows that exist within larger contemporary media structures have greatly transformed the way that audience viewers understand themselves, relate to characters on screen, and make sense of their social realities (Grindstaff & Turow, 2006). Television shows serve as a metaphorical reflection of the culture and society in which they are produced (Bogart, 1958; Hunt, 2004).

Though television appears to have meaningless social implications on our lives, research suggests audiences who have little exposure to non-normative social groups—such as sexual, ethnic, or racial minorities—often interpret and navigate relationships to them based on media exposure (Hunt, 2004; Sreberny, 2005). Mass media's characterizations of racial and ethnic groups influence how people construct relationships with racial and ethnic minorities. Theorists also suggest that media reinforces hierarchical relationships of power (Collins, 2000; Hunt, 2004). The recent visibility of South Asian origin actors on television shows such as *30 Rock*, *Community*, *The Office*, *Outsourced,* and *The Mindy Project* (henceforth *TMP*) fuel the interest of this study that questions the representation and positioning of South Asian

American identity on mainstream media and how these depictions relate to, reinforce, and subvert the existing racial structure.

In this chapter, I apply the theoretical purview of "color-blind racism" to the representation of South Asian American identity on *TMP*. Specifically, I explore how television media articulate a racial ideology through the inclusion and representation of Mindy Kaling and *TMP* on FOX, a mainstream television network. *TMP* is a romantic comedy sitcom starring Indian American actress Mindy Kaling. Not only is Kaling an ideal subject for this research because of her unique role as the show's creator, producer, protagonist, and occassional writer, but she is also a particularly interesting case study because of how her more pronounceable stage name "Mindy Kaling" gets more spotlight than her birth name "Vera Chokalingam." *TMP* depicts relationships between the protagonist Mindy Lahiri—a self-described "chubby" obstetrician/gynecologist (OB/GYN) of Indian descent—and her coworkers, friends, and romantic partners.

I begin the literature review by examining the formative representations of ethnic and racial groups, specifically minorities, on television. Next, I examine those representations over time, highlighting the implications that racial justice campaigns have had on minority representations. Finally, I discuss research on mass media's representations of people of South Asian origin. Following the literature review, I outline my conceptual approach by defining color-blind racism and Bonilla-Silva's ideological frames (2010). Goffman's concepts of "dramaturgy" and "presentation of self" (1959) are relevant here because of Mindy Kaling's role as a producer, writer, and actor. Next, I discuss my methodological approach and the process I utilized to collect data from *TMP* episodes, online articles, and interviews with Kaling. In the results section, I present and analyze the significance of the data as they relate to color-blind racism's ideological frames. I conclude by discussing the larger implications that *The Mindy Project* has in society, including how it relates to the existing racial hierarchy and the relationships of contemporary South Asian immigrant communities to other racial groups in America.

Literature Review

United States Media's Racist Origins

Since its inception in the early 20th century, U.S. television has utilized negative representations, images, and symbols to portray people of color, notably indigenous people and Blacks, as inferior to people of European descent. Researchers who have looked at racial representations in mass media find that, since its formation, television has reinforced the existing racialized power structure—a structure founded on anti-Black racism. For example, Dates and Barlow found that, since the era of slavery, "the ultimate yield of the negative image of African people in various media has been to cement the superordinate/subordinate power relationship, Whites over Blacks" (1993, p. 110).

Additionally, researchers who have studied depictions of women in media share similar findings: mass media objectify women and portray them in subordinate roles to reinforce the social order (Pozner, 2010). Mulvey (2009) emphasized producers' and writers' use of "the male gaze" to uphold men's dominance over women. Collins' (2000) research on mass media's representation of Black women found that the existing White supremacist structure exports "controlling images" such as the "mammy," "matriarch," "welfare queen," and "jezebel" to various social institutions—such as schools, the Internet, news media, and government agencies—to preserve dominant racial and gender ideologies.

Researchers have also looked into the effects that racial justice campaigns have had on contemporary representations of minorities in mass media. Hunt's (2004) research on the channeling of Blackness found that people of African descent have always resisted U.S. media's racist portrayal of Blacks; for instance, the National Association for the Advancement of Colored People (NAACP) initiated campaigns in the 1960s that highlighted how the representation of Blacks in "ghetto," "hypersexualized," and "unprofessional" roles perpetuated racial oppression. Racial justice campaigns petitioned U.S. media to produce shows that captured a wider variety of Black representations in television and film.

Scholars have looked at how the representation of Blackness has transformed over time—analyzing the historical trajectory through shows such as *Amos 'n' Andy*, *Beulah*, *The Jeffersons*, and *The Cosby Show*. Gray (1995) finds the contemporary images of African Americans are anchored by three types of discursive practices: assimilationist (invisibility), pluralist (separate by equal), and multiculturalist (diversity) ones. Researchers have found that while contemporary representations of Blacks are more diverse and complex than in previous decades, the mere inclusion of a few positive images is not enough to subvert a historically racist structure (Gray, 1995; Hunt, 2004).

In addition to being cast in superior roles to minority racial and ethnic groups, researchers have found that White men dominate the industry as writers, directors, and producers for prime-time television shows (Hunt, 2004; Mulvey, 2009). Whites account for 94% of writers for non-ethnic sitcoms and 54% of ethnic sitcoms (Hunt, 2004). These scholars' findings illustrate how a racialized and gendered oppressive structure continues to color mass media's representation of marginalized groups. These findings also reveal a significant research gap: few researchers have studied the depiction and role of Non-Black people of color in mass media productions.

Beyond Black and White: Multicultural and Minority Media

Researchers who have analyzed the representation of Non-Black people of color and other marginalized groups in mass media recognize that television shows, news programs, and advertising agencies began diversification processes to include people of various racial, ethnic, and sexual orientation backgrounds several decades ago. Scholars have also found that while general diversity has increased over the years, the representations of these minorities lack depth and diversity (Alsultany, 2012; Hamamoto, 1994; Linneman, 2008; Monk-Turner, Heiserman, Johnson, Cotton, & Jackson, 2010; Sreberny, 2005). In their in-depth analysis of prime time television shows on ABC, NBC, CBS, and FOX, Monk-Turner and colleagues (2010) found that prime-time television networks still portray socially constructed images of minority characters and fail to provide counter-stereotypical portrayals of them. Srerberny (2005) found that, even when media outlets attain their diversity quota, they depict racial and ethnic minority groups through a lens of "cultural fixity." Similarly, Linneman's (2008) research on the portrayal of homosexuality in prime-time television found that, regardless of whether a gay character on *Will & Grace* embodied hegemonic masculine (think Will Truman) or effeminate (think Jack McFarland) traits, the show consistently feminized gay characters in every social interaction. In her study analyzing post-9/11 representations of Arabs and Muslim Americans in TV dramas, news reports, and non-profit advertisements, Alsultany (2012) finds that despite the presence and circulation of more diverse, even positive and sympathetic images of Arab Americans and Muslim Americans in media sources, these images alone do not solve the problem of racial stereotyping; in fact, the seemingly positive images often produce meanings that justify exclusion and inequality.

Contemporary Depictions of South Asians in the U.S.

South Asian Americans are witnessing greater visibility in mass media and popular culture. Researchers who have studied the depiction of South Asian Americans in mainstream media find that although mainstream U.S. institutions portray some authentic characteristics of South Asian culture, they tend to exaggerate South Asian Americans' more noticeable ethnic markers and portray the most orthodox cultural elements. As Prashad suggests, "The norm that appeals to the guardians of multiculturalism is often a collection of the most orthodox cultural elements […]. Indian culture, for instance, is typically identified as a sort of Hindu culture, and it is the male orthodoxy that is given license to speak for the culture's norms" (2008, p. 5). The majority of South Asian representations in the public sphere fail to showcase this ethno-racial group's immense diversity by socioeconomic status, educational background, religious affiliation, and national origin, and often reinforce hegemonic ideological understandings of South Asian Americans as a monolithic group (Davé, 2013; Gottschlich, 2011).

Both Gottschlich's (2011) and Davé's (2013) work on the representation of Indian Americans found that the characterization of the popular character Apu Nahasapeemapetilon (who is voiced by a White actor) on *The Simpsons* validates Davé's theory of the "brown voice." Davé argued that the presence and performance of a monolithic brown voice by multiple

South Asian characters in American culture perpetuates the racialization of South Asians as perpetually foreign, inherently intelligent, and culturally privileged (Davé, 2005). In addition to having a thick South Asian accent, Apu works diligently in menial occupations to attain the "American Dream" despite attaining advanced educational degrees. The producers perpetuate stereotypical understandings of South Asians through assigning Apu an exaggeratedly lengthy surname and through reinforcing the "myth of the model minority" (Chou & Feagin, 2008).

Thakore's (2014) research builds on analyses of 21st century South Asian representations in popular television by questioning how South Asian characterizations are produced. Thakore finds that producers utilize the external political economy and its racial ideologies to replicate characterizations that "reflect how South Asians are already perceived in the U.S."— often as characters who aspire toward a "model minority" identity and desire assimilation into a mainstream (White) "American" identity (2014, p. 152). Through promoting a narrative of South Asian immigrants who are economically successful and culturally assimilated, these representations buttress the existing political economy (Thakore, 2014).

Researchers illustrate how despite attempts to include people of color in mainstream media, both as characters and producers, a "White male gaze" (Mulvey, 1975) dominates the meaning-making process of how audience members are invited to construct their relationships to people of color. While existing research finds that stereotypical ethnic identification markers continue to characterize the portrayal of people of color in mainstream media, scholars have not yet analyzed how South Asian Americans in "positions of power" interact with these representations and with existing racial ideologies. Mindy Kaling is the first South Asian American to produce her own show, which was broadcast on FOX the first three seasons and moved to Hulu for season 4. This study looks at how Kaling negotiates this existing racial hierarchy.

Conceptual Framework

In this study, I utilize the frames of color-blind racism to examine how mass media perpetuate dominant racial ideologies on television shows. Critics of color-blind policies identify "color-blind racism" and the "White racial frame" as modern phenomena used to justify racial inequality (Bonilla-Silva, 2010; Brown et al., 2003; Carr, 1997; Feagin, 2006, 2010). Bonilla-Silva (2010) uses color-blind racism to explain how an oppressive White-on-Black structure is normalized in modern day interactions through (1) discourse, and (2) the quality of interactions and relationships across different racial groups. Color-blind racism employs four frames to reinforce the White supremacist status quo: (1) abstract liberalism, (2) naturalization of racism, (3) cultural racism, and (4) minimization of racism (Bonilla-Silva, 2010, pp. 26–30). The frames encourage Whites to form relationships with Non-Whites in a "post-racial" manner.

In this chapter, I utilize abstract liberalism and minimization of racism to analyze the representation of Mindy Lahiri on *TMP*, the self-representation of Kaling off-air, and the greater implications these representations have on South Asian identity and racial positioning. Abstract liberalism reinforces the White supremacist status quo by (1) obscuring the structures that laid the foundation for a dehumanizing racial order, (2) encouraging Americans to unquestionably accept liberalism's principles as just, and (3) ignoring the contemporary racialized structures that perpetuate the White-on-Black racial order (Bonilla-Silva, 2010). The minimization of racism frame encourages Whites to believe present-day discrimination is not so bad; Whites utilize it to emphasize the illusion of progress, to accuse Non-Whites who call attention to racism as being "hypersensitive," and to silence the experiences of Non-Whites (Bonilla-Silva, 2010).

Bonilla-Silva purports that color-blind racism encourages Non-Whites to adopt its frames. Bonilla-Silva suggests the employment of color-blind racism's rhetoric by high achieving Non-Black people of color has led society to categorize them as "honorary Whites." Society uses this intermediary group's success to reinforce anti-Black values and to emphasize liberal, meritocratic policies.

Goffman's (1959) research on the "presentation of self" demonstrates how an ideology maintains its power over subjects not simply through coercion but also through "dramaturgy." In an interpretation of Goffman's theory, Ritzer posits that when individuals interact with the outside world, they consciously elect "to present a certain sense of self that will be accepted by others" (2007, p. 372). I employ presentation of self and dramaturgy to analyze how Kaling utilizes her power and agency as a producer. Bamberg (2006) contends that in addition to understanding how individuals perform their identity through the stories they produce, it is equally significant to analyze how individuals present themselves outside of the larger meta-narratives they construct and how they relate their stories to an audience. Bonilla-Silva discusses the stylistic elements—or the "peculiar *linguistic manners* and *rhetorical strategies*" that individuals employ to fortify color-blind racism (2010, p. 53). Strategies include the propensity to avoid using direct language related to race and the use of diminutives when discussing race.

In an era when a South Asian American woman produced and starred in her own romantic comedy sitcom on network television, I posit that scholars must simultaneously analyze how mass media utilizes color-blind racism to justify inequality, how people of color utilize honorary White narratives to assimilate and align themselves with Whites, and how the interaction of both these trends reinforces anti-Black racism.

Methodology and Data

Both Weber (1990) and Linneman (2008) agree that content analysis is a useful method for identifying the overarching patterns in various media sources. Julien purports that researchers can utilize content analysis to identify "conscious [sic] and unconscious messages communicated by text" and to study an extensive range of textual data, including, but not limited to, narratives, speeches, interview transcripts, and media images and videos (2008, pp. 120–122). I utilize content from episodes of *TMP* and interviews to analyze the role that mass media play in shaping our perception of and relationship to particular racial and ethnic groups.

TMP is a prime-time television show that began airing on the FOX Broadcasting Company in September 2012. Up until April 2015, it averaged approximately 3.5 to 4.5 million weekly viewers. In 2015, FOX canceled *TMP*; however, Hulu quickly picked up the show for its fourth season (Littleton, 2015). *TMP* serves as a particularly valuable data set because its cast consists of one character of South Asian descent, one Black character, and multiple White characters. Much of the show is set in New York City at an OB/GYN medical office. Kaling's character, Dr. Mindy Lahiri, serves as the protagonist. With her are coworker and later boyfriend Dr. Danny Castellano (Chris Messina), coworker Dr. Jeremy Reed (Ed Weeks), and two nurses, Morgan Tookers (Ike Barinholtz) and Tamra Webb (Xosha Roquemore). Other former and recurring characters include Dr. Peter Prentice (Adam Pally); Lahiri's ex-boyfriend Josh (Tommy Dewey); Brendan (Mark Duplass), a midwife who Lahiri used to date; receptionist and former nurse Beverley (Beth Grant); Lahiri's former ex-fiancé Casey (Anders Holm); Lahiri's best friend Gwen (Anna Camp); former receptionists Betsy (Zoe Jarman) and Shauna (Amanda Setton); and Lahiri's brother Rishi (Utkarsh Ambudkar).

Using the aforementioned frames of color-blind racism, I analyze verbatim quotes and the nature of characters' social relations from the first three seasons of the show (67 episodes total). In the following sections, I discuss (1) Lahiri's monologues, (2) Lahiri's relationships and interactions with other characters on the show, and (3) Kaling's "presentation of self" in interviews. First, I focus on representations of Lahiri as a character, and then I focus on representations of Kaling as a producer.

Results and Analysis: *The Mindy Project*

Language

The data in this section focus on the significance of naming, language, and discursive rhetoric. In several episodes, including the "Pilot," Lahiri affirms her connection to European-American culture by remarking how she has always idolized actors such as Tom Hanks and Sandra Bullock. Additionally, she makes numerous references to other pop culture idols such as Meg Ryan and Elle Woods. Take, for instance, the episodes titled "Harry and Sally" (season 1, episode 13) and "Harry and Mindy" (season 1, episode 14), a play upon the popular romantic comedy film *When Harry Met Sally*. In the episode "Danny Castellano is My Gynecologist," (season 1, episode 5), Danny asks Mindy whether she plans to start a family in the future (Kaling, 2012–2015). Lahiri informs Danny that she plans to have four children, whose names will be "Jaden, Madison, Brie, and Piper," names that carry a linguistic connection to White America, not South Asia.

Contrasting Lahiri's regard for European names and White actors and actresses, her references toward people of Asian and African ancestry embrace a different tone. For example, in the "Thanksgiving" episode (season 1, episode 6), when she meets a former blind date's new Indian girlfriend Gita, Lahiri instantly distances herself from sharing a connection with Gita and is disappointed when the globe that she spins predicts she will live in India. Similarly, in the episode "The One That Got Away" (season 1, episode 16), Lahiri's references to Afghanistan, Al Qaeda, and Osama Bin Laden reinforce stereotypes that associate Muslims with extremist terrorist. While Lahiri does not delineate intentional malignance toward South Asians and people of color and even wears an Indian sari in the season 3 finale "Best Man" (episode 21), her references to South Asian identity and toward people of color are often characterized by superficiality and disembodiment.

In the episode "In the Club" (season 1, episode 3), Lahiri and her coworkers go to a New York City nightclub. When Shauna informs Lahiri that NBA players hang out there, Lahiri exclaims,

MINDY: Oh my God! I'm going to be at a club where NBA guys are. This is amazing because Black guys love me.
SHAUNA: Whoa ... Keep your racism voice down.
MINDY: That is not racist. It's a scientific fact that Black guys love Indian girls. And Black guys also love ass, which I happen to have a lot of, thank you very much, so I'm gonna work my ass up to the VIP if you know what I mean.

When Lahiri receives an invitation to the VIP lounge, she affirms to Shauna, "See I told you Black guys love me." Ironically, Lahiri later realizes that Josh—a White, sports attorney who represents professional athletes and whom she dates in later episodes—invited her. In the lounge, Lahiri converses with Josh's clients, including professional basketball stars Amar'e Stoudemire and Dr. J. She forgets her pashmina next to Stoudemire when she leaves and does not hear Stoudemire yell out to inform her. When Lahiri says goodbye to Josh later in the episode, she remarks, "Hey, I think that Amar'e Stoudemire might have stolen my pashmina." While Lahiri's interaction with Gita and comments about Stoudemire can be seen as comical, one may also interpret Kaling and the writers to be making tongue-in-cheek references that reinforce stereotypes about Asian Americans' "perpetual foreigner" status (Fong, 2007) and Black men's inherent criminality.

Relationships

In this section, I discuss data that relate to the workplace and to Lahiri's social, mostly romantic, relationships with other characters on *TMP*. As a licensed OB/GYN who works with a team of physicians at a private practice, Dr. Lahiri occupies a position of power within her staff. She works as a supervisor to Betsy, Beverley, Morgan, Shauna, and Tamra. Drs. Danny Castellano and Jeremy Reed, both White males, work as equal partner colleagues to Lahiri. While a few episodes highlight the struggles that Lahiri exhibits as a woman with two White male colleagues in the workplace, the show does not portray her as experiencing overt discrimination with her partners. In the first few episodes of season 1, Lahiri and Jeremy are sexual, but do not formally date. Throughout the first two seasons, Lahiri dates several men. Initially, Lahiri's relationship with Danny can be seen as combative though the two clearly exhibit romantic feelings for each other. Their romantic relationship becomes "sealed with a kiss" in the season 2 finale "Danny and Mindy" (episode 22).

Until the practice hires Tamra near the end of season 1, all of Lahiri's coworkers are White. At first, Lahiri's relationship with Tamra is less cordial than her relationship with other coworkers. While they are not enemies, Tamra and Lahiri do not seem to share commonalities. In the episode "Girl Crush" (season 2, episode 18), Lahiri remarks on her identity as a woman of color and commonalities with Tamra in working at a White- and male-dominant work environment, but Tamra does not take this remark or Lahiri's other attempts at feigning solidarity seriously, perhaps because such comments are made in jest. These attempts often reemphasize Lahiri's power over rather than her identification with Tamra. In "Mindy Lahiri is a Racist" (season 2, episode 9), Tamra accuses Lahiri of being racist. When Lahiri acknowledges her use of a condescending tone with Tamra, Tamra ultimately drops her accusations. While this reference can be also interpreted as comical, it is one of the few interactions that Lahiri has with Non-Whites on *TMP* and reinforces the power dynamic between Lahiri and Tamra.

Lahiri's interactions with people of color outside the workplace setting are minimal. Throughout season 1, all of Lahiri's non-familial social relationships are with characters of White European descent. Lahiri's best friend from college, Gwen, is White, skinny, blond, and married with a child. Gwen's successful marriage and nuclear family symbolizes what Lahiri desires. The sitcom characterizes Lahiri as a single workaholic who desires a family life but is too inexperienced, dramatic, and unstable to attract marriageable mates. Of the 13 men whom Lahiri dates or has sexual relationships with during the first two seasons, all are White. In the "Mindy Lahiri is a Racist" episode (season 2, episode 9), Lahiri suggests to her colleagues, "I'm Indian; I can't be racist." Danny responds, "Oh please, you only hook up with White guys" (Kaling, 2012–2015). While Lahiri's colleagues poke fun at her bias toward dating White men, the humorous remark does not actually confront her prejudice tendencies in a disruptive tone. Lahiri continues to date from a pool of White men.

Lahiri's choice of rhetoric and social relationships support the structure of color-blind racism. The minimal attention given to Lahiri's racial and ethnic background plays into how she develops her relationships with friends, coworkers, and intimate partners. The abstract liberalism frame helps explain how Lahiri's ability to assimilate, culturally and economically, is seemingly guided by her independent free will as opposed to structural ideologies and policies. Accordingly, the audience is invited to believe that Lahiri acquired her relationships through her personal efforts, individualized merits, and work ethic. Furthermore, in a society that is "blind" toward color and supposedly sees all human beings as one race, the differences between South Asian and Whites are assumed to be insignificant; those who notice racial differences are the ones who are racist. By focusing on her commonalities with Whites, Lahiri plays into her honorary White placement. Lahiri jokingly highlights differences in a couple scenes of the show. For example, Casey jokes about his racist family meeting her Indian relatives in "All My Problems Solved Forever …" (season 2, episode 1); in the "L.A." episode (season 2, episode 13), Lahiri ridicules Danny for his ignorance toward her identity as a Hindu. However, these differences do not set Lahiri—a professional doctor who has no issues dating White men— back from social, economic, and cultural assimilation. The focus on Lahiri's commonalities with Whites happens at the expense of a focus on similar connections to people of color.

The show also affirms Bonilla-Silva's minimization of racism framework. *TMP* only creates a space for Lahiri to express her racialized experience as a person of color in a comedic manner. If *TMP* were to develop a plot line that addresses Lahiri's racialized experiences, then the show's focus would shift toward highlighting Lahiri's Non-White identity and would likely be less appealing to the mainstream White viewer. Consequently, *TMP* depends on the frames of color-blind racism for its survival, its positive ratings, and "success" in the television industry.

Results and Analysis: Kaling as a Producer

Ritzer's (2007) reiteration of dramaturgy and Bamberg's understanding of presentation of self suggest the importance of understanding how entertainers represent and perform their identity off the air. This section observes Kaling's off-screen presentation of self in American culture. Lahiri's references toward Black culture place Blacks in a racial category markedly different than her own, reinforcing how the racial binary contrasts Whiteness to Blackness. I purport that Kaling's commitment to a discursive rhetoric of Whiteness on air mimics her commitment to a similar rhetoric off air. For example, Kaling identifies with a stage name that is more common and more easily pronounced than "Chokalingam." Though her character's surname is recognizably Indian, Kaling's stage name, similar to Lahiri's ideal children's names delineate her assimilationist inclinations. Kaling's efforts to distance herself from her birth name also demonstrate the pervasiveness of White racial ideology and the normative influence of cultural assimilation on Non-Whites.

In July 2012, journalist Alan Sepinwall interviewed Kaling at the TV critics press tour. Sepinwall asked Kaling about what it means for her to be "an Indian-American woman fronting her own sitcom."

KALING: If I'm like trailblazing accidentally, then great and I should probably not say "accidentally." I don't really think of my work in political terms. [...] Even over the course of *The Office*'s eight years, when I started, Aziz (Ansari), Danny (Pudi) weren't there yet. So I've seen an incredible amount of change and to NB's credit, they've put us on these shows. But this is the first time I'm being a lead and front and center [...]. *I don't feel daunted by it because I think, "Okay, Tina did it, Amy did it, Sarah did it, Lena is doing it and all the other people." But then again I don't think of myself so much as in terms of being Indian. So if that's another thing that Americans see me as, we'll have to see.* [...][emphasis added]

SEPINWALL: I think that's what is good about it is that it's not about you being Indian. It's just about you playing this part.

KALING: *I hope so. I think that we're in a time when it doesn't have to actually be about those things* [emphasis added]. Although, maybe they'll come up in an interesting way.

(Sepinwall, 2012, para. 41–44)

In addition to not thinking of her work in political terms, Kaling mentions White actresses in Hollywood as her role models, noting that she does not think of herself "in terms of being Indian." Kaling also remarks on living in an era when her racial-ethnic identity carries less significance, recognizing the move of certain segments of the population to view our society as one that is post-racial.

In a separate commentary at PaleyFest 2013, Kaling expressed, "I try not to rely on it or deny the fact that I'm Indian. I mean, you turn on the show, and you'll know that I'm Indian. I can't hide that." While she feels honored to inspire South Asian American fans, she also does not want to take on the burden of representing all Indian American women; she notes that White male actors do not feel compelled to serve as representations for their race because of their dominance in media.

Kaling seems willing to draw attention to her South Asian identity if it benefits her. However, given that her South Asian identity carries little influence on how she produces her show and plays her character, it seems as if "race" does not matter to her. The findings from *TMP* illustrate how Lahiri embodies a rhetoric and racial grammar of color-blind racism. By avoiding authentic discussions about how she represents her Non-White identity, Kaling reinforces her belief that we live in a post-racial era.

In this analysis, I argue that Kaling disembodies her Indian identity and writes herself as an honorary White both off and on the air of *TMP*. Kaling disembodies her Indian identity in order to survive on air. Further, when

Kaling calls on her woman of color or Indian identity, it is at times that she thinks it may benefit her ratings. Similarly, Lahiri manipulates her South Asian—or Indian—identity by calling upon it in times when it leverages her to a higher position of power. The Indian identity shows up to tokenize Kaling as a producer and Lahiri as a character; these momentary identifications with her South Asian heritage make Whiteness more visible.

In an era when President Barack Obama made history as the first U.S. president of African descent, many Americans use his victory as proof that we live in a post-racial society (McWhorter, 2008; Millhiser, 2015). Similarly, within the contemporary media structure, the ideology of color-blind racism necessitates that the depiction of Whiteness be normalized and that the depiction of Non-Whites be an inconsequential signifier of one's identity. Mainstream media networks, such as FOX, operate within the context of a political economy that seeks to utilize entertainers who embody this post-racial ideology. These mainstream media networks do not seek characters and producers who seriously call attention to the existing racial, class, caste, or gender inequalities. FOX is not narrating the stories of South Asian Muslim families' experiences with hate crimes and FBI surveillance, Dalit people's resistance to caste-based oppression, or working-class immigrant taxi drivers' experience with post-9/11 discrimination, hate crimes, and FBI surveillance. As Thakore (2014) noted, such stories do not uphold the modern political economy's narrative of the honorary White or model minority. FOX tells the story of the successful Indian doctor because such a "bootstraps" narrative validates the American Dream and justifies cultural assimilation. Accordingly, even if Kaling wanted to write in working-class Non-White characters that date Non-Whites and call attention to post-9/11 racism, FOX may refuse to broadcast such a show. The representations of Kaling and Lahiri illustrate how dominant racial ideologies within the contemporary media structure prevent Non-Whites from constructing characters that counter stereotypical images, even when Non-Whites are in a position of relative power.

Conclusion

While *TMP* does not avoid discussions on Mindy's racial identity altogether, *TMP* presents Mindy Lahiri as "race-less." As Bonilla-Silva (2010) claims, color-blind racism encourages people to utilize rhetoric and "racial grammar" that identify racism as a thing of the past. Moreover, in line with the "honorary White" theory, *TMP* utilizes a rhetoric that understands people of South Asian identity to be nearly similar in speech, action, and values to White Europeans. Why may a show like *TMP* evade a discussion of Lahiri's noticeable Non-White identity? To such a question, I respond by inquiring, would a show like *TMP* be on a mainstream broadcasting company such as FOX if it highlighted Lahiri's Non-White identity? Mindy's disembodiment of her Indian identity is directly connected to its popularity and success with mainstream viewers. In a society that is easily lured by the notion of a post-racial society, Kaling must appeal to the norm, attitudes, and humor of a mostly White, "post-racial" audience. Kaling chooses to disembody her Indian identity because her success as a producer and actor depends on her ability to affirm the White supremacist status quo. As a larger implication, Kaling demonstrates how Non-Black, Non-White immigrants experience privilege in their ability to manipulate their racial identity to gain access to White culture and economic success.

Currently, Kaling's work on *The Mindy Project* reinforces "color-blind racism" and the notion that South Asian Americans are the honorary Whites. Some viewers may argue that the character of Lahiri subverts the status quo by inviting audience members to laugh at her comical attempts to culturally assimilate into White norms. However, if Kaling truly wished to address racism, she would produce a show that directly challenges the racial status quo as opposed to one that simply responds to the challenges of cultural assimilation. Similar to how stand-up comic Hari Kondabolu and writer Eddie Huang (in his memoir, and now ABC series, *Fresh Off the Boat*[1]) invite critiques on colonialism and racism in their narratives, Kaling can utilize *TMP* to offer solutions to social injustices. Now that Hulu has picked up *TMP* for season 4, Kaling has an opportunity to use her creative power, wit, and intellect to complicate the representation of South Asian identity on air by calling attention to issues that affect marginalized members of the community and constructing complex relationships between herself and other people of color. Perhaps shifting her strategy will challenge the show's success with mainstream audiences. Nonetheless, a more complex depiction carries the potential to honor people of color's racialized experiences and subvert the existing racist media structure.

Note

1. While Huang's memoir calls attention to his racialized experiences as a Chinese American, Huang critiques how the content is catered to a mass audience since its development into a television show.

References

Alsultany, E. (2012). *The Arabs and Muslims in the media: Race and representation after 9/11*. New York, NY: New York University Press.
Bamberg, M. (2006). Stories: Big or small: Why do we care? *Narrative Inquiry*, 16(1), 139–147.
Bogart, L. (1958). *The age of television*. New York, NY: Frederick Ungar.
Bonilla-Silva, E. (2010). *Racism without racists: Color-blind racism and the persistence of racial inequality in America*. Lanham, MD: Rowman & Littlefield.
Brown, M. K., Carnoy, M., Currie, E., Duster, T., Oppenheimer, D. B., Shultz, M., & Wellman, D. (2003). *Whitewashing race: The myth of a color-blind society*. Berkeley, CA: University of California Press.

Carr, L. G. (1997). *"Color-blind" racism.* Thousand Oaks, CA: Sage Publications.
Chou, R. S., & Feagin, J. R. (2008). *The myth of the model minority: Asian Americans facing racism.* Boulder, CO: Paradigm Publishers.
Collins, P. H. (2000). *Black feminist thought.* New York, NY: Routledge.
Dates, J. L., & Barlow, W. (Eds.). (1993). *Split image: African Americans in the mass media.* Washington, DC: Howard University Press.
Davé, S. (2005). Apu's Brown Voice: Cultural inflection and South Asian accents. In L. Nishime, T. Oren, & S. Davé (Eds.), *East main street: Asian American popular culture* (pp. 313–336). New York, NY: NYU Press.
Davé, S. (2013). *Indian accents: Brown voice and racial performance in American television and film.* Urbana, IL: University of Illinois Press.
Feagin, J. (2006). *Systemic racism: A theory of oppression.* New York, NY: Routledge.
Feagin, J. (2010). *The White racial frame: Centuries of racial framing and counter-framing.* New York, NY: Routledge.
Fong, T. P. (2007). *The contemporary Asian American experience: Beyond the model minority.* New York, NY: Pearson.
Goffman, E. (1959). *The presentation of self in everyday life* (1st ed.). New York, NY: Anchor.
Gottschlich, P. (2011). Apu, Neela, and Amita stereotypes of Indian Americans in mainstream TV shows in the U.S. *Internationales Asien Forum. International Quarterly for Asian Studies, 42*(3), 279–298.
Gray, H. (1995). *Watching race: Television and the struggle for "Blackness."* Minneapolis, MN: University of Minnesota Press.
Grindstaff, L., & Turow, J. (2006). Video cultures: Television sociology in the "new TV" age. *Annual Review of Sociology, 32,* 103–125.
Hamamoto, D. Y. (1994). *Monitored peril: Asian Americans and the politics of TV representation.* Minneapolis, MN: University of Minnesota Press.
Hunt, D. M. (Ed.). (2004). *Channeling Blackness: Studies on television and race in America.* New York, NY: Oxford University Press.
Julien, H. (2008). Content analysis. In L. Given, *The SAGE encyclopedia of qualitative research methods.* Thousand Oaks, CA: SAGE Publications. Retrieved from http://knowledge.sagepub.com/view/research/n65.xml.
Kaling, M. (Writer, Producer). (2012–2015). *The Mindy Project* [Television series]. Los Angeles, CA: FOX Broadcasting Network.
Linneman, T. J. (2008). How do you solve a problem like Will Truman? The feminization of gay masculinities on *Will & Grace. Men and Masculinities, 10*(5), 583–603.
Littleton, C. (2015, August 9). "The Mindy Project" celebrates new creative freedom at Hulu. *Variety.* Retrieved from http://variety.com/2015/tv/news/the-mindy-project-hulu-mindy-kaling-fox-1201566383/.
McWhorter, J. (2008, December 30). Racism in America is over. *Forbes.* Retrieved from http://www.forbes.com/2008/12/30/end-of-racism-oped-cx_jm_1230mcwhorter.html.
Millhiser, I. (2015, June 18). When John Roberts said there isn't enough racism in America to justify the Voting Rights Act. Retrieved from http://thinkprogress.org/justice/2015/06/18/3671107/two-years-ago-supreme-court-said-isnt-enough-racism-justify-voting-rights-act/.
Monk-Turner, E., Heiserman, M., Johnson, C., Cotton, V., & Jackson, M. (2010). The portrayal of racial minorities on prime time television: A replication of the

Mastro and Greenberg study a decade later. *Studies in Popular Culture*, 32(2), 101–114.

Mulvey, L. (1975). Visual pleasure and narrative cinema. *Screen*, 16(3), 6–18.

Mulvey, L. (2009). *Visual and other pleasures* (2nd ed.). New York: Palgrave Macmillan.

PaleyFest. (2013, March 8). *The Mindy Project: In person*. Paley Center for Media, Beverly Hills, CA.

Pozner, J. L. (2010). *Reality bites back: The troubling truth about guilty pleasure TV*. Berkeley, CA: Seal Press.

Prashad, V. (2008). My hip-hop life. In A. Nair & M. Balaji (Eds.), *Desi rap: Hip-hop and South Asian America* (pp. 3–16). Lanham, MD: Lexington Books.

Ritzer, G. (2007). *Sociological theory*. New York, NY: McGraw-Hill.

Sepinwall, A. (2012, September 4). Mindy Kaling on "The Mindy Project," "The Office" and more. Retrieved from http://www.hitfix.com/whats-alan-watching/mindy-kaling-on-the-mindy-project-the-office-and-more.

Sreberny, A. (2005). "Not only, but also": Mixedness and media. *Journal of Ethnic and Migration Studies*, 31(3), 443–459.

Thakore, B. K. (2014). Must-see TV: South Asian characterizations in American popular media. *Sociology Compass*, 8(2), 149–156.

Weber, R. P. (1990). *Basic content analysis*. Los Angeles, CA: Sage.

Part III
Visual Representations of Contention

8 Drifting for Whiteness
Hollywood Representations of Asian Americans in the Twenty-First Century

John D. Foster

In May 2015 a bit of a ruckus ensued when some media outlets criticized the casting of Emma Stone, a White American actress with blond hair and blue eyes, as a multiracial character named Allison Ng in the Hollywood film *Aloha* (2015). The character was portrayed as half White and half Asian—more specifically, one-quarter native Hawaiian and one-quarter Chinese. The director of the film, Cameron Crowe, later issued an apology for the decision to cast Stone for the part. The miscasting was considered to be the cherry on top of the sundae of a lousy film, which was almost universally panned by film critics.

While some (rightly) pointed out how it is perfectly possible for an American of such a descent to have such phenotypical features (and that, according to Crowe, the real-life Allison Ng was a "red head"; Crowe, 2015), the important point is that, once again, Hollywood had effectively, if unintentionally, whitewashed a character literally created as "Asian American" (or as *hapa*, or half Asian). This action by Crowe and Sony Pictures denied yet another lead role for an actor of Asian-Pacific descent. What was the reasoning behind the casting decision? It could not have been for a lack of Asian American actresses available. What actress would turn down the opportunity to co-star alongside Bradley Cooper and Rachel McAdams in a romantic comedy directed by the director of *Jerry McGuire* and *Say Anything*? Perhaps one reason for the casting of a White woman to portray an Asian American character was an attempt to avoid charges of racism for the condescending treatment of native Hawaiian culture in the film. Even more important was the way the film used the character and her cultural traditions to strengthen a White man's ego.

The decision to whiten or even erase a film character of Asian-Pacific descent is nothing new. Other films such as *The Last Airbender* (2010) or *21* (2008) have also been criticized for casting White actors in roles of Asian American characters, particularly for lead roles. Far too often characters of Asian-Pacific descent are in the background, little more than props to broaden a film's appeal to a more racially diverse audience while maintaining its White support. Inserting any Non-White character in the spotlight causes too many White viewers to ghettoize the film and call it a "Black" or "Indian" movie (Chaisson, 2000). Who are the filmmakers that make these decisions to keep Non-White actors in the woodwork while continuing to place Whites in the spotlight? The answer might surprise some: I should mention that, while Crowe and Robert Luketic, director of *21*, are both White (Crowe is American and Luketic is from Australia), *The Last Airbender* was directed by M. Night Shyamalan, an Indian American. Meanwhile, Clint Eastwood—a man whose conservative views are well known—cast Hmong American actors to play lead roles in his film *Gran Torino* (another film included in this study).

While the portrayal of Asian Americans, including those who are half-Asian, in Hollywood films is welcome, how they are depicted matters even more. Perhaps Asian Americans can no longer be excluded, but the old habits of the blatantly racist past too often continue to rule the day in Hollywood. Even more important, filmmakers can employ Asian American characters to assist in the maintenance of the White hegemonic social order, whether intended or not. Despite this kind of Orientalist renewal, however, there are also challenges to the "old" Hollywood that even receive (at least limited) support from Hollywood itself. This challenge comes from a variety of Asian American filmmakers, as well as some Whites who, whether intended or not, challenge the racial order in U.S. cinema that has lasted for generations. My focus in this chapter is on the representation of Asian Americans in Hollywood films in the new century, and what impact (if any) Asian American filmmakers have had in this endeavor.

The Perpetual Stranger

Despite people of Asian descent in America for more than two centuries, Asian Americans continue to occupy the social status of what Georg Simmel (see Levine, 1971) called the stranger, or one "who comes today and stays tomorrow." While other ethnoracial minorities have been or are on the margins of U.S. society, the Asian American remains the quintessential stranger. In fact, the very conception of "Asian American" is disputed (Kibria, 1998). I posit that the term "perpetual stranger" is a more fitting than "forever foreigner" (Tuan, 1998) or "perpetual foreigner" (Wu, 2002) in that Asian Americans are indeed Americans, not sojourners or tourists. Palumbo-Liu (1999) describes the peculiar social position of Asian Americans this way: "Asia/America resides *in transit*, as a point of reference on the horizon that is part of *both* a 'minority' identity and a 'majority' identity'" (p. 5; emphasis in original).

Following the lifting of immigration restrictions in 1965, more people from Asian countries were able to claim residency in the United States. As the proportion of Latinos and Asian American continues to grow, the formation of a tri-racial social system (Bonilla-Silva, 2004) seems increasingly possible. The racialized social system unique to the United States did not transpire by accident; it was created by and for powerful White men in an attempt to maintain their privilege and dominance in U.S. society. Media outlets assisted in the transmission of this message, including Hollywood movies (Fuller, 2010; Locke, 2009).

A "New" Orientalism?

Orientalism, a concept coined by the late Edward Said, is "a style of thought based upon ontological and epistemological distinction made between 'the Orient' and (most of the time) 'the Occident'" (Said, 1978, p. 2). According to Said, the Orient does not exist in the literal sense, but is rather an Occidental or Western (predominantly British, French, and American) creation for the purpose of domination and self-aggrandizement. The European perception of the Orient and "Orientals" differs somewhat from the American one, in that Americans tend to focus on China and Japan rather than the Middle East (e.g., Turkey, Syria, Lebanon, etc.) or India, although this has changed in recent years. The American version has traditionally homogenized Asians and Asian Americans into one of these two groups (Chinese or Japanese), whereas other groups have been either excluded entirely or assumed to be identical to those from China or Japan.

Hollywood has traditionally depicted Asians and Asian Americans as interchangeable and malleable, capable of turning from good to evil in an instant. A good example of this interchangeability includes the flip-flop of good Asian/bad Asian characters following World War II, when the "evil Jap" became the "evil Red Chinese" and the benign and "mysterious" Chinese became the "meek" and submissive Japanese (Shah, 2003). Furthermore, seemingly "good" images of Asian/Americans are typically depicted as docile, meek, and submissive to White masculinist authority (Chou & Feagin, 2008).

Depictions of Asians and Asian Americans in U.S. media have not always been negative. Depending upon the social realities at a given moment, Hollywood filmmakers and other creators of U.S. dominant culture have used Asians in ways to achieve certain desired ends, whether such images were positively or negatively charged. For instance, more "positive" portrayals of Asians have been utilized to counteract the actions other racial minorities, particularly African Americans. Still, whether the portrayals were positive or negative, Asians (and Asian Americans) were (and continue to be) depicted as fundamentally different from "us" or incapable of becoming fully "American." Finally and most important (while often overlooked by analysts), White filmmakers have used images of ethnoracial "others" as a method of propping up Whiteness, while expressing "true" interests or values. Consequently, Non-Whites are given the task of doing the "dirty work" of cinema in which White purity and innocence is maintained while otherness is further degraded.

Images of Fu Manchu, Madame Butterfly, and other images of the past as portrayed in history books, films, oral narratives, ceremonies, and other sociocultural products are copied and mass produced in today's capitalistic postindustrial societies, which creates a kind of political Orientalism (Tchen, 1999). The effects can be devastating: on one hand, members of the dominant group come to believe that Asians and Asian Americans are really like the way they are depicted in popular culture; on the other hand Asian Americans feel isolated, degraded, segregated, and discriminated against by these images (Shah, 2003). Worse, these images can affect the way members of the oppressed view themselves, and can even assist in their own oppression, thereby engaging in symbolic violence (Bourdieu, 1993).

In more recent years (particularly since the turn of the century) images of Asian Americans have "softened" for a number of reasons. First, demographically Asian Americans (and Americans of color more generally) have become more visible, especially in particular regions of the country. Second, the work of watchdog organizations such as the MANAA (Media Action Network for Asian Americans) help to expose the misrepresentations of Asian Americans in Hollywood films and other forms of media, which can apply pressure on Hollywood filmmakers and studios to change their ways. In fact, a press release by MANAA criticizing the film *Aloha* for the casting decision was what had sparked interest in the issue (at least in large part). Third, the taste for more blatant forms of racist imagery of White Americans has waned in recent years, preferring more subtle imagery that maintains White supremacy under the pretext of racial tolerance and multiculturalism (Hughey, 2009; Park, 2010). The ways that Hollywood filmmakers, including Asian American filmmakers, "drift for whiteness," while ostensibly painting a picture of racial and ethnic solidarity, is the task of this chapter.

Method

This study is a content analysis of Hollywood representations of Asian Americans that takes a phenomenological-interpretive approach (Liberato, Rebollo-Gil, Foster, & Moras, 2009). Utilizing such an approach enables analysts to critically assess the ways filmmakers characterize society and its inhabitants. In addition, this approach assists in the exposure of the processes through which these cultural products are formed and legitimized, which is crucial for making critical readings of cultural products.

The data used for this chapter consist of 10 Hollywood films released between 2002 and 2013 (see Table 8.1 for the list of films). The criteria for films used in the analysis had two primary characteristics: First, these films were "mainstream" Hollywood productions that were critically acclaimed, commercially successful, or both. The box-office performance for each film was looked up at the website *Rotten Tomatoes*, and identified by ratings on the "Tomatometer" (which measures the percentage of film critics who liked the movie). The second criterion was that the films depicted Asian American characters in roles that are central to the film's storyline. Since the number

Table 8.1 Sample of Films, 2002–2013

Film	Tomatometer Rating (Percent)	Box Office (in Millions)
Better Luck Tomorrow (2002)	81	$3.7
The Fast & the Furious: Tokyo Drift (2006)	37	$62.5
Fast & Furious (2009)	28	$155.0
Fast Five (2011)	78	$209.8
Fast & Furious 6 (2013)	69	$238.7
Gran Torino (2009)	79	$148.1
Harold & Kumar Go to White Castle (2004)	74	$18.2
Harold & Kumar Escape from Guantanamo Bay (2008)	53	$38.1
A Very Harold & Kumar Christmas (2011)	68	$35.0
The Namesake (2006)	87	$13.7

Notes: The "Tomatometer" is the percentage of film critics approved by Rotten Tomatoes who gave the movie a positive review. The figures cited for box office performance is for domestic performance only; it does not include international earnings. Box office numbers were cross-checked at www.imdb.com.

of Hollywood films featuring Asian American characters in their stories is scant, finding such films was difficult, partially given to the rise in recent years of the "multiculti" action film, in which a crowded cast is utilized to broaden its appeal while maintaining a White (usually male) lead at the center of attention (Beltrán, 2005). While the four *Fast & Furious* films fit squarely into this film genre, one Asian American character takes a more pivotal role, at least in the first film of the series in which he appears (*The Fast & the Furious: Tokyo Drift*); thus, this particular film in the series is given the most attention (referred to hereafter as *Tokyo Drift*).

The search for these films generally centered on the filmographies of well-known Asian American actors such as John Cho or Kal Penn, and a kind of snowball sample emerged. Unfortunately, many films were excluded from the analysis because they lacked the criteria necessary. For example, characters played by Keanu Reeves in films such as *The Matrix: Reloaded* (2003) tend to be Whitewashed, with essentially no reference to an Asian American identity. Although there is little to no reference to the character Han's ethnoracial background in the *Fast & Furious* films, these films were included because his character's identity had been established in the previously released *Better Luck Tomorrow*. Another reason many films were excluded from the analysis was because they were indies (i.e., movies financed independently without any support from a Hollywood studio). Thus, not only were these films financed by Hollywood, they also appeared to turn a profit for their respective distributors.

Results

Despite the diversity of films used for the analysis, I found three common themes that emerged from all or most of the films. The first theme dealt with the quest for identity, often coupled with a general desire for multiculturalism or transnationalism. This theme was most noticeable in the *Fast & Furious* films, *Better Luck Tomorrow*, and *The Namesake*. The second theme consisted of Asian American characters being used as fodder to strengthen the power of the film's White male lead. This theme appeared in *Gran Torino* most notably, though it appeared in other films, including *Tokyo Drift*. The third dominant theme was the struggle of the Asian American characters dealing with White racism while navigating within a White-dominated society. This theme appeared most in the *Harold & Kumar* films, particularly in *Harold & Kumar Go to White Castle* (referred to hereafter as *White Castle*).

Multiculturalism and the Struggle for Identity

One of the dominant themes that emerged from the films was the struggle of the Asian American characters to establish an identity and to find where they belong in U.S. society. The most common solution to their dilemma in these films is to embrace multiculturalism and, more generally, to intermingle with ethnoracial others (especially Whites) to "fit in" and achieve "success." In contrast, those characters who did not embrace multiculturalism were punished. For instance, in *Tokyo Drift* the primary antagonist of the plot named D.K. (an acronym for "Drift King"), who resembles a kind of Fu Manchu character (intelligent but evil and androgynous), chastises his girlfriend Neela for refusing to accept her inferior position in the Japanese social order (her mother was a call girl from Australia). He is ultimately defeated on his own turf by a White American named Sean who has learned Japanese customs (by the end of the film he is speaking some Japanese) and uses a hybrid car to defeat him (a Ford Mustang with a Nissan engine), and Neela leaves him for Sean.

Color-blindness is advocated for in the *Fast & Furious* films, while racial difference is trivialized. For example, in *Tokyo Drift* considerable time is devoted to deconstructing the Japanese concept of *gaijin* (meaning "outsider" more generally or a neutral term for "foreigner"). The film misrepresents this term, perhaps unintentionally, by treating it as a kind of ethnic slur on par with ethnophaulisms such as "nip" or "gook." While it is considered a slur to use this term in reference to a hapa (or half Japanese), it is not used the way D.K. does when speaking to Sean, in which the film seems to imply that D.K. is using it as a kind of slur. A cinematic move such as this one appeals to many within the White American audience that views this as an instance of "reverse racism." In one scene, Sean tells Neela how he can relate to her experience as an outsider, despite his Whiteness, and takes it a step further by making it a personal choice: "I kind of made myself an outsider, you know, without even thinking about it. But I realize now, outsider or insider it doesn't really matter. All that matters is knowing what you really want and going after it." In effect, Sean compares his own experience to Neela's status in contemporary Japan. While the comparison defies logic in that race is a social fact and not simply left to personal choice, she appears to concur with his analogy. This point of view lacks an understanding of the structural realities of racialized social systems and can be deployed to blame minorities for failing to "succeed" due to a lack of initiative (Bonilla-Silva, 2001). Regardless of intentions, "drifting" for color-blindness fails to challenge the racial order with Whites on top.

The intended audience of a film can make a major difference in how filmmakers portray various people and locales. With the exceptions of *Gran Torino* and *The Namesake*, the sample of films for this study targeted predominantly young males. The desire for multiculturalism and color-blindness continued with the portrayal of women in these movies. The aforementioned Neela from *Tokyo Drift*, along with Giselle from the other *Fast & Furious* films (who develops an intimate relationship with Han), could both pass as White and possess "White" features. Meanwhile, in *White Castle* Harold expresses disinterest in Cindy, a fellow Korean American who leads Princeton's East Asian group, and prefers Maria, a fair-skinned Latina, who lives in his apartment building. Over the course of the film, Harold suffers from low self-confidence, and at one point tells Kumar "I'm gonna end up with Cindy whether we like it or not," as if he would be settling if he wound up with her. Similar to the *Fast & Furious* films, the desire for multiculturalism and a melting pot appears to be a façade for a continued promotion of the White aesthetic, generally giving thin, fair-skinned women the most screen time, and they are the most valued and sought after by men (Beltrán, 2005).

Among all the films in the sample, the greatest contrast existed between the competing messages stemming from Justin Lin's *Better Luck Tomorrow* and Mira Nair's *The Namesake*. In *Better Luck Tomorrow*, the primary characters are punished for failing to have a more diverse circle of friends, thereby echoing the theme of multiculturalism in the *Fast & Furious* films: characters that possess an ability to cross ethnoracial lines and navigate a multicultural world succeed, while those who lack such skills do not. Conversely, in *The Namesake* Nair neither punishes nor rewards the second-generation children for their boundary crossings; the film is not a rejection of U.S. culture (though it is subtly critical of it) but an embrace of transnationalism and individualism. *Better Luck Tomorrow*, while still somewhat subtle, is more forceful in its indictment of U.S. culture, including suburbanization and segregation, the education system, ethnic stereotyping (namely, model minority), societal definitions of "success," and even the American Dream itself.

Better Luck Tomorrow is meant to disturb and provoke discussion, as Lin had pointed out during an interview (Aderer, 2001) following the film's release. One of the points not discussed around the film was the subtle yet significant anti-Blackness, as well as its implicit presentation of a tri-racial system in U.S. society. Following a scene in which one of the main characters pulls a gun on a bigoted White student at a party, they are shown driving alongside a group of four young men who I contend are ethically, if not racially mixed. The young man in the passenger seat (who has the darkest skin tone of the four) brandishes his Uzi to the monoracial, Asian American boys, and then they drive off. The protagonists had violated a "golden" rule of sorts, and that is to avoid adopting a "gangster mentality," as Lin referred to it, or in other words, to be associated with Blacks (or at least one particular element of Black culture). Paradoxically, these two scenes show how limited this group of Asian Americans is due to their lack of diversity within.

While *Better Luck Tomorrow* provides an example in which the children of immigrants fail to adjust to the larger society, *The Namesake* portrays the opposite. Most attention is given to Gogol, the son of Bengali immigrants who struggles to establish his own identity. By the time he is an adolescent, he begins to reject his parents' customs and by young adulthood spends most of his time with his White girlfriend and her family. After Gogol's father dies, the pendulum swings in the opposite direction as he tries to live according to the ways *he thinks* his parents would want him to (as his aunt told him before going off to college: "Have as much fun as you want. But marry a Bengali!"). Indeed, there is a desire to maintain knowledge of one's roots (as the trip to India underscores). However, there is also a desire to be happy, even if happiness requires actions that defy conventional practices, including interethnic and/or interracial marriage. Ultimately, with his marriage to a Bengali American in tatters, Gogol has found his equilibrium: "For the first time in my life, I actually feel free." Unlike *Better Luck Tomorrow*, *The Namesake* demonstrates both the importance of knowing where you came from as well as navigating this society in the present.

Assisting the (Re)Establishment of White Domination

Another theme commonplace in these Hollywood movies was the use of Asian American characters to assist White characters in achieving their goals. While many films from the previous century have also done this, the films used for this study on the surface come across as more progressive (e.g., the portrayals of Asian Americans are often more humanizing and less stereotypical). This shift in representation of Asian Americans is in part due to the greater distaste for blatantly racist imagery; hence, a "new" racism was born (Bonilla-Silva, 2010). By the late 1990s, such portrayals of Asian/Americans had fallen out of style. Nonetheless, the need to glorify White Americans continued; thus, *cinethetic racism* (Hughey, 2009) emerged in order to reproduce stereotypes of racial minorities and to normalize Whiteness, all under the guise of racial harmony and cooperation.

Among the films in the sample for this study was this theme generated more than by Clint Eastwood's *Gran Torino*. While the film was generally well received by critics, few recognized the film's defense of the racial status quo and, more specifically, the role Asian Americans play in defending it. In addition to directing, Eastwood stars as Walt Kowalski, a "White ethnic" male at the center of attention experiencing an identity crisis due to his age, poor health, estrangement from his family, and his inner demons haunting him from his service during the Korean War. Kowalski is an unabashed bigot who educates viewers on nearly every ethnic slur targeting Asians and Asian Americans over the last 50 years. Initially he is repulsed by the Hmong neighbors next door, but spends time with them over the course of the film. After an unsuccessful attempt to thwart a threat from a Hmong gang, Kowalski presumably sacrifices his life for them.

As Roche and Hösle (2011) point out, *Torino* is a film about redemption, and that "Walt is a Christ figure" (p. 662). However, their reading is limited because it misses a critical point of the film: that Whiteness is presumably in crisis, and Walt sacrifices himself for it. While the audience is expected to credit Kowalski for his innumerable "gifts" to the Hmong family, in fact everything Walt does for them in the film is for redeeming and fulfilling himself. The point of *Gran Torino*, then, is to restore one's faith in White supremacy, not in Catholicism. Indeed, *Gran Torino* is yet another instance of the "White messiah" film in which a White male "saves" racial others from themselves (Hughey, 2014; Vera & Gordon, 2003).

Gran Torino stands out from the other films for this analysis because it seems to be from an earlier era, a swan song for modernity. For instance, there is no love for multiculturalism here: racial boundaries are clearly drawn between Whites, Blacks, Latinos, and the Hmong. Furthermore, *Gran Torino* is another example of pitting Asian Americans against Blacks and Latinos, a key component to the construction of the model minority. The Vang Lors are deemed deserving in *Torino*. Unlike the *cholos* or Black gang members portrayed in the film, the Hmong are allowed opportunities to prove their worthiness. More specifically, they are deserving of assistance from White Americans, though not government assistance, since one of the main tenets of the model minority myth is self-affirmative action (Palumbo-Liu, 1999). Meanwhile, other youth of color are depicted (albeit mostly in fleeting and superficial ways), but they are underserving of Whites' attention, much less assistance. In fact, *Torino* is as much about Blacks (and to a lesser extent Latinos) as it is about the Hmong; while the former are lost causes, the latter has potential to assist Whites in "taking back our streets," as Pat Buchanan once said back in 1992. However, not all Hmong (and thus Asian) Americans are deemed deserving: Thao and Sue's cousin Fong and his gang are given no opportunity to redeem themselves in this film; in other words, they are a lost cause because they are "soiled" (as Kowalski describes himself to Thao). The gang members are used by Walt to save himself and his ego as the White messiah of Non-White people—yet, ironically, Walt needs them for his own salvation.

While it is weak Asian American characters that assist in the redemption of a White man in *Gran Torino*, it is a strong character that helps a young

White man establish his dominance in *Tokyo Drift*; the roles reverse but the goal remains the same. In *Gran Torino*, Walt takes Thao under his wing and teaches him the ways of racist America; in *Tokyo Drift*, Han (one of the main characters from *Better Luck Tomorrow*) plays a 21st century version of Mr. Miyagi as he trains Sean to become a drift racer. In fact, Han actually makes a reference to *The Karate Kid* (1984) when he tells Sean "There's no 'wax on, wax off' about drifting. Learn by doing it." Despite the character differences, Han performs the same function for White men that Mr. Miyagi did a generation earlier: he helped a young White man realize his potential to dominate.

Fighting White Racism in a White-Dominated Society

The third major theme I found permeating throughout these films was the struggle to resist racism in U.S. society. Films like the *Fast & Furious* movies and *The Namesake* generally called for more subtle responses (if any), while the *Harold & Kumar* films were generally more forceful in both their recognition of, and response to, racist acts. For this analysis I focus primarily on the first two films of the trilogy, *White Castle* and *Harold & Kumar Escape from Guantanamo Bay* (referred to hereafter as *Guantanamo Bay*), since *A Very Harold & Kumar Christmas* (referred to hereafter as *Christmas*) is little more than a poor imitation of the first two.

While *Better Luck Tomorrow* was a parody of both teen and gangster movies, the *Harold & Kumar* films were parodies of the stoner and gross-out comedies (Hillenbrand, 2008). Structurally *White Castle* was groundbreaking because it co-starred John Cho (Korean American) and Kal Penn (Indian American), providing a more complete view of Asian Pacific Americans today, while promoting a pan-ethnoracial alliance (albeit implicitly). Too often in U.S. society "Asian American" has been conceptualized as people with *East* Asian ancestry, particularly China, Japan, and Korea, and to a lesser extent Southeast Asian counties such as the Philippines and Vietnam. A common misconception is to equate color with race, so that Black is associated with Africa, White is associated with Europe, and yellow is equated with Asia; such a categorization defies logic due to the racial diversity on all the world's continents, including Asia. The *Harold & Kumar* films expose and mock these misconceptions: for example, in *Christmas* the daughter of a Ukrainian mobster remarks to Kumar that "I don't date Black men," making reference to his dark skin tone. A similar instance in which ignorant Whites misrecognize the diversity among Asian/Americans is in *Guantanamo Bay* when the deputy chief of Homeland Security misidentifies Kumar and his parents as Arabs, while he also equates Harold's Korean ancestry with North Korea. While the example from *Christmas* lacked any relation to larger social issues (like most of the ethnic jokes in the film), the instances of misrecognition shown in *Guantanamo Bay* made reference to the post-9/11 racist hysteria and the ill-conceived "War on Terrorism."

Few Hollywood films present the cumulative effects of racism, both for its victims as well as the unjust enrichment (Feagin, 2000) enjoyed by its perpetrators. At the beginning of *White Castle*, Harold's White coworker complains to another White banker that he has a lot of work to complete over the weekend. At the behest of his White colleague, he pushes the work onto Harold, and Harold agrees to do the work. The two are then shown leaving the bank, laughing at how their little scheme succeeded, and rationalize it by saying they had probably made Harold's weekend to give him extra work. In a different scene, Kumar is being interviewed for medical school when the professor interviewing him struggles with his race talk (Foster, 2013): "We played in the name of the famous colored, uh, Negro, uh, basketball squad. Black. African American. You know, people of … colors." Though the awkward statement may well expose the limitations of the term "people of color" as a method to bunch all Non-Whites into one category (Gillota, 2012), it also chides Whites (particularly older ones) for their inability to speak coherently about race matters.

Similar to the primary characters in *Better Luck Tomorrow*, both Harold and Kumar contradict the model minority stereotype in a variety of ways, including their pot smoking and other deviant behavior, Kumar's resistance to attend medical school, and Harold's disinterest in East Asian tastes and customs. The *Harold & Kumar* films challenge the notion that there is a monolithic, overarching definition of what it means to be "Asian American." Unlike *Better Luck Tomorrow*, the *Harold & Kumar* films do a better job of representing this diversity, though they also present a tri-racial social system in which Asian Americans benefit from the White racism perpetrated against African Americans (Gillota, 2012).

While the *Harold & Kumar* films were groundbreaking in many respects, they also had some problems. Satire is always dangerous because the skit could potentially reinforce the very stereotype the filmmakers are trying to subvert. Most of the multiethnic humor tends to lack the grounding needed to avoid reproducing such stereotypes; perhaps the filmmakers figured the majority of the film's viewers would know not to take it seriously. Meanwhile, the solution to stop White racism emanating from *White Castle* and *Guantanamo Bay* seemed to be based on the individual: in *White Castle*, the message was that Harold was too uptight and needed to stand up for himself (like Kumar would), and in *Guantanamo Bay* you need to know the right people (e.g., the president of the United States who can grant you a pardon). At least the solution in *Guantanamo Bay* is so ridiculous that it could encourage support for structural efforts to end racism, but that is probably a stretch.

Discussion

In this chapter I provide an analysis of the ways Hollywood films have portrayed Asian Americans in lead roles since the turn of the century. After identifying three dominant themes from the sample of 10 films, I conclude that, in conjunction with Hughey (2014, 2009), these films are not as progressive as one may think. Since the amount of screen time for Non-White characters has increased, I concur with Ono (2012) that "inclusionary progress" has occurred. Furthermore, these films appear to better represent Asian Americans, at least compared to films of the previous generation. Moreover, I assert that the films of this sample directed by Asian American filmmakers present, on the whole, more humanized and developed Asian American characters. For example, the relationship on screen between Han and Giselle in the *Fast & Furious* films is one to behold, given the emasculation of Asian American men in Hollywood films traditionally (Marchetti, 1993). Still, Feng (2002) points out that Asian American filmmakers like Justin Lin have to "give in" to a certain extent in order to challenge such racist storylines. While working on the set of *Tokyo Drift*, Lin may well have fought with studio executives to change some of the original script and Orientalist *mise-en-scène* (King, 2010) to appear less stereotypical (Beltrán, 2013), but the structure of the story conformed to the typical "white man wins" script.

Despite a progressive veneer, these films do little to challenge the White patriarchal order. Rather than seeing more recent films such as *Torino* as representing some new, progressive change in American cinema, they represent instead a kind of "new" Orientalism in that, in reality, they return to older tropes used by Whites to pit minorities against each other. The images portrayed in *Torino* resemble those images of Asian Americans promoted during the riots of the 1960s, as well as by neoconservatives in the 1980s (Lee, 1999). Palumbo-Liu (1999) points out that "[a]s in 1966, in the coverage of the Rodney King incident Asians are again used as a fulcrum inserted between ethnic groups to leverage hegemonic racist ideology" (p. 188). *Gran Torino* ultimately does the same thing: situating the Hmong between Whites and Blacks (and Latinos) to "defend" the cities. In other words, the Hmong in *Gran Torino*, like the media-peddled image of Korean Americans in south Los Angeles circa 1992, are the "frontline forces of the White bourgeoisie" and "the buffer zone between the core of a multiethnic ghetto and White middle-class America" (Palumbo-Liu, 1999, p. 186).

In accordance with critical race theory, a certain amount of value convergence has resulted with these "new" images of Asian Americans. While films such as *Gran Torino* or *White Castle* provide opportunities for Asian American actors, the films fail to offer structural solutions to challenge systemic racism in U.S. society. In fact, casting practices for these films have often undermined the ability of Asian American actors to find lead roles in Hollywood films (as the casting decision for *Aloha* in the introduction illustrates). In accordance with Beltrán (2013), I stipulate that contemporary Hollywood images of Asian Americans in films such as the *Fast & Furious* films:

> [mobilize] notions of race in contradictory ways. [They] reinforce Hollywood traditions of white-centrism, reinforcing notions of White

mastery while also dramatizing the figurative borders crossed daily by culturally competent youth ... who fuel race-car and other commercial youth cultures. (p. 77)

Moreover, the sample of films for this study largely presented Asian Americans as the "middleman minority" within a tri-racial social system in which they assist the group on top (Whites) in their mission to maintain superiority over the group on the bottom (Blacks).

Finally, media representations do not occur in a vacuum; in fact, often there is inconsistency in the portrayal of racial minorities. In the 1980s the gook image dominated the silver screen, while in print media it was the image of the model minority. However, by the 2000s these representations largely switched so that as Charlie Chan images inundated the movies (e.g., Han in *Tokyo Drift*), and the dominant image of Asian men in news media turned negative. Still, what remained the same was that, whether deemed threatening or not, Asian Americans remain, in the words of Sau-Ling Cynthia Wong, "permanent houseguests in the house of America" (from Espiritu, 1997, p. 100).

References

Aderer, K. (2001). Justin Lin: Getting better all the time. *AsianAmericanFilm.com*. Retrieved from http://www.asianamericanfilm.com/archives/000029.html.

Beltrán, M. C. (2005). The new Hollywood racelessness: Only the fast, furious, (and multiracial) will survive. *Cinema Journal*, 44(2), 50–67.

Beltrán, M. C. (2013). Fast and bilingual: *Fast & Furious* and the Latinization of racelessness. *Cinema Journal*, 53(1), 75–96.

Bonilla-Silva, E. (2001). *White supremacy and racism in the post-Civil Rights era*. Boulder, CO: Lynne Rienner.

Bonilla-Silva, E. (2004). From bi-racial to tri-racial: Towards a new system of racial stratification in the USA. *Ethnic & Racial Studies*, 27(6), 931–950.

Bonilla-Silva, E. (2010). *Racism without racists*. Lanham, MD: Rowman & Littlefield.

Bourdieu, P. (1993). *The field of cultural production: Essays on art and literature*. New York, NY: Columbia University Press.

Chaisson, R. L. (2000). *For entertainment purposes only?: An analysis of the struggle to control filmic representations*. Lanham, MD: Lexington Books.

Crowe, C. (2015). A comment on Allison Ng. *The Uncool*. Retrieved from http://www.theuncool.com/2015/06/02/a-comment-on-allison-ng/.

Chou, R. S., & Feagin, J. R. (2008). *The myth of the model minority: Asian Americans facing racism*. Boulder, CO: Paradigm.

Espiritu, Y. L. (1997). *Asian American women and men: Labor, laws, and love*. Thousand Oaks, CA: Sage.

Feagin, J. R. (2000). *Racist America: Roots, current realities, and future reparations*. New York, NY: Routledge.

Feng, P. X. (2002). *Identities in motion: Asian American film and video*. Durham, NC: Duke University Press.

Foster, J. D. (2013). *White race discourse: Preserving racial privilege in a post-racial society*. Lanham, MD: Lexington Books.

Fuller, K. R. (2010). *Hollywood goes Oriental: CaucAsian performance in American film*. Detroit, MI: Wayne State University Press.

Gillota, D. (2012). "People of colors": Multiethnic humor in *Harold and Kumar Go to White Castle* and *Weeds*. *The Journal of Popular Culture, 45*(5), 960–978.

Hillenbrand, M. (2008). Of myths and men: *Better Luck Tomorrow* and the mainstreaming of Asian American cinema. *Cinema Journal, 47*(4), 50–75.

Hughey, M. W. (2009). Cinethetic racism: White redemption and black stereotypes in "magical Negro" films. *Social Problems, 56*(3), 543–577.

Hughey, M. W. (2014). *The white savior film: Content, critics, and consumption*. Philadelphia, PA: Temple University Press.

Kibria, N. (1998). The contested meaning of "Asian American": Racial dilemmas in the contemporary U.S. *Ethnic & Racial Studies, 21*(5), 939–958.

King, H. (2010). *Lost in translation: Orientalism, cinema, and the enigmatic signifier*. Durham, NC: Duke University Press.

Lee, R. G. (1999). *Orientals: Asian Americans in popular culture*. Philadelphia, PA: Temple University Press.

Levine, D. (Ed.). (1971). *Georg Simmel: Individuality and social forms*. Chicago, IL: University of Chicago Press.

Liberato, A. S. Q., Rebollo-Gil, G., Foster, J. D., & Moras, A. (2009). Latinidad and masculinidad in Hollywood scripts. *Ethnic and Racial Studies, 32*(6), 948–966.

Locke, B. (2009). *Racial stigma on the Hollywood screen from World War II to the present: The Orientalist buddy film*. New York, NY: Palgrave MacMillan.

Marchetti, G. (1993). *Romance and the "yellow peril": Race, sex, and discursive strategies in Hollywood fiction*. Berkeley, CA: University of California Press.

Ono, K. A. (2012). "Lines of flight": Reterritorializing Asian American film and media studies. *American Quarterly, 64*(4), 885–897.

Palumbo-Liu, D. (1999). *Asian/American: Historical crossings of a racial frontier*. Stanford, CA: Stanford University Press.

Park, J. C. H. (2010). *Yellow future: Oriental style in Hollywood cinema*. Minneapolis, MN: University of Minnesota Press.

Roche, M. W., & Hösle, V. (2011). Cultural and religious reversals in Clint Eastwood's *Gran Torino*. *Religion and the Arts, 15*(5), 648–679.

Said, E. W. (1978). *Orientalism*. New York, NY: Vintage.

Shah, H. (2003). "Asian culture" and Asian American identities in the television and film industries of the United States. *Simile, 3*(3), 1–10.

Tchen, J. K. W. (1999). *New York before Chinatown: Orientalism and the shaping of American culture, 1776–1882*. Baltimore, MD: Johns Hopkins University Press.

Tuan, M. (1998). *Forever foreigners or honorary whites: The Asian ethnic experience today*. New Brunswick, NJ: Rutgers University Press.

Vera, H., & Gordon, A. (2003). *Screen saviors: Hollywood fictions of Whiteness*. Lanham, MD: Rowman and Littlefield.

Wu, F. H. (2002). *Yellow: Race in America beyond black and white*. New York, NY: Basic Books.

9 Consuming Black Pain
Reading Racial Ideology in Cultural Appetite for *12 Years a Slave*

Jennifer C. Mueller and Rula Issa

Reviewing a film most peers considered "brilliant," even "essential" (Rotten Tomatoes, 2013), Black film critic Armond White pulled no punches. *12 Years a Slave* (2013) claimed dozens of honors, including the Oscar for Best Picture; still, White was unflinching. Among other charges, White (2013) claimed the film's director had grossly depicted "slavery as a horror show," continuing:

> … [Steve] McQueen has made the most unpleasant American movie since William Friedkin's 1973 *The Exorcist*. That's right, *12 Years a Slave* belongs to the torture porn genre with *Hostel*, *The Human Centipede* and the *Saw* franchise but it is being sold (and mistaken) as part of the recent spate of movies that pretend "a conversation about race."

Known for acrimonious reviews, White appeared extraordinarily enflamed by this "race hustle," and the Black director himself. So disturbed, White dropped the last straw months later heckling McQueen as he accepted an award from The New York Film Critics' Circle. White's outburst cost the one-time president his membership as peers expelled him from the organization a week later (Gleiberman, 2014).

Though many have used the weight of spectacle to delegitimize White, his critique raises questions worth considering. Far from the usual parade of horrors featuring imaginary innocents and psychopaths, *12 Years a Slave* (henceforth, *12 Years*) recounts the true story of Solomon Northup (played by Chiwetel Ejiofor), a Black man born free in New York, but kidnapped and sold into slavery in the antebellum Louisiana south. What accounts for the popular appeal of a film featuring grotesque White-on-Black torture grounded in historical truth? Moreover, what inspires praise that *12 Years* is "essential" viewing? And, *why now*—what do contemporary audiences gain from this media exercise surrounding the past? Finally, *to which audiences* does this film speak?

In this chapter we analyze *12 Years* alongside various data—online film reviews and reader comment threads, public Twitter and Instagram postings, Amazon.com DVD reviews, and director and screenwriter commentary—to explore these questions. We use this case to argue that, similar to sensational illusions projected in films like *The Human Centipede*, contemporary representations of racial history and Black suffering, even seemingly liberal ones, can enable deep fantasies, too; ideological mystifications that co-opt and whitewash Black pain and suffering. Our analysis elevates four means by which media, as a system of cultural production, distribution, and consumption, can provide cover for White supremacy: segregating White supremacy, qualifying Black victimization, mystifying material determinism, and politicizing "knowing" as sufficiently antiracist. We describe the dimensions of each maneuver to demonstrate how even allegedly liberal media can reinforce an epistemology of ignorance (Mills, 1997, 2007) that suppresses and distorts critical understanding of systemic White supremacy.

Media, Ideology, and the Epistemology of Ignorance

All hierarchical orders are undergirded by powerful, rationalizing ideologies. Critical scholars have worked to link prevailing logics and structural elements of White supremacy (Bonilla-Silva, 1997; Jewell, 1993; Moore, 2014; Omi & Winant, 2014). While many mark distinctions of post-civil rights era discourse (Bobo, Kluegel, & Smith, 1996; Bonilla-Silva, 2010; Doane, 2006), we focus instead on a historical continuity that unites seemingly disparate racial ideologies—ignorance.

To operate in the service of power, hegemonic ideologies must hide domination by misrepresenting the world. In other words, successful racial ideologies achieve purchase through grounding in social processes that facilitate widespread *not knowing*—what critical race philosopher Charles Mills (1997, 2007) refers to as epistemologies of ignorance. Unlike private ways of knowing, epistemologies of ignorance are *social epistemologies*, structured into the rhythms of institutions and everyday practices alike (Mills, 2007; Mueller, 2015). Because they ignore and distort the mechanisms by which racial reproduction occurs, epistemologies of ignorance are deeply implicated in the persistence of White supremacy.

Amid looming evidence of disparities and resistance among people of color, epistemologies of ignorance develop an economy of (mis)understanding that makes racial domination psychically palatable. Utilizing cognitive strategies that produce racial ignorance—or *white*[1] *epistemic maneuvers*—Whites can foreclose critical understanding and reframe their own involvement in the "terrible ordeal of creating and maintaining inequality" (Bonilla-Silva, 2010, p. 26; Mueller, Forthcoming). Patterns of ideological hegemony further encourage people of color to internalize the oppressive logics produced by epistemologies of ignorance (Bonilla-Silva, 2010; Mills, 2007). In this sense, broad *"misunderstanding, misrepresentation, evasion, and self-deception on matters related to race"* is far from accidental; White supremacy requires far-reaching internalization of such maneuvers (Mills, 1997, p. 19; original emphasis).

Media is a vital site for examining cultural production of ignorance given its "main sphere of operations is the production and transformation of ideologies" (Hall, 2003, p. 89). Movies enjoy a particularly wide discursive reach as a result of steady access and persistent popularity (Entman & Rojecki, 2000; hooks, 2008; Hughey, 2014; Moore & Pierce, 2007). While White supremacy structures the backdrop of all film, films themed around race lay bare mechanisms of racial ignorance most readily. Valuable analyses have demonstrated excessive reliance on stereotypical tropes of pathological Blackness (Bogle, 1973/2005; Guerrero, 1993; Jewell, 1993) and messianic Whiteness (Hughey, 2014; Moore & Pierce, 2007; Vera & Gordon, 2003). We push further "left" by focusing our analysis on a paradox: Can Black-centered film intended to confront brutal realities of racial domination actually facilitate racial ignorance? Focusing on this puzzle is at once provocative and strategic; by interrogating media that is purportedly liberal we surface White supremacy's most covert dimensions (Bracey, 2015).

A final word on approach: films embody a range of political discourses, set in an equally politicized economy of production, distribution, and consumption (Kellner, 1995; Moore & Pierce, 2007). Likewise, films resonate and are decoded across different audiences and politics of understanding, like those shaped by racial ideology and social location (Hall, 2006). As such, we are less intent on defining what *12 Years* "says" to an illusory universal audience, than on surfacing ways the film may limit and obstruct critical racial consciousness.

White Epistemic Maneuvers

Using theory-focused discursive analysis, we searched the data for evidence of representational "dysfunctions (which are psychologically and socially functional)" (i.e., those that could ease and support racially ideological interpretations) (Mills, 1997, p. 18), and identified four maneuvers: (1) segregating White supremacy, (2) qualifying Black victimization, (3) mystifying material determinism, and (4) politicizing "knowing" as sufficiently antiracist. While presented here as discrete, maneuvers often overlapped and bolstered one another in effect, patterns we have attempted to highlight. Our analysis demonstrates that media can operate as a system of cultural meaning-making to reinforce racial ignorance, even through projects designed to reveal Black suffering.

Segregating White Supremacy

Segregating White supremacy emerged as a prominent maneuver, appearing in discourse that functionally isolated White supremacy in discrete "social locations" (e.g., in problematic people, and/or particular places and times), implying by relation social locations where White supremacy does not exist. For example, *12 Years* draws a consistent division between the racially harmonious North and the "racist" antebellum South. Scenes portraying a well-dressed Solomon and family, living in relative luxury and freely traversing upstate New York, contrast starkly with the misery of southern plantation life he experiences following capture.

In one salient scene, Solomon and family enter a general store in Saratoga Springs to purchase a bag for his wife, who will soon travel to a job away from home. The shop owner immediately and warmly greets the family upon entrance; to Solomon's request for a "fresh carry-all for my missus," he gleefully replies, "I have just the thing! Something to suit your style, and yet sturdy enough for the 40-mile round trip." During the two men's lighthearted quibbling over price, a Black man enters the shop looking confused and stunted. The shopkeeper, unaware the man is actually a slave who has traveled north with his owner, cheerfully turns attention from Solomon and his wife: "Forgive me, Solomon, Forgive me, Mrs. Northrup. A customer waits ... Welcome, sir!" Solomon mocks the expense of his wife's bag by joking with the slave, "Shop well, sir, but mind your wallet." This comfortable exchange is disrupted when the enslaved man's owner enters the store, yelling "Jasper!" and startling everyone in sight. When he turns to the storeowner to apologize for his slave's "intrusion," Solomon responds immediately by staring *directly* at the man and proclaiming "No intrusion." The slave owner appears dismayed, but overruled by Solomon's unabashed declaration. He tips his hat bidding "good day" to the White shopkeeper, and quickly demands "Jasper! Out!"

Solomon appears entirely self-determining here, inhibited neither by the detriments of Blackness nor White supremacy more broadly. Indeed, the total scene intimates an equal status positioning of Whites and Blacks in the North—an assumption foreign to the enslaved man, but so internalized by Solomon that he feels compelled to confront the White slave owner and establish the deviance of his racist behavior. More than geographically imposed, this segregation appears embodied *within* Solomon; as one reviewer suggested, "even while he was inside slavery—physically, psychologically, emotionally—part of him remained intellectually and culturally at a remove" (Dargis, 2013). In this way, racism *and* oppression appear personified in individuals rather than defined by structures of social relations. Racist Whites (and obsequious Blacks) may make their way *into* the North, but these characters find themselves out of place in a 19th century normative climate oddly fetishized as color-blind.

To the extent *12 Years* acknowledges structural elements of White domination, these are neatly confined *within* the institution of slavery, which unjustly structures social relations but only in regionally specific places. Ironically, the North appears perpetually disconnected from slavery: there are neither indications that slavery ended in New York just a decade prior to the period covered in the film, nor that Northrup's father had been a slave (Delton, 2013). Beyond place, White supremacy *qua* slavery is further sequestered by time, suggesting tidy beginnings and ends to Black suffering.

For example, the film resolves with Solomon's return to his family, with little made of the fact that slavery persisted in the South for another 12 years, or that White supremacy can exist beyond the bounds of this "peculiar institution."

Collectively, segregating maneuvers minimize the extent of White supremacy, facilitating fantasies that racism may exist *in* the world, but should not be regarded as characteristic *of* the world. The resulting logic suppresses understanding White supremacy as structuring all institutions, group relations, and interests, and persisting across time and space (Bell, 1992; Bonilla-Silva, 1997; Bracey, 2015; Feagin, 2014). Segregating maneuvers urge further faith in a "future" somehow *always* and *inevitably* more just and less racist; and the possibility that both people of color and Whites can successfully "escape" racism, or, when necessary, extract it like a cancerous tumor. Imagining people, places, and times where White supremacy does not exist is particularly effective in shielding White viewers from relationally understanding all Whites derive benefits from structural positioning. Notably, trust in Western institutions and culture remains undisturbed, despite the fact that all are grounded in and by the logics of White supremacy (Bracey, 2015; Feagin, 2014). White racism "appears" in the antebellum South, but vanishes up North. White racism "materializes" in characters' complicity with slavery, but is relieved with Solomon's return. In other words, though not infallible, White institutions and people are always redeemable and thus remain appropriate ideals, as the next theme captures further.

Qualifying Black Victimization

In an NPR interview, John Ridley, the film's Black screenwriter shared his interest in Solomon's story:

> [Solomon was] a man who used every part of himself to survive—his wits, his guile, his physicality—but never gave into bitterness, never gave up his faith in other people and the system that completely let him down. ... I just said, if I were trying to show ... what I thought the character ... of an American man, of a man of color—that's what Solomon was when I read this book.
>
> (Inskeep & Montagne, 2014)

Ridley's comments suggest he was not simply captured by the circumstances of Northrup's enslavement, but also exceptionalities embodied in Northrup. The next maneuver—*qualifying Black victimization*—works to similar effect, tacitly distinguishing Black victims. In practice, this maneuver discursively "asterisked" Solomon's virtuous character and distinctive suffering, with a subtext of comparison to other Black victims.

As Ridley's description suggests, life and death appear to rest in Solomon's internalization of an extraordinary blend of sensibilities for a

Black man—measured temperament, indomitable spirit, savvy but not-overbearing rationality, and sustained faith in White-normed institutions and culture despite harms suffered. Idealistic filmmakers may search for relatable characters and messages in an effort to secure audiences and funding, particularly in the face of "challenges" (e.g., foregrounding Black leads and unpleasant "race issues"). Northrup's "extraordinariness" is thus arguably most vital to attracting White audiences, presumed important but unwittingly ignorant and apathetic about racial matters; assumptions often follow that these viewers require pseudo-experiential inroads to Black suffering in order to develop empathy. And indeed, *12 Years* goes to great lengths emphasizing distinctive harms Northrup endured by virtue of his experiences as a "free man." Throughout the film many Whites and other enslaved Blacks witness Northrup's exceptional talents; even his first owner proclaims him "a marvel." Nonetheless, nearly all attempt to dissuade Northrup from the foolish boldness these traits might inspire, encouraging he habituate to life as a slave instead. Northrup remains unyielding if at times only internally, regularly marking his unique status with the claim "I'm not supposed to be here" (i.e., *in* slavery—again, neatly segregated). Still, these continual references raise an ideologically hidden question: Who *is* supposed to find themselves enslaved?

This convention highlights an exceptional offense visited on an equally exceptional Black man, securing stronger buy-in than more quotidian characters might. Clarifying the resonance of this message, NPR interviewer Terry Gross (2013) shared that it was "especially easy" to put oneself "in the shoes of Solomon Northrup ... whether you are descended from a slave or not" because "he starts as a free man"; "[Y]ou're a free person, he was a free person, and imagine what it would be like to suddenly be a slave!" Searching "#12YearsASlave" on Twitter turned up similar comments, like "Could you imagine being a free person then kidnapped and made into a slave??!" and "To find yourself a slave as Solomon Northrup did. Horrific." Similarly, an Amazon.com consumer wrote: "To be free and then be enslaved would have to be the most demeaning of attacks on the human spirit. ... [S]uch an ordeal would consume many, yet somehow Northup found the determination to manage under such horrible circumstances."

Here, the odiousness of slavery appears *uniquely harsh* for Solomon *because* he wasn't supposed to "be there." Solomon's exceptionality is then further marked by his even more remarkable response to unimaginable conditions. One of the most commonly tweeted quotes was "I don't just want to survive. I want to *live*!"—a retort Solomon offers in reply to two other enslaved men who urge him to "keep [his] head down" and hide his true identity or risk death. That audiences appeared so taken by these elements— and this quote in particular—suggests the remarkable "character" Ridley hoped to capture indeed reverberates.

Arguably, most egregious is the subtle subtext of blame directed toward more "typical" victims. Solomon's steady positioning as an exceptional person who, more than implicit Black others, is "supposed" to be free implies he not just understands liberty better, but *longs* for it in a way other enslaved people cannot. Ordinary Black characters are presented as foolhardy and thus doomed in their resistance, or prone to hopeless, inconsolable despair—so much so that one female character, Patsey (played by Lupita Nyong'o) begs Solomon to kill her. Armond White charged McQueen was repulsively devoted to "nihilistic trope[s]," like "Patsey's completely unfathomable longing for death" (White, 2013). Though severely tested, Solomon by contrast retains wits and, as one reviewer argued, an "unmistakable desire for freedom" (Dargis, 2013).

Discursive asterisks of exceptionality do more than distinguish Northrup from adversaries, passive bystanders, and sympathetic but feeble Black victims alike. Hughey (2009) suggests "magical negroes" as a common film trope where stereotypically "lower-class, uneducated, and magical black characters … transform[ing] disheveled, uncultured, or broken white characters into competent people" (p. 543). That delivery is foreclosed, however, in a story where "brokenness" extends beyond individual White characters. Moreover, because slavery is more normatively condemned today, apologists cannot easily delegitimize historical Black victims (e.g., as is common today with targets of police brutality). As such, to remain ideologically useful, a film this racially "exposing" must go beyond magical Black characters.

Qualifying Black victims works toward that end. Companion embodiment to segregating White supremacy in deviant Whites, this maneuver implies racial deliverance also resides in individuals. Though *12 Years* incorporates several, "White saviors"[2] are not centered as heroes. Focus remains instead on a Christ-like Black who never gave up during the very worst of times; who proved himself willing to exhaust all *legitimate* efforts for survival while resisting the rage that often accompanies intolerable cruelties; and who maintained faith in White institutions, culture, and by extension people. Christ-like Black victims provide assurance that when individual Whites and White institutions fall short of justice, exceptional people of color with enough resolve *can* survive the harshest punishments and neglect. In this sense, Solomon's Christ-like character tacitly absolves Whites' culpability for Black suffering by proving deliverance remains available to exceptional-enough Blacks; his character also works to sustain faith in White-normed institutions, and by extension Whites' humanity, morality, and worth, despite the indisputable tarnish that slavery, colonialism, and contemporary neglect imply. In this sense, Whiteness again appears eternally redeemable.

Mystifying Material Determinism

If segregating maneuvers minimize the *extent* of White supremacy, the next—*mystifying material determinism*—distract from its *essence* as a system grounded in material exploitation. This maneuver manifested in discursive tactics that ignored or obscured the material foundation of racialized slavery. In many respects this appears the most paradoxical maneuver: How does one escape material underpinnings in a film focused on industries clearly grounded in material exploitation, namely, chattel slavery and plantation production? The film arguably included what one reviewer referred to as "insistent (if subtle) reminders" (Adams, 2013). For example, when Northrup is led from a slave ship in one scene, the shot pulls back to reveal dozens of ships docked behind, suggesting the industry's expansiveness. Similarly, several scenes depict Solomon's highly sadistic second owner, Epps (played by Michael Fassbender), evaluating cotton picked by his slaves and exacting punishment for inadequate production.

New Yorker reviewer Richard Brody (2013) believed McQueen had "cannily" utilized subtle conventions like these, drawing on "the public's knowledge" regarding the "general historical fact of slavery in America" and the fact that Northrup was "a real person":

> It's as if McQueen himself were standing beside the screen with a pointer, calmly but frankly filling in the barest outlines of common knowledge with the staggeringly painful particulars of Northup's story and, therefore, of American history.

Despite such trust, recognizing material dimensions rests almost entirely on audiences' prior understanding that material exploitation formed the basis of slavery. In this respect, the "staggeringly painful particulars" to which Brody refers—extraordinary violence, heartless cruelty, desperate and unyielding anguish, all elements White (2013) believed comprised "torture porn"—may distract from exposing how Whites' investment in material domination enflames racist ideology, violence, and cruelty, not the reverse.

Reviews and social media attention indeed centered on the film's horrors, eclipsing slavery's materiality almost entirely. Many appeared to suggest *12 Years'* very legitimacy rested in willingness to "bravely, unshrinkingly" render the grotesque (Brody, 2013). Reviewer Vadim Rizov (2013) remarked "McQueen [didn't] shirk" when it was "time for brutalizing violence." From his perspective viewers *needed* something to disrupt "comfortably settled images of slavery in the national imagination[;] it's important to make sure this isn't high school classroom-friendly stuff." While we explore this emphasis further below, it is worth underscoring how common such views were, far surpassing commentary on material dynamics.

For his part, McQueen believed the contemporary material residue of slavery life should be "obvious":

> I mean, all you've got to do is walk down the street, and you see the evidence of slavery in everyday life. ... You know, why are [sic] the prison population of Black males so huge? Why is poverty in that community so huge? Why is mental health, why is education so poor,

why? ... [I]t all leads down to what happened in slavery because ... once it has stopped, you know, everyone was left to get on with their own devices but without a platform, without a leg up. And there you have the evidence of slavery, ... which I feel needed a platform.

(Gross, 2013)

McQueen rightly identifies slavery is not just historically significant, connecting it to enduring racial inequality; nonetheless neither reviews nor comment threads suggested the platform of "brutalizing violence" worked "to polemically link past and present in ... thoughtful or galvanizing ways" (Rizov, 2013).

Rare commenters who sensed contemporary symbolism were frequently defensive. For example, on one article comment board (Stevens, 2014), @matteroffact[3] argued "people who have never enslaved anyone ever are being made to feel as if they owe other people who were never enslaved." Others jumped on @matteroffact's position:

@DOMINOJOE: Speak for yourself, @matteroffact. It sounds like you have deeper hangups that are unrelated to slavery (or movies about slavery). The rest of us don't carry that baggage when we walk into a theater.
@MATTEROFFACT: and I suppose you have been anointed as the spokesperson for 'the rest of us'?
@DOMINOJOE: I speak for everyone who can watch a movie about slavery in the U.S. and not immediately tie it to modern racial politics. ... And yes, there are probably more of us than there are of you.
@JACKSONVILLE: @matteroffact ... I don't know who made you feel the way you do, but dude, you shouldn't feel accountable for slavery. It would be ridiculous to blame the atrocities of centuries past on the people of today.

Evaluating defenses deployed against the idea that contemporary White "debts" *could* be inferred from the movie is telling. Note how these ostensibly liberal critics rely on segregating maneuvers; like most contemporary Whites, these writers assume a massive social distance between themselves and the relics of "real" racists, as well as between prior eras structured around *de jure* White supremacy and the meritocratic structure presumed today. This ideological pattern appears supported by the film rather than challenged. Alongside abundant coverage of horrifying particulars, the lack of explicit material focus enables racially liberal but nonetheless ideological positions like those articulated by the commenters. Many such viewers conceded slavery part of a "difficult history" involving "horrible circumstances," but seemed to believe these terrors had been surpassed.

Indeed, an interviewer who spoke with screenwriter Ridley suggested it was easier to face the "difficult" task of "look[ing] back at a difficult history" knowing "you have overcome horrible circumstances" (Inskeep & Montagne, 2014). Ridley himself was adamant viewers not let the big picture of "where we've come as a country ... get lost" in the everyday horrors covered. He thought there should "be a sense of pride that we have come this far," both "for the individuals whose families survived all of this," but also "for those individuals who look at, if my family was like this, I am not." He shared further concerns for this latter, implicitly White group:

> [I]t's very important for people to not go into it going: Oh, if my family did that 160 years ago, that's me. You know, as opposed to, you know, why don't we find out what happened ... how we got to a point now where our kids or our grandkids are in the same school, enjoying the same privileges, that we are citizens in the same country and can actually talk about this—as opposed to being afraid or horrified about what happened.
>
> (Inskeep & Montagne, 2014)

Ridley appears as convicted as everyday commenters that contemporary Whites not ruminate on connections to slavery nor Whites of bygone eras. To support his claim, Ridley asserts an outright fantasy—a contemporary U.S. society where racialized resource disparities no longer exist.

These examples illuminate how segregating maneuvers take on stronger significance when combined with material mystification. Resultant logics sustain White ignorance about ongoing intergenerational mechanisms that have reproduced White supremacy over time, up to and including today. Shockingly, Ridley erases even the obvious significance of legal-slaveholding, which propelled Whites' unjust enrichment in the U.S. for nearly 250 years before transitioning to similar patterns for nearly a century more under legal segregation (Feagin, 2014; Mueller, 2013). Nonetheless, it is this very materialism—and the associated possessive investment this system sustains among Whites—that contours the racial violence and resultant suffering endured by people of color under White supremacy regardless of what sadistic, or more symbolic or "gentle" forms such violence takes. In the film's context, material mystification thus does double duty, disregarding the material dynamics of White supremacy while substituting the impression that White supremacy is generated *from* an ideology of White superiority. Slavery appears driven by Whites' sadistically ideological impulses—which contemporary White audiences can disavow—as opposed to material interests all Whites share by virtue of structural positioning. Encouraging such viewers to identify with Solomon rather than problematic White characters further diminishes the likelihood of developing a critical relational understanding. Further still, by substituting ideological emphases, material mystification inevitably distorts practical solutions, a theme we extend next.

"Knowing" as Antiracism

Though their views on the contemporary significance of slavery differed, McQueen and Ridley appeared to agree that creating a "platform" to penetrate the "deafening silence" surrounding slavery should be a central goal of the film (Gross, 2013). Imagining the main cleavage dividing Blacks and Whites today as a failure to communicate, the creators' appeared bent on finally confronting the country's deep wounds, helping viewers face illogical and unnecessary fears about inventorying how White superiority and anti-Blackness once played out as ugly racial ideologies. In his review, Armond White (2013) threw a wet blanket over such idealistic hopes, ridiculing, "[s]ome of the most racist people" he knew were "bowled over" by the movie because they could "congratulate themselves for 'being aghast at slavery.'" The final maneuver—*politicizing "knowing" as sufficiently antiracist*—surfaces the substance of White's inflammatory claim. This maneuver found expression in statements that implied the moral and socio-political significance of the film, both broadly and for individual viewers.

Analyzing public reactions to even mildly disparaging critiques is again illuminating. Slate movie critic Dana Stevens' (2014) offered a largely positive review. Though she disagreed that McQueen had sought "to make White people feel good about their own guilt," she reluctantly conceded there might be "a grain of truth" in White's claim about the film being "torture porn." She worried using "body horror" to approach this subject might serve to shut out audiences, rather than "make them think, feel, and engage," and recalled the "grand, elemental simplicity" of the scene where Solomon and family reunite:

> Watching that ending in a packed theater with an audience that was, almost to a person, crying, felt like a welcome if painfully incomplete catharsis, one that was maybe only reachable after the cinematic crucible we had all been through together.

Reaction was swift and morally condemning. One article commentator mocked,

> Dana, are we to understand that you are uncomfortable with any emotion that isn't heartwarming and joyful, and your version of dealing with strife isn't confronting true pain and misery, but the "kumbaya" moments of reflecting on it? We get it. Your life is pretty sanitized, and your threshold for human suffering is pretty low. But that says a lot more about you than about the movie or its faithfulness to the particular range of human experience that is called suffering.

As suggested earlier, many thought *12 Years'* brutalizing violence was necessary to eradicate revisionist ideas about slavery once and for all. Indeed, reviewers often lauded *12 Years* presumed authenticity in relation to older films that appeared disingenuous and fraught with romanticized trappings by comparison.

Another of Steven's detractors scolded her for missing the seemingly obvious, "Oh, you don't like watching it? It makes you uncomfortable? It turns your stomach? That. Is. The. Whole. Point." Everyday commentators again and again reinforced the significance of "knowing" about Black suffering in a pseudo-experiential way, no matter how uncomfortable. Some viewers were even anticipatory, like one seemingly White Instagram user who posted a "selfie" of her holding the DVD case with the comment, "my Friday night sorted, let's see how long it takes before I'm booing my eyes out." Others established the film's value by emotional responses invoked. For instance, a Twitter user who also appeared to be White declared, "probably the best movie I've seen in a long time! #12yearsaslave had me crying 3 times." Moreover, viewers implied reactions to the film were revealing of character; as @loverofmusic tweeted, "If one can watch #12yearsaslave and come to the end unmoved, I'm not sure that is a person I can trust."

McQueen's desire to facilitate audiences' ability to "experience" the brutality of slavery betrays an implicit privileging of White viewers and their ostensibly greater ignorance and empathic oversights. Comments on Black Twitter highlighted how differently African American audiences sit in relationship to this film. Black actor Laz Alonso attended a public screening sharing, "I was emotionally devastated after the film. Couldn't even stay 4 the Q&A." Comments from many everyday Black users revealed a similar trauma and anger. For instance, one woman tweeted, "12 minutes into #12YearsaSlave for the 1st time. Pissed already. This [is] why it takes me so long to watch these films." After sharing a disturbing quote from the film, another anxiously worried "OMG I don't know if I can do this." Still others were equally if not more upset by the film's politics of representation, like @Trina1292, who announced "I will never ever watch #12yearsaslave again. Too many n[-word] bombs the whipping just all of the film WS ..." "WS" is a likely a reference to the content aggregating video blog, *World Star Hip Hop*. Well known for circulating "viral videos" of Black people involved in violent fights and lewd public acts, many decry the site's role in promoting stereotypical views of the Black community. This Twitter user thus appeared to be signaling her opinion that offensive, stereotypical representations in *12 Years* rivaled those of World Star's. Unlike a White user who tweeted, "No matter how many times I watch #12YearsASlave, it remains as riveting and emotional as the first viewing," @Trina1292 had no such intentions of subjecting herself to the film again.

One "disheartened" commentator testified she "didn't appreciate how terrible slavery was until I saw it." She wondered how making audiences "feel how truly horrible slavery really was" could "be a bad thing?" (Stevens, 2014). Drawing on the aforementioned data points to what some scholars have called the "slipperiness of empathy" (Hartman, 1997, p. 18; Razack,

2007). Hartman (1997) suggests it is regularly assumed that overcoming Whites' "commonplace callousness to Black suffering" requires the White body "be positioned in the place of the Black body" to make Black suffering "visible and tangible." Nonetheless, through this convention Whites' pain can only come into existence by reifying the objectification of Black people, as conduits for Whites' moral redemption (Razack, 2007). The comparative reactions of White viewers' are telling in this regard. In accepting the invitation to "look at Solomon and see themselves,"—as McQueen hoped audiences would, "regardless of their race or ethnicity" (Mitchell, 2013)— White viewers are relieved from having to imagine themselves in the position of "morally compromised" Whites, including the passive bystanders that inevitably propelled racial reproduction during slavery, as well as today.

Some White viewers appeared to believe willingness to submit to a saddening, but all-too-facile identification with Solomon was reassurance of their moral goodness. Here we see most readily how maneuvers converge with and amplify one another to mystify the racial reproduction that sustains White supremacy over time. While many read readiness to know (at least some things) about White supremacy as promising, this willingness can itself be used as a segregating maneuver, allowing liberal Whites to exempt themselves from more "problematic," conservatively racist positions. Worse, as discussed earlier, in the context of a film that fails to unpack the materiality upon which White supremacy rests, it is unlikely most White viewers take away meaningfully antiracist ideas about the contemporary significance of slavery, let alone an understanding that challenging contemporary structural racism will require a countervailing antiracist praxis that extends beyond "knowing" (Mueller, 2015). Instead, too many are emboldened to imagine baring (and pseudo-experientially *bearing*) the torture of Black bodies contributes meaningfully to a more just and unified world, disregarding this fate ultimately rests on altering the patterns of unjust impoverishment and unjust enrichment set into motion during slavery and sustained today.

Conclusion

Seventy-five years prior to *12 Years'* Oscar win, the Academy honored another film centered in U.S. slavery—*Gone with the Wind* (1939). Steve McQueen responded to questions about the historical significance of his victory by relation:

> Well, it obviously is a mark of development. ... The background characters are now in the foreground, and their history, and their lives— how they lived—are being recognized in a way more than before. ... I think it's indicative of what's going on now. ... [P]eople are ready for this narrative.
>
> (Horn, 2014)

144 *Jennifer C. Mueller and Rula Issa*

For McQueen, *12 Years'* mainstream success was a hopeful sign. As the director saw it, it was "understandable ... people had difficulty coming to terms with [slavery] or visualizing it via cinema" for so long; slavery was "horrendous, violent, vicious, nasty." Still, he thought people were uniquely "receptive" today: "People are wanting to engage in that history in order to go forward more than any other time" (Horn, 2014).

It is not hard to understand why many believe *12 Years* represents not just cinematic but broader racial progress. As one reviewer extoled, *12 Years* made it "impossible for American cinema to continue to sell the ugly lies it's been hawking for more than a century" (Dargis, 2013). To be sure, by foregrounding the banality of evil *12 Years* gave lie to romanticized fantasies that made *Gone with the Wind* a beloved classic—"the paternalistic gentry with their pretty plantations, their genteel manners and all the 'fiddle-dee-dee' rest" (Dargis, 2013). Nonetheless, in a society still contoured by structures that sustain Whites' possessive investment in racial privilege and domination, we must remain on guard against ideological trappings of our own era. Here, drawing on the conceptual lens of ignorance proves invaluable. Grounding media analysis in the concept of an epistemology of ignorance shifts focus, foregrounding what is *not* there as opposed to what is. This critical adjustment brings the maneuvers by which "*misunderstanding, misrepresentation, evasion, and self-deception on matters related to race*" occur into sharp relief (Mills, 1997, p. 19; original emphasis; Mueller, Forthcoming).

Using this method to analyze *12 Years* reveals that even media intent on raising racial consciousness and validating the suffering of people of color can participate in ideological mystification. Further, the lens of ignorance exposes continuities across cultural products that otherwise appear wildly different. Racial ideologies—and thus forms of ignorance—must adapt and change as structural conditions evolve. During slavery and legal segregation, White supremacy required a racial epistemology that legitimized mythical racial difference as "real" and discrimination morally just (Mills, 1997). Films like *Gone with the Wind* and *Birth of a Nation* thus fulfilled related White fantasies that racial domination was necessary or at minimum benign. Today hegemonic ideologies rest in color-blind illusions that mystify the covert and highly institutionalized mechanics driving White supremacy today (Bonilla-Silva, 2010; Doane, 2006; Mills, 2007). Nonetheless, contemporary fantasies span political divides, from conservative representations that blame people of color for their diminished status and ignore the role of race in shaping life chances, to neo-liberal representations that appear to acknowledge race and even structures of racial hierarchy while simultaneously rescuing whiteness, mystifying the material and relational basis of race, and elevating anemic ideas about antiracism.

Positioning our read of the film in relation to formal reviews, everyday social media, and director and screenwriter commentary, our analysis also suggests ideological ignorance is best thought of as an accomplishment that takes place recursively, between White-normed/instrumentally controlled institutions and everyday individuals. Though we focus here on cultural production, distribution, and consumption within media, epistemologies of ignorance guide the logic and practice of many institutions and the actors within (see, e.g., Malewski & Jaramillo, 2011; Moore, 2014; Steinberg, 2007). The epistemic authority of institutions like law, education, and media, serves to embolden everyday racial ignorance further still, a problem liberal racial projects are not likely to escape (Mills, 2007). Indeed, in illuminating the evidence of White supremacy in *12 Years a Slave*, our analysis clarifies just how strategic racial progressives must be in developing critical, oppositional projects if media is to serve as a countervailing force for racial justice.

Notes

1. We utilize the label "White" to qualify how ways of knowing, knowledge, and action are related to structural *White supremacy*; not to indicate these phenomena as confined to *White people*.
2. While we do not revisit the "White savior" trope in our analysis (see, e.g., Hughey, 2014; Moore & Pierce, 2007; Vera & Gordon, 2003), it is worth noting *12 Years'* buffering characters, such as the general storekeeper and Samuel Bass (played by Brad Pitt).
3. All actual names and social media handles have been replaced with pseudonyms.

References

Adams, S. (2013, October 18). "12 Years a Slave" dissenters raise questions worth answering. *Indiewire.com*. Retrieved from http://blogs.indiewire.com/criticwire/12-years-a-slave-dissenters-raise-questions-worth-answering.

Bell, D. (1992). *Faces at the bottom of the well*. New York: Basic Books.

Bobo, L., Kluegel, J., & Smith, R. (1996). Laissez faire racism: The crystallization of a "kinder, gentler" anti-Black ideology. In S. Tuch & J. Martin (Eds.), *Racial attitudes in the 1990s* (pp. 15–42). Westport, CT: Praeger.

Bogle, D. (2005). *Toms, coons, mulattoes, mammies, and bucks*. New York, NY: Continuum. (Original work published 1973).

Bonilla-Silva, E. (1997). Rethinking racism: Toward a structural interpretation. *American Sociological Review, 62*(3), 465–480.

Bonilla-Silva, E. (2010). *Racism without racists*. Lanham, MD: Rowman & Littlefield.

Bracey, G. E. (2015). Toward a critical race theory of state. *Critical Sociology, 41*(3), 553–572.

Brody, R. (2013, October 21). Should a film try to depict slavery? *The New Yorker*. Retrieved from http://www.newyorker.com/culture/richard-brody/should-a-film-try-to-depict-slavery.

Dargis, M. (2013, October 17). The blood and tears, not the magnolias: "12 Years a Slave" holds nothing back in show of suffering. *New York Times*. Retrieved from http://www.nytimes.com/2013/10/18/movies/12-years-a-slave-holds-nothing-back-in-show-of-suffering.html.

Delton, J. (2013, December 12). Film gives taste of false luxury. *Times Union*. Retrieved from http://www.timesunion.com/opinion/article/Film-gives-taste-of-false-luxury-5059991.php.

Doane, A. (2006). What is racism? Racial discourse and racial politics. *Critical Sociology, 32*(2), 255–274.
Entman, R., & Rojecki, A. (2000). *The black image in the white mind*. Chicago, IL: University of Chicago Press.
Feagin, J. R. (2014). *Racist America*. New York, NY: Routledge.
Gleiberman, O. (2014, January 13). Why Armond White got kicked out of the New York Film Critics Circle. *Entertainment Weekly*. Retrieved from http://insidemovies.ew.com/2014/01/13/armond-white-kicked-out-of-ny-critics/.
Gross, T. (2013, October 24). "12 Years a Slave" was a film that "no one was making" [Interview]. *NPR Fresh Air*. Retrieved from http://www.npr.org/templates/transcript/transcript.php?storyId=240288057.
Guerrero, E. (1993). *Framing Blackness*. Philadelphia, PA: Temple University Press.
Hall, S. (2003). The whites of their eyes: Racist ideologies and the media. In G. Dines & J. M. Humez (Eds.), *Gender, race, and class in the media* (pp. 89–93). Thousand Oaks, CA: Sage.
Hall, S. (2006). Encoding/decoding. In M. G. Durham & D. Kellner (Eds.), *Media and cultural studies* (pp. 163–173). Malden, MA: Blackwell.
Hartman, S. V. (1997). *Scenes of subjection: Terror, slavery, and self-making in nineteenth-century America*. New York, NY: Oxford University Press.
hooks, b. (2008). *Reel to real*. New York, NY: Routledge.
Horn, J. (2014, March 4). Oscars: "12 Years a Slave" puts spotlight on Hollywood's approach to race. *Los Angeles Times*. Retrieved from http://www.latimes.com/entertainment/movies/moviesnow/la-et-mn-oscar-race-20140304-story.html.
Hughey, M. W. (2009). Cinethetic racism: White redemption and Black stereotypes in "magical negro" films. *Social Problems, 56*(3), 543–577.
Hughey, M. W. (2014). *The white savior film*. Philadelphia, PA: Temple University Press.
Inskeep, S., & Montagne, R. (2014, January 16). "12 Years a Slave" inspires "true conversations" about slavery [Interview]. *NPR*. Retrieved from http://www.npr.org/templates/transcript/transcript.php?storyId=262946971.
Jewell, K. S. (1993). *From mammy to Miss America and beyond*. New York, NY: Routledge.
Kellner, D. (1995). *Media culture*. New York, NY: Routledge.
Malewski, E., & Jaramillo, N. (Eds.). (2011). *Epistemologies of ignorance in education*. Charlotte, NC: Information Age Publishing.
Mills, C. W. (1997). *The racial contract*. Ithaca, NY: Cornell University Press.
Mills, C. W. (2007). White ignorance. In S. Sullivan & N. Tuana (Eds.), *Race and epistemologies of ignorance* (pp. 13–38). Albany, NY: State University of New York Press.
Mitchell, E. (2013, October 7). Steve McQueen. *Interview*. Retrieved from http://www.interviewmagazine.com/film/steve-mcqueen-1/.
Moore, W. L. (2014). The legal alchemy of white domination: Embedding white logic in equal protection law. *Humanity & Society, 38*, 7–24.
Moore, W. L., & Pierce, J. (2007). Still killing mockingbirds: Narratives of race and innocence in Hollywood's depiction of the white messiah lawyer. *Qualitative Sociology Review, 3*(2), 171–187.
Mueller, J. C. (2013). *The social reproduction of systemic racial inequality* (Doctoral dissertation). Texas A&M University, College Station, TX.

Mueller, J. C. (Forthcoming). Producing color-blindness: Everyday mechanisms of white ignorance. *Social Problems*.

Omi, M., & Winant, H. (2014). *Racial formation in the U.S.* New York, NY: Routledge.

Razack, S. H. (2007). Stealing the pain of others: Reflections on Canadian humanitarian responses. *The Review of Education, Pedagogy, and Cultural Studies, 29*, 375–394.

Rizov, V. (2013, October 17). NYFF critic's notebook: *12 Years a Slave, Blue is the Warmest Color, Like Father, Like Son. Filmmaker Magazine*. Retrieved from http://filmmakermagazine.com/76665-nyff-critics-notebook-12-years-a-slave-blue-is-the-warmest-color-like-father-like-son/#.VQdT0kLZr8E.

Rotten Tomatoes. (2013). 12 Years a Slave. Retrieved from http://www.rottentomatoes.com/m/12_years_a_slave/.

Steinberg, S. (2007). *Race relations: A critique*. Stanford, CA: Stanford University Press.

Stevens, D. (2014, January 17). My problem with *12 Years a Slave. Slate*. Retrieved from http://www.slate.com/articles/arts/the_movie_club/features/2014/movie_club_2013/_12_years_a_slave_my_problem_with_steve_mcqueen_s_harrowing_film.html.

Vera, H., & Gordon, A. (2003). *Screen saviors: Hollywood fictions of whiteness*. Lanham, MD: Rowman & Littlefield.

White, A. (2013). Can't trust it. *City Arts*. Retrieved from http://cityarts.info/2013/10/16/cant-trust-it/.

10 Racial Ideology in Electronic Dance Music Festival Promotional Videos

David L. Brunsma, Nathaniel G. Chapman, and J. Slade Lellock

Opening Act

Electronic dance music (EDM) has seen a meteoric rise in worldwide popularity. Emerging from the discotheques of the 1960s, the clubs of the 1970s, the house parties of the 1980s, and the warehouse raves of the 1990s, EDM became highly commercialized and festivalized in the mid-2000s to rapidly become one of the most popular forms of music worldwide. EDM and its attendant cultures surfaced out of the confluence of complex socio-historical changes in the technologies of production and dissemination of popular music, aesthetic shifts in various dance-oriented music genres, the transformation of music scenes, and changes in audience consumption practices.

EDM is strongly tied to college-age demographics (McGrath, 2013). According to a Nielsen (2014) study, EDM listeners are 55% male, 45% female, and nearly two-thirds (63%) White. DJs and promoters often gear their tours and festivals to these audiences. Since Daft Punk's 2006 performance at Coachella, EDM has broken into Top 40 radio (Bogart, 2012) and has received institutional legitimation through having its own Billboard chart. The popularity of EDM is well established and appears to be growing, with an economic impact valued in the billions (McGrath, 2013), especially given the festivalization of EDM culture. Some reports suggest that the global EDM industry is worth over $6 billion, of which $1.03 billion is generated by festivals alone (Hampp, 2014).

Despite the amazing popularity of this musical phenomenon, there has been sparse social science scholarship on EDM asking very basic questions (e.g., what is the demographic makeup?), scarce critical scholarship asking deeper questions (e.g., what kinds of experiences are had, and by whom?), and even less attention from critical scholars of race inquiring about the racial dynamics of EDM phenomena. Given that EDM emerged from and has been deeply inspired by the music of people of color (e.g., disco, hip-hop, etc.), we begin interrogating EDM by investigating its racial representations and ideologies through promotional videos. Our work is theoretically undergirded by recent work in color-blindness as racial ideology (Bonilla-Silva, 2010), research on narratives of Whiteness (Hughey, 2014), and theories of racialized aesthetics in late capitalism (Desmond & Emirbayer, 2009).

The central motivating ideological apparatus of EDM festival culture is widely recognized as the cultural ideals of PLUR—Peace, Love, Unity, and Respect (Lorenz, 2014). Given the reigning ethos of PLUR, the continuously rising significance of the EDM festival phenomenon, as well as the paucity of critical scholarship interrogating the ideals of PLUR, particularly as it relates to dynamics of race and ethnicity, we analyze promotional videos for one of the most popular U.S.-based EDM festivals—Electric Daisy Carnival (EDC). Beginning as a small festival in Los Angeles with 5,000 fans coming together for one day in 1997, EDC has now expanded to various cities (some international) with events lasting several days and drawing well over 300,000 attendees. Modern EDM is strongly connected to the festival experience (Feinstein & Ramsay, 2012).

In their consideration of the male-dominated EDM industry and DJ/club cultures in Germany, Sweden, and the UK, Gavanas and Reitsamer (2013, p. 51) herald a clarion call of sorts when they state:

> It is not sufficient to simply and matter-of-factly conclude that there is (and always has been) a gender imbalance in [EDM] culture without analysing what this fact means to DJ culture as a whole ... it is important to analyse the (self-) representations of women in EDM culture in relation to the specific characteristics of male bias within that culture.

In this chapter we conduct, in some ways, a unique parallel analysis to their gendered call. Previous research has increased our understanding of how gender operates in the experience and promotion of EDM; however, analyses regarding how race organizes the EDM experience are almost non-existent. With this in mind, we begin to craft critical sociological understandings of the experience of EDM, its marketing, and the racial ideologies embedded within the promotion of EDM festivals, aiding scholars in theorizing how race is represented in EDM. We begin to theorize how race and racial representations are utilized to market an experience to an 18- to 34-year-old, color-blind generation through promotional YouTube videos, and contribute to the scholarship on the political economy of media production by asking: What kinds of experiences are being sold by EDM festival promotion videos, to whom, and through which racial lens? What experiences are being promoted and to whom? What narratives do promotional videos convey? Finally, how is race represented in these narratives? Our data consist of promotional videos for Electric Daisy Carnival, an electronic dance music festival.

Rave, PLUR, and the Modern Electronic Dance Music Festival

From its 1960s disco origins to its current state in the 2010s, all forms of EDM foster an environment that encourages losing one's self in the music, embracing dance, and the values of PLUR. PLUR is central to EDM culture and is manifested in myriad ways through material artifacts (e.g., kandi) and embodied rituals (e.g., gestures) (Lorenz, 2014; St. John, 2006). The central ritual in the EDM festival experience is dance. Upbeat tempos and familiar musical structures of EDM put participants in a trance-like state often aided by the use of drugs such as ecstasy. Hughes (2014), studying raves, notes that in such settings, "dancing is a form of submission to [the] overmastering beat" (p. 149). Rietveld (2011) refers to this as a "shared experience of surrender" in which a DJ produces a "specific group subjectivity that, even temporarily, effaces everyday social stratifications on the darkened dance floor" (p. 8). In Tomlinson's (1998) view, rave and modern EDM are seen as something you immerse yourself in with other people, it is an experience that provides participants with an escape or catharsis much like disco did in the 1970s (pp. 203–204). As this scholarship emphasizes, raves like contemporary EDM festivals can be characterized by a collective experience that involves embodied rituals, drug use, and the creation of a temporary liminal social space where PLUR flourishes.

EDM festivals are larger, more produced versions of raves. Festivals, according to Richards (2011), "may be arts events, community celebrations, or political or commercial events designed to promote a particular idea or specific products" (p. 259). The modern EDM festival can be viewed as a celebration of a community that shares the values of PLUR. Richards notes that modern festivals have gradually become "more external to the communities that produce them" (p. 260). Trent Wolbe (2014) contends that "[m]odern EDM festivals, like EDC, are massive productions that dwarf their predecessors: most "laptop" artists and DJs were, until recently, lucky to have shoddy projections on a poorly hung bedsheet as their visual backup. But when Daft Punk brought their massive LED-coated pyramid to Coachella in 2006, things started to change." While there were many festivals prior to 2006, this year marked a significant shift in the production and overall experience of EDM festivals.

Gauthier (2001) has noted that the dance experience of the clubs and underground raves approximates the festival ritual. These festivals have become globally commonplace. As the popularity of EDM increases, so does the scale of production, as seen in mega-events that draw in crowds of over 300,000 attendees. Kiendl (2013) notes that "attendance at the top twenty global festivals jumped from 1.9 million in 2009 to over 3.4 million in 2013." These larger festive gatherings represent what V. Turner (1982) refers to as a "timeless zone, a space of disorder and indeterminacy where dancers (neophytes and experienced) are licensed to experiment with their other selves" and that the "rave is an explosive importation of the carnivalesque into the contemporary—a popular mode of subversive play, of the 'subjunctive mood'" (p. 83). These carnivalesque elements are manifested in many ways: "'freaky' costumes, skillful acrobatic displays and fire-twirling, kaleidoscopic light shows, and elaborately constructed soundscapes and art spaces" (Tramacchi, 2006, p. 140). All of these factors contribute to create a unique and marketable experience.

These festival experiences represent a scaling up of the underground raves of the 1990s. Festival producers benefit from increased global popularity of EDM festivals and attempted to create experiences that harken back to the days of the club, but also represent a new, more modern iteration of EDM. Modern EDM festivals push the boundaries of sensory experience using state-of-the-art sound and lighting technology, pyrotechnics, carnival rides, performance art, and a plethora of other sensory experiences. Gauthier (2004) suggests that the festival takes on a life of its own "by opening up to creativity, by staging an otherly, unlicensed, temporary world, the festive need only contain itself. Disengaging from temporality, the festive bursts into an 'eternal'—or, to be more precise, 'indefinite'—present" (p. 69). St. John (2006) notes "such experiences potentiate the transgression of imposed morality, exemplifying the expression of 'passional' or 'orgiastic' behavior" (p. 6). These types of experiences promote the carnivalesque while also maintaining the ethos of PLUR that the culture values above all else. Gauthier (2004) contends that the modern, or techno-rave, "participates in a cultural resurgence of the festive, providing new avenues for experiences of the sacred in an atomized society" (pp. 68–69). Further, Gauthier (2004) asserts that the modern techno-festal culture "implicitly seeks forgetfulness, selflessness, and oblivion. What this implies is that the promoted effervescence is sought after for itself and in itself. In other words it is its own purpose and reason" (p. 69).

The EDM festival is a modern manifestation of the values of a club culture that promotes PLUR. Festival producers attempt to create unique experiences that highlight these values while also fostering an atmosphere of entertainment and the carnivalesque. These festivals exist as temporary worlds in which fans of EDM, avid club goers, and perhaps curious outsiders can escape the perceived problems of society and lose themselves in an immersive experience that they share with thousands of other festival-goers. As the scale, size, frequency, and locations of these events have shifted over time, one theme remains constant: PLUR. PLUR suggests that everyone should engage in peaceful behavior, love their fellow festival-goer, and respect the differences between people. As EDC and its PLUR-centered fans are fond of repeating, "Come one, come all, come in peace or don't come at all."

While there is a scarce amount of literature on the dimensions of race at U.S. EDM festivals or at other rave and EDM events, there has been some research outside of the U.S. context. Fraser (2012) argues "there is an inevitable politics of space within EDM," and further that "these issues call into question the too-often taken-for-granted notion that EDM is about PLUR" (p. 503). One of the issues creating tension in EDM spaces, particularly in international EDM tourism contexts, as observed by Fraser (2012) is the racist attitude of some "Goa Freaks," (those who prefer Goa and trance forms of EDM, toward Indian tourists in EDM cultural destinations) (p. 53). Saldanha (2005, p. 710) adds that these racist attitudes lead to "sensuous configurations" of race, class, sexuality, ethnicity, and region, within hedonistic EDM spaces (also see Fraser, 2012). Fraser (2012) further suggests that these configurations are "generative of exclusion as well as inclusion, closure as well as openness" (p. 503).

Because scholarship on the racial dynamics and the ideals of PLUR has been largely focused on rave and club contexts outside of the U.S., we suspect that PLUR may be contextually distinct, socio-historically situated, and, as such, shaped by racial dynamics. By investigating what major promoters, like Insomniac, consider important to promote as well as how it is promoted, may give us insight as well into the potential contextuality of PLUR. In the following section, we prop up these ideas against color-blind ideology in an attempt to show how EDM festivals are promoted as White spaces and how the values of PLUR may additionally promote racial exclusivity.

Color-Blind Ideology and the Promotion of Electronic Dance Music Festivals

In *Racism without Racists: Color-Blind Racism and the Persistence of Racial Inequality in the United States,* Bonilla-Silva (2010) asks: How is it possible to have such tremendous racial inequality in a country where most Whites claim that race is no longer relevant? The answer to this question in the 21st century, according to Bonilla-Silva, is color-blind ideology. Color-blind ideology explains racial inequality as the outcome of non-racial dynamics (as opposed to Jim Crow, explicit, in-your-face racism). This has also been referred to as the "new racism," subtle, institutional, and, according to its proponents, non-racial.

Bonilla-Silva's (2010, pp. 26–30) analysis focuses on the central "frames" of color-blindness (set paths for interpreting received racial information): abstract liberalism (the belief in equal opportunity, choice, and individualism where discrimination is understood as no longer a problem, and any individual who works hard can succeed), naturalization (reframes ongoing inequality as the result of natural processes rather than social ones allowing Whites to explain away racial phenomena by suggesting that they are natural occurrences), cultural racism (suggests inherent cultural differences are the cause of inequality today), and minimization of racism (highlights that we now have a fairly level playing field, everyone has equal opportunities to succeed, and that racism is no longer a real problem). This ideology, part of the institution of race, blocks Whites from seeing themselves as racialized, as active agents in the racialized social structure, as group-advantaged, and thus seeing any benefit to them (Whites) of even discussing race. It also disengages them from understanding that racism affects us *all*. Such color-blind set paths of interpreting information or frames have been investigated primarily as speech acts, narratives, "race talk," and varieties of mass mediated narrative structures such as film (Hughey, 2014), broadcast and journalistic news (Drew, 2011), and even music lyrics (Rodriquez, 2006), among others.

Through the ever-growing research on color-blind racism, it is becoming clear that Whites, in general, are well versed in color-blind rhetoric and expect its soothing voice to lull them into another generation of continued structural racism without individual racists.

Given the empirical evidence of color-blind racism in virtually every facet of American society, the strategies of advertising, marketing, and promoting products, experiences, and events like EDM festivals in general, and EDC in particular, would also surely be impacted by such ideological frames. Such an analysis of how color-blind ideology is manifested within visual texts is rare, yet such an analysis is important for theoretically developing our understanding of both color-blind racism as well as EDM (see S. Turner & Nilsen, 2014, for a recent exception). We use Bonilla-Silva's four frames of color-blindness to understand the racial ideologies embedded within promotional videos for one of EDM's premier music festivals—Electric Daisy Carnival. We ask: Whose voice is here? Whose is not? Whose gaze is catered to? Who is visible? Who is not? Who is active? Who is not? We analyze color-blind ideology and rhetoric in visual representations of race in EDM promotional videos in "post-racial" United States.

Electronic Dance Music Promotional Videos: A Visual Content Analysis

As Schnettler and Raab (2008) argue, the interpretive analysis of visual data in the social sciences, particularly audiovisual data (e.g., video), has been remarkably underutilized, inadequately theorized, and, thus, largely neglected as a viable mode of inquiry by researchers. Part of this analytic aversion stems from social scientists' historically rote emphasis on textual data. Interpretive analyses of visual data should not occupy such a marginal place in scholarly pursuits given the powerful ideological features embedded in audio-visual cultural objects. As Morrison (2012) notes, however, it can be particularly problematic to filmically represent what is, by nature, a sonic and social experience such as music festival participation. Bearing this cautionary insight in mind, we proceed in our analysis with the following epistemological caveat: what is promoted (represented) in EDM videos may not necessarily represent the grounded realities and lived experiences of EDM festival participation. Consequently, our analysis is inherently limited in that we can only make claims about the particular aspects of PLUR and color-blind racial ideology as they are evident in EDM promotional videos.

We selected a subset of official promotional videos produced by Insomniac Events (a leading company in EDM festival promotion) for Electric Daisy Carnival. We captured the promotional videos from the official YouTube channel of Insomniac Events. Despite EDC's origins in the mid-late 1990s, we could not locate any promotional videos for the festival until its 2006 event. As such, 2006 is the first video in our analysis. While we examined videos through 2014, we did not analyze from 2011 onward as we felt saturation had been met. Our sample consists of promotional videos from years 2006, 2007, 2009, and 2010.[1]

We conducted a multistage visual content analysis of a subset of these promotional videos. In stage 1, we watched all the promotional videos in their entirety drawing "sensitizing concepts" from the scholarly literature on EDM and EDM festivals. We also placed a lens over the data from Bonilla-Silva's (2010) dominant frames of color-blind ideology, operationalizing these visually. We began by individually writing narrative "gestalts" for each entire video. Gestalts provided an overall feeling of the video, its affect, its flow, its feel, its sound, as well as the various elements that resonated with each of us in our first viewing. This strategy produced a bird's-eye view of the data. Further, our gestalts allowed us to identify common thematic elements and also how these elements changed over time. During this process, our attention was initially drawn to the striking representations of gender and sexuality. For this analysis, however, we hone in on the codes that are most closely resonant with the demographics of DJs, EDC performers (e.g., professional dancers hired to perform on stage and among the crowd), and attendees as well as other elements that can be understood by Bonilla-Silva's color-blind ideology. We then developed a coding scheme based on the themes we identified.

In stage 2, we methodically examine each video for evidence of those concepts and frames. To do this, we assigned 10-second intervals as the unit of analysis given the rapid displays of immense amounts of visual and aural content. This resulted in 39, 10-second intervals across all four EDC videos. We looped each 10-second interval in order to exhaustively code for these concepts and frames. We allowed our deep coding to be relatively open during this process so as to avoid precluding emergent findings or ideas. Coding for each minute of video playback took roughly 1 hour to complete. In the final pass, we carry out a critical discourse analysis as described by van Dijk (1993).

Findings

The purpose of each of these videos is to promote the upcoming year's EDC festival. In our sample we observed promotional videos as having two distinct forms: the informative promotional video, and the hyper-produced, thematic, and narrative promotional video. The videos from 2006 and 2007 are much shorter in length averaging 45 seconds. These videos are more basic and informational, and forgo many high-tech production elements. Each video featured narration and on-screen text that provided basic information including the date of the festival, where to purchase tickets, the location, and the artist lineup. The videos from 2009 and 2010 followed a formulaic structure: establishing time-lapse shots that showed the stadium slowly filling with fans, the artists and the festival itself, the intensity of the EDM backing music paralleled the action/affect in the video, lighting and visual effects becoming more intense, a later emphasis on the night where the intensity of the music and much of the shots are much quicker, pulsating, and ramped-up. Each video contained footage from the previous year's festival as if to entice the festival-goer into attending again with the promises of a much larger experience the coming year.

Gestalts as Snapshots of Electric Daisy Carnival Promotional Videos

We noticed several significant differences between the videos. There were indeed changes across time in how Insomniac's production team chose to represent and market EDC to potential attendees; there were also many similarities across these four videos. Key elements emerging from the cross-gestalt analysis reveals that from 2006 to 2010 these videos consistently emphasized certain imagery, content, and structural elements. These recurring elements are the focus on EDM itself as the backing-track, DJs either as stills or performance shots (the vast majority of these are White men), the use of individual daisies (possibly signifying EDC attendees) and fields of daisies (possibly signifying EDC itself), imagery of Ferris wheels and amusement park rides, intense usage of colors and pulsating lights, the focus on women's bodies and female sexuality, and, relatedly, if there was a narrator of the promotional video it was a woman, and if there were lyrics to the backing track it was a man. All of these elements were established in the earlier videos (2006 and 2007).

While we are still unaware of why the 2008 EDC promotional video remains unavailable, there were striking additions post-2008 in the promotion of EDC. While all of the elements mentioned earlier remained constant through the videos in 2010 and beyond, all elements were intensified in powerful ways. Over time, EDC promotional videos have had several noteworthy changes. First, the production value of the videos increases with each passing year. Second, there is a newfound sense of pacing and plotting, of flow and structure, to these promotional videos: starting slowly, building to a climax, and ending. Third, the carnivalesque, the burlesque, the hyper-festivalization, and the emergence of costuming, staging, and props are enhanced in a visually urgent manner with each passing year. Fourth, there is an intensification of female sexuality, women's barely covered bodies, and sexual innuendo, evidenced by close-up shots of individual or small groups of dancing women, presumably for the heterosexual male gaze. Fifth, there is a seemingly unresolved tension between the increased focus on the individual over time while simultaneously emphasizing the collective, mass dancing, huge crowd experience. Sixth, the videos are increasingly stimulating both visually and sonically over time.

Race and Representation in Electronic Dance Music Promotional Videos

In *Racial Domination, Racial Progress*, Desmond and Emirbayer (2009, pp. 359–368) discuss the "White aesthetic" and the "racist aesthetic" in artistic, filmic, and other mediated cultural forms. Detecting a White aesthetic in art "often means paying attention to absences ... seeing the unseen, listening to the silences ... [asking] What-or who-is missing?" (p. 359). Whiteness, in the White aesthetic, is the norm in this frame. Non-Whiteness, if it appears, must be located in a socio-historical-cultural imaginary (jungle, kabuki, etc.) in order to be comprehended. As such, the racist aesthetic—often epiphenomenal to the White aesthetic, or White racial frame (Feagin, 2010)—depicts Non-Whites in distorted, stereotypical, and negative ways. The White aesthetic ignores people of color, and the racist aesthetic represents them. Furthermore, despite the appearance of Non-White bodies (however scarce) within the artistic field, it is a prime articulation and constant reminder that Non-Whites have yet to gain full control over the representation of themselves. Our findings regarding the presence of Non-Whites within the EDC promotional videos dovetail very closely to an operation of a White aesthetic with an accompanying racist aesthetic. Such an aesthetic frame serves the political economy of media production centrally by speaking directly to the color-blind yet stereotypical language to those who spend the enormous sums of money to attend these festivals—Whites.

Across the segments of the videos, our codes allowed us to account for Non-White presences across three different primary roles that comprise an EDC event: DJs, EDC professional performers, and EDC attendees. Across the four videos, the DJs were all male and overwhelmingly White. While it is difficult (and inherently subjective) to identity Non-White presences among the hundreds of thousands of EDC attendees, one approach is to simply acknowledge that across 39, 10-second segments of video, there were only 10 (or 25.6%) segments with any Non-White participants close-up. This, however, is not a very accurate or even adequate understanding of the demographic makeup of the EDC crowd, either in reality or in the promoted "reality." Watching these promotional videos gives an overwhelming sense that this is a vastly White event with a predominantly White aesthetic at play. When Non-Whites are presented on the screen, they are displayed in transient, quick, and limited ways—this is especially true of the EDC professional performers.

The 2006 and 2007 videos did not focus at all on the paid EDC professional performers who are an increasingly important part of the EDC experience. But, beginning in 2009, and certainly in 2010 (and in the years following), the promotional videos did indeed draw attention to these dancers. Of the 19 segments in the 2010 video including EDC professional dancers, all were female, and the vast majority (17; 89.5%) were White women donned in a wide variety of unique costuming—no doubt chosen specifically by the promoters—including, but not limited to: White-wigged, burlesque, painted-face women with 60s mod-boots; a bikinied, acrobat woman spinning in a hoop; White, face-painted catwomen with small black hats; people in full-bodied orange rubber suits; bikini-clad cage dancers; yellow-wigged, painted-faced women with pink tutus; a White woman with dreadlocks in a robot-bikini; fishnet-wearing, striped-bikinied ballerinas; mini-skirted women en masse on stage; and colorful clown women with wigs and colored nose balls. The two Non-White EDM professional performers were an Asian American woman whose face was painted White in a Japanese Kabuki style, with make-up in addition to highlight eye slant, twirling a yellow umbrella, with yellow streaks in her black hair, smelling a handful of daisies as she turns to reveal tattooed shoulder blades. The other was a Black woman, on stage during the night, silhouetted with a yellow bikini and doing a fast-paced tribally influenced dance for the attendees. Stereotypically, the Asian American woman is portrayed as alluring and submissive, while the Black woman is portrayed as intensely and aggressively dancing. In EDM promotional videos, embodied gender and sexuality are stereotypically racialized in their depictions that seem to serve a particular White, heteronormative gaze.

Color-Blind Ideology and Color-Blind Framing in Electronic Dance Music Promotional Videos

The EDC promotional videos had some general patterns branding EDC, told a similar narrative within each video, had a clear lack of racial and ethnic diversity in its promotion, focused largely on the White aesthetic while also engaging in stereotypical representations of the few Non-White bodies. These videos are overwhelmingly White, predictable, hyper-sexualized, with intense scenes of a collective effervescence beholden to the master beat. These videos are clearly made for the White gaze and its attendant White imaginary and aesthetic. Surely EDM and these EDC promotional videos exist within and engage with the dominant frames of color-blindness in this supposedly "post-racial" America. Bonilla-Silva's four frames of color-blind ideology can also be applied to these promotional videos to help illuminate the ways in which they may circumvent the potential racial utopia, implied by PLUR, through rhetorical and visual devices of color-blind ideological representations.

The most evident frame used in these videos is the rhetoric of abstract liberalism. This frame asks us to look for the ways that highlight individualism, individual choice, notions of universalism, and ideals of meliorism that express (Whites') desires, needs, and hopes for societal goals (peace, harmony, the end of racism, etc.). There is no doubt that EDC promotes to its audience a strident and fervent individualism, where attendees can be anything they want to be, dress anyway they wish to dress, make any choice they wish to make, express their individual desires while maintaining a collective connection to the beat. The 2010 narrator sums up this frame by saying: "A new day is dawning. A place built of love and light and sounds that touch the places in our hearts that long for something true. We come together united under the electric sky." At this point in our analysis one must interrogate what "new day is dawning"? For whom? Whose truth? Who is the "we" referent that is "united" during EDC? Perhaps there is a racial futurism at play here, a vision of a White utopia, one where there are no people of color at all.

Bonilla-Silva's second frame of color-blind ideology is also apparent in these promotional videos. For color-blindness to work in a post-racial White aesthetic, one moves away from explicitly engaging with race and racialized rhetorics, per se, and instead focuses the audience's attention toward cultural ways to identify difference in the White aesthetic. Thus, we observe in the EDC promotional videos a filmic focus on the sea of White masses enraptured in their individualistic (but deeply united collectivist) connection to the experience of EDC with very limited, and always stereotypical, images of Non-Whites (especially among the EDC professional dancers who are part and parcel of the constructed spectacle that is EDC). One is also struck by the fact that Whiteness is actually actively engaged in a drag/minstrel performance of sorts—a doing of race—while at the same time culturally appropriating the musical products the Non-White experiences in the United States. Scholars of popular culture and popular music see this kind of cultural co-optation as a result of the hyper-commercialization of cultural products and the resultant commodification of style and identity (Kotarba, Merrill, Williams, & Vannini, 2013). This is evident in EDC.

Indeed, EDC promotes an upfront minimization of race, and, by extension, recognition of racism or structures of inequality—despite its myopic ideological tunnel vision of PLUR. Color-blindness demands that, ideologically, as well as visually and affectively, one does not (and should not) see or discuss race or racism. A color-blind, PLUR-based EDC would certainly diminish the acknowledgement of race (e.g., who attends and/or who "should" attend EDC), racial inequalities (e.g., who can afford EDC; is this raced, classed, etc.; who is misrepresented at EDC), and racisms (e.g., who drives the master beat, cultural appropriations, etc.).

Finally, the naturalization frame of color-blind ideology promotes a White EDC experience by engaging in (il)logics that rationalize the low Non-White presence, the lack of DJ headliners of color, the overarching Whiteness of EDC as "just the way things are." Looking more closely, when one recognizes that these are *promotional* videos, designed to sell a product, a ticket, and experience, perhaps a particular subjectivity, it becomes clear that EDC is, despite the framing within a naturalization frame, driven by market processes, social processes, and, indeed racial processes. Yet, color-blindness demands that the promotion keeps these factors invisible.

Encore (or How to Promote PLUR in a Twenty-First Century Electronic Dance Music Festival)

Through an analysis of EDC promotional videos, we now have a more refined understanding of how race and racial representations are used to market the EDM experience to an 18- to 34-year-old, color-blind generation in the U.S. If asked how does one promote the central organizing principle of PLUR and the experience of EDM festivals, our analysis of the promotional videos of a massively popular festival, EDC, one significant component of the answer, apparently, is through a White aesthetic and a color-blind visual rhetoric.

The videos we analyzed are clearly promoting an event: an event where *all* are invited to meet, for several days, and to be united as one. There is no doubt that this event brings Non-White bodies to the dance floor. Indeed, Insomniac and EDC clearly *hire* some "diversity" performers, who are almost the only Non-White bodies of any kind of visual focus in these promotional videos. Yet, what is promoted, and how the promotion is packaged, lends some evidence to the idea that EDC, as but one EDM festival of many, caters its experience of PLUR to the White gaze, via a White aesthetic, with a White racial grammar/logic orchestrated and underwritten by color-blind ideological frames. Whiteness, as Desmond and Emirbayer (2009) aptly highlight, is a collective and "deep yearning to be included among the 'beautiful people' … Art that fails to include Non-Whites represents the world as a White world … and if Non-Whites do not exist, neither does racial domination" (p. 361). EDM and its central tenet, PLUR, organize the festival experience around the world—whether in Germany, Sweden, U.K., Japan, or Australia. However, the U.S., with its particular contemporary yet socio-historical racialized social structure, and its reigning racial ideology, will contextually shape PLUR in recognizable ways for Whites and Whiteness. Analyses of these videos begin to highlight the contextuality of PLUR in EDM scenes and how it interfaces with racial inequalities.

In his study of White savior films, Matthew Hughey (2014) concludes that we have seen the promotion, production, and dissemination of White savior films in this "post-racial," "color-blind" moment in history for five basic reasons: (1) hope and desire for a societal change to an authentically egalitarian society absent of racial prejudice and discrimination; (2) embrace of individualism and individualist approaches to achieving such utopia; (3) shared belief in the cultural and moral dysfunctions of people of color; (4) impatience with or disinterest in race-based discussions; and (5) downplaying and minimizing racism and racial inequality (p. 165). These conclusions are equally resonant with our analysis of the promotional videos of EDC. For, despite prevalent representations of EDM festival spaces as harmonious, inclusive, and integrated social spaces, largely through social and cultural assumptions about the meaning and universal operation of Peace, Love, Unity, and Respect, our findings caution us to be cognizant, as scholars of popular culture and race, of the ways that PLUR is mediated and ideologically interpreted through Whiteness and color-blindness, leading to perhaps, EDM as electronic/experiential/exclusionary dance music.

Note

1. The promotional video for Electric Daisy Carnival 2008 was not available online at the time of data collection. We contacted Insomniac Events via e-mail requesting the missing video, but our request was not granted.

References

Bogart, J. (2012, July 10) Buy the hype: Why electronic dance music really could be the new rock. *The Atlantic*. Retrieved from http://www.theatlantic.com/entertainment/archive/2012/07/buy-the-hype-why-electronic-dance-music-really-could-be-the-new-rock/259597/.

Bonilla-Silva, E. (2010). *Racism without racists*. Lanham, MD: Rowman & Littlefield.

Brown, H. (2014, July 29). Festival deaths on the rise in EDM culture. *Billboard Magazine*. Retrieved from http://www.billboard.com/articles/6188652/festival-deaths-edm.

Desmond, M., & Emirbayer, M. (2009). *Racial domination, racial progress: The sociology of race in America*. New York, NY: McGraw Hill.

Drew, E. M. (2011). "Coming to terms with our own racism": Journalists grapple with the racialization of their news. *Critical Studies in Media Communication, 28*(4), 353–373.

Feagin, J. (2010). *The White racial frame: Centuries of racial framing and counter-framing*. New York, NY: Routledge.

Feinstein, D., & Ramsay, C. (2012, November 8). The rise of EDM. *Huffington Post*. Retrieved from http://www.huffingtonpost.com/danny-feinstein/electronic-dance-music_b_2094797.html.

Fraser, A. (2012). The spaces, politics, and cultural economies of electronic dance music. *Geography Compass, 6*(8), 500–511.

Gavanas, A., & Reitsamer, R. (2013). DJ technologies, social networks and gendered trajectories in European DJ cultures. In B. Attias, H. Gavanas, & H. Rietveld (Eds.), *DJ culture in the mix: Power, technology, and social change in electronic dance music* (pp. 51–76). London, UK: Bloomsbury.

Gauthier, F. (2001). Consumation. La religiosité des raves. *Religiologiques, 24*, 175–197.

Gauthier, F. (2004). Rapturous ruptures: The "instituant" religious experience of rave. In G. St John (Ed.), *Rave culture and religion* (pp. 65–84). London, UK: Routledge.

Hampp, A. (2014, May 21). EDM biz worth $6.2 billion. *Billboard*. Retrieved from http://www.billboard.com/biz/articles/6092242/edm-biz-worth-62bn-report.

Hughes, W. (2014). In the empire of the beat: Discipline and disco. In A. Ross & T. Rose (Eds.), *Microphone fiends: Youth music and youth culture* (pp. 147–187). New York, NY: Routledge.

Hughey, M. (2014). *The white savior film: Content, critics, and consumption*. Philadelphia, PA: Temple University Press.

Kiendl, W. (2013, December). The economics of EDM. *The Music Business Journal*. Retrieved from http://www.thembj.org/2013/12/the-economics-of-the-electronic-dance-industry/.

Kotarba, J. A., Merrill, B., Williams, J. P., & Vannini, P. (2013). *Understanding society through popular music*. New York, NY: Routledge.

Lorenz, N. (2014). *The power of PLUR: EDMC as a reflection of a new generation*. Senior project. California Polytechnic State University, San Luis Obispo.

McGrath, M. (2013, November 4). EDM-obsessed millennials boost SFX entertainment outlook. *Forbes*. Retrieved from http://www.forbes.com/sites/maggiemcgrath/2013/11/04/edm-obsessed-millennials-boost-sfx-entertainment-outlook/.

Morrison, S. A. (2012). "Clubs aren't like that": Discos, deviance and diegetics in club culture cinema. *Dancecult: Journal of Electronic Dance Music Culture, 4*(2), 48–66.

Nielsen. (2014, July 10). Who is the electronic music listener? *Nielsen*. Retrieved from http://www.nielsen.com/us/en/insights/news/2014/who-is-the-electronic-music-listener.html.

Richards, G. (2011). The festivalization of society or the socialization of festivals? The case of catalunya." In G. Richards (Ed.), *Cultural tourism: Global and local perspectives* (pp. 257–280). New York, NY: Routledge.

Rietveld, H. C. (2011). Disco's revenge: House music's nomadic memory. *Dancecult: Journal of Electronic Music Culture, 2*(1), 4–23.

Rodriquez, J. (2006). Color-blind ideology and the cultural appropriation of hip-hop. *Journal of Contemporary Ethnography, 35*(6), 645–668.

Saldanha, A. (2005). Trance and visibility at dawn: Racial dynamics in Goa's rave scene. *Social & Cultural Geography, 6*(5), 707–721.

Schnettler, B., & Raab, J. (2008). Interpretative visual analysis developments: State of the art and pending problems. *Forum: Qualitative Social Research, 9*(3). Retrieved from http://www.qualitative-research.net/index.php/fqs/article/view/1149/2556.

St. John, G. (Ed.). (2006). *Rave culture and religion*. London, UK: Routledge.

Tomlinson, L. (1998). This ain't no disco ... or is it? Youth culture and the rave phenomenon. In J. Epstein (Ed.), *Youth culture: Identity in a postmodern world* (pp. 195–211). Malden, MA: Blackwell.

Tramacchi, D. (2006). Entheogenic dance ecstasis: Cross-cultural contexts. In G. St. John (Ed.), *Rave culture and religion* (pp. 125–144). London, UK: Routledge. Turner, S., & Nilsen, S. (2014). *The color-blind screen: Television in post-racial America*. New York, NY: New York University Press.

Turner, V. (1982). *From ritual to theatre: The human seriousness of play*. New York, NY: Performing Arts Journal Publications.

Van Dijk, T. A. (1993). *Elite discourse and racism*. Thousand Oaks, CA: Sage.

Wolbe, T. (2014, July 1). Shut up and spend: Inside the electronic music money machine. *The Verge*. Retrieved from http://www.theverge.com/2014/7/1/5857152/shut-up-and-spend-inside-the-edm-electronic-music-money-machine.

Part IV
Perpetuating Contentious Ideologies

11 The Rise of the Racial Reviewer, 1990–2004

Bianca Gonzalez-Sobrino, Devon R. Goss, and Matthew W. Hughey

In 2002, Norman Denzin wrote "the media and the cinematic racial order are basic to the understanding of race relations in any society" (p. 244). This cinematic world that encompasses the films, writers, and production crews also includes the critics that validate or invalidate a particular film's worthiness of viewership. Film reviewers are often understood as neutral authorities in the world of movies. This conceptualization of the film critic operates on the assumption that professional film reviewers exist outside of the social structures and cultural ideologies that guide layperson interpretations. Hence, critics are often understood as "objective" evaluators of film—as helpful guides that show us the dispassionate and right way to understand and interpret specific films. This is especially the case with acclaimed films that take on hot-button topics—such as race, racial inequality, and racism. For example, recent films with problematic racial characterizations have been heralded and even rewarded, like *Gran Torino* (2008), *The Blind Side* (2009), and the remake of *The Karate Kid* (2010).

In this chapter, we demonstrate how the assumptions of film reviewers are driven by the dominant racial ideologies of the times, which in turn affect their interpretations of racialized films. Taken together, these reviews are a reflection of the dominant racial meanings of the time period, not mere artistic expressions or intellectual appraisals of individual reviews. Using a mixed methods approach and following the methodological steps employed in Hughey's (2014) analysis of "White Savior" films, we trace the dominant racial ideologies by examining the index of discussions on race relations printed in *The New York Times* over a 15-year period (1990–2004). Following Hughey (2014), we correlate that data with a content analysis of the reviews from mainstream news outlets for the highest grossing racialized movie of each respective year (1990 to 2004).

For this analysis, we define "racialized films" as cinema that has explicit or implicit racial characters and/or storylines in which race is a determinant of how the film is understood and consumed. These racial meanings can be completely apparent in the storyline of the film, while others can be a part of the music, the setting, and the characters, among other things. For example, *Maid in Manhattan* (2002), starting Jennifer Lopez, was largely framed as a movie about class and upward mobility, yet the main character,

Marisa Ventura, is a woman of color, presumably Puerto Rican and from the South Bronx. Her ethnic/racial background is never explicitly mentioned in the film. However, it is noteworthy that this storyline would be irrevocably altered if the race of this character was different. Given the already understood stereotype of people of color—especially Latinas—as domestic service workers in the United States, the character's Latina racial identity helped solidify the character and storyline as authentic, plausible, and legitimate. The racial identity of the character and her placement in a Horatio Alger-uplift myth would fail to tap into the national collective consciousness concerning race if *Maid in Manhattan* dealt with a White maid falling in love with a White politician. Rather, that storyline would be more about a class-based, rags-to-riches love story, in the context of a White woman's rightful and just escape from "undignified" domestic servitude that is essentially beneath her, instead of a social commentary on the "White man's burden" of saving a Latina from work that defines her so that she may reach her true potential in a White-run world on the arm of a White man. Accordingly, this chapter aims to map out the relationship between the dominant racial ideologies in society and how film reviewers are constrained and enabled by these ideologies as they engage in public interpretations of racialized films.

Background

As United States' popular culture is inevitably influenced by broader social forces, it should be no surprise that race and racism have longstanding impact on the media imagery that Americans consume. From Hattie McDaniel's Academy Award-winning role as the outspoken housemaid Mammy in *Gone with the Wind* (1939), to Octavia Spencer's eerily similar Academy Award-winning character Minny in *The Help* (2011), the possibilities for a wide range of roles are still limited for Black actors. Moreover, the majority of cinematic opportunities for people of color are largely based on the era's racial stereotypes.

Racial stereotypes have been a mainstay in media imagery for many years. If we start with D.W. Griffith's *Birth of a Nation* (1905), motion pictures have a long-standing record as a potent platform for the dissemination of racialized meanings and social propaganda. These ideologies run the gamut. While the turn of the 20th century saw rationalizations for Jim Crow and White supremacist backlashes toward equality, Black power and Black pride messages began to radiate through theaters during the Civil Rights Movement, as witnessed by the introduction of the "blaxploitation" genre in the 1970s (also a marketing ploy to get dissatisfied Blacks to attend the movie theater) (Hughey, 2014). In both cases, these movies reinforced popular notions of people of color as violent, aggressive, and sexual—even as these meanings were deployed for, ostensibly, very different political ends.

Racism in the United States has become increasingly subtle and concealed, as Bonilla-Silva (2010) has described: "In contrast to the Jim Crow era, where racial inequality was enforced through overt means ... today racial practices operate in a 'now you see it, now you don't fashion'" (p. 3). In order to explain this new type of racial discrimination, Bonilla-Silva introduced the idea of "color-blind racism." Color-blind racism undergirds structural racism and rationalizes the contemporary status of minorities as the product of market dynamics, naturally occurring phenomena, and their own cultural limitations (Bonilla-Silva, 2010). Through color-blind racist ideals, many racial groups, but especially Whites, are able to deny the existence of racism and racial discrimination, while maintaining, rationalizing, and legitimating racist worldviews and structural arrangements.

Utilizing this color-blind racist ideology, there was an explosion of theatrical films in the 1980s that dealt with historical racial events through the motif of inter-racial redemption. Two particularly powerful racialized movie tropes include the "Magical Negro" film and the "White Savior" film. Magical Negro films, in which lower-class, mystical, and powerful Black characters work to change damaged and broken-down White characters back into proper forms of hegemonic Whiteness, aiding in reaffirming the racial status-quo that places Whiteness on the top of the racial hierarchy (Glenn & Cunningham, 2009; Hughey, 2009). Examples of this movie trope include *The Green Mile* (1999) and *The Matrix Trilogy* (1999, 2003, 2003).

This type of race film is contrasted by the White Savior film, wherein good-hearted White individuals cross the color line in order to inspire and ease the suffering of people of color, often despite the White Savior enduring suffering themselves (Hughey, 2010). Examples of White Savior films include *The Blind Side* (2009), *Freedom Writers* (2007), and *The Help* (2011). Both of these tropes highlight the concept of what has been called "cinethetic racism"—a synthesis of the dynamics of stereotypical and racist representations of people of color and the normalization of Whiteness through representations of White individuals (Glenn & Cunningham, 2009; Hughey, 2009, 2010). While the vast majority of the research on such films focuses on the content of the media itself, we draw attention to how critics decode and understand these racialized messages in film.

These cinematic racial stereotypes function within what Collins (2000) termed "controlling images"—images that hold special meanings through elite systems of domination and control. Controlling images mark people of color as "the other" and help viewers to justify race and gender-based dominance. Moreover, these images do not only maintain the U.S. White/Black color line, but also relate to all racial groups, including East Asian Americans (e.g., Espiritu, 1997; Pyke & Johnson, 2003) and South Asian Americans (e.g., Purkayastha, 2006; Sharma, 2010). These racial ideologies work to naturalize racism by positioning racial minorities as a quintessential dangerous and/or dysfunctional "other" that is culturally and/or socially inferior to Whites.

Film and Film Critics

We understand the production of media as an organized and collective activity whereby the content directly echoes the author's intentions, the resources of the production industry, and the normalized conventions of the industry and culture in which the media was produced (Holz & Wright, 1979). In this paradigm, media is understood as a reflection of wider cultural meanings and societal ideologies and act as a vehicle to introduce and frame topics to a wider audience (Glassner, 1999).

Film, as a media product that reflects wider cultural meanings, is a central part of North American life and culture. Sixty-eight percent of the American and Canadian population went to the movies at least once in 2013, bringing in $10.9 billion into the box office (Motion Picture Association of America, 2014). Additionally, new films are no longer available only in theaters, but are also widely accessible for home viewing through services such as Netflix, Hulu, and Movies on Demand. Moreover, due to the racial homogeneity of the United States, White Americans often have little interaction with people of color, with 75% having no person of color in their social network (Public Religion Research Institute, 2014). Therefore, racial portrayals in the media may be the dominant source of information that many Americans utilize to understand their intergroup relations (hooks, 1995).

One of the ways that meanings are ascribed and reproduced in the watching of film is through film critics. Although critics play important roles in other industries, including publishing, art, and technology, scholars have also identified the essential role of these experts within the film industry (Eliashberg & Shugan, 1997). Film critics act as conduits between the producers and consumers of media; they serve as cultural intermediaries (Bourdieu, 1984). Researchers have shown that film reviewers aid audiences in understanding film content and deciding which films to see (Basuroy, Chatterjee, & Ravid, 2003; Gemser, Van Oostrum, & Leenders, 2007). However, it is essential to understand that film critics do not exist in a vacuum. Film critics rely on normative cultural frameworks in order to reproduce or contest dominant racial logics within their reviews, constituting a "racialized interpretive community" (Hughey, 2010, p. 475).

Data and Methodology

For this study, we implemented a mixed methods approach using a measure of mainstream perceptions of racial conflict from 1990 to 2004 and a content analysis of the film reviews for 15 "racialized" films that were released between 1990 and 2004. The measure of mainstream perceptions of racial conflict was taken from descriptions of events involving race listed in the *New York Times Index*, 1987–2004. The film reviews were gathered through a systematic search of The Movie Review Query Engine (henceforth MRQE).

As a way of gauging the dominant perceptions of racial conflict, we used the index to measure the frequency of racial conflict. Racial conflict was operationalized by coding for 48 categories related to race relations in the index. Afterward, we arranged the three major racial discourses found in the index: (1) group awareness, (2) group relations, and (3) group threat. While it seems that perceptions of racial conflict have been declining, these different discourses give us a nuanced understanding of diverse meanings attached to the overall racial conflict discourses. Group awareness discourses measure instances where racial groups were mentioned, thus serving as an indicator of awareness of the racial group in the public sphere. The group relations type measures focus on the awareness of interests of racial groups. Third,

Table 11.1 Top Racialized Film per Year, 1990–2004

Film	Year	Distributor	Box Office Ranking	Gross U.S.
Dances with Wolves	1990	Orion	3	$184,208,848
Boyz N the Hood	1991	Columbia Pictures	23	$57,504,069
White Men Can't Jump	1992	20th Century Fox	16	$90,753,806
Cool Runnings	1993	Walt Disney Pictures	15	$154,856,263
Above the Rim	1994	New Line Cinema	94	$16,192,320
Pocahontas	1995	Walt Disney Pictures	4	$364,000,000
A Time to Kill	1996	Regency Enterprise	10	$108,766,007
Amistad	1997	DreamWorks Pictures	50	$44,229,441
Rush Hour	1998	New Line Cinema	7	$141,186,846
The Green Mile	1999	Warner Brothers	12	$136,801,374
Crouching Tiger, Hidden Dragon	2000	Sony Classics	12	$128,078,872
Save the Last Dance	2001	Paramount	25	$91,057,006
Maid in Manhattan	2002	Sony Revolution	26	$94,011,225
Pirates of the Caribbean: The Curse of the Black Pearl	2003	Buena Vista	3	$305,413,918
Man on Fire	2004	20th Century Fox	34	$77,911,774

Source: Data from Box Office Mojo.
Note: $N = 15$.

group threat focuses on overt racial threat between groups. These measures fluctuate greatly over time, thus debunking the common belief that perceived racial conflict has steadily declined with time.

To examine the meanings in the reviews of racialized films, we created a database of film reviews collected from the MRQE for the top-grossing racialized film from each year spanning from 1990 to 2004. Table 11.1 lists the films for each year, the production company, the box-office ranking for the year, and the gross domestic box-office revenue. The preliminary search for reviews for the 15 films yielded a total of 1,694 film reviews. After selecting reviews that appeared in top news outlets (print and electronic), we identified 138 reviews for analysis.[1] Each review was coded in three stages. First, we read every individual review and took notes inductively to trace patterns and themes in the data. Second, we created a coding schema from our inductive review of the data. Third, we coded the data, where the themes were only marked present when it was clear. In the next section, we will discuss the findings and the relationships between the dominant racial logics of the times and the themes in the film reviews.

Results

Figure 11.1 is a frequency distribution of the racial ideologies present in the *New York Times Index* from 1987 to 2004. Overall, the mentions of racial tension in the index shows a decline. While this trend seems to align with the incorrect dominant notions of the "declining significance of race" (Wilson, 1980), when we examine Figure 11.1 a different trend emerges. The three discourses (group awareness, group relations, and group threat) vary across time, thus undermining the common belief of steady progress in race relations and racial insignificance. We can observe how racial threat continues to have a steady presence in the media, while racial group relations have nearly disappeared. On the other hand, group awareness greatly fluctuated between 1987 and 2004. While these frequencies serve as an indicator of numeral changes, these changes in trend present three discursive time periods. These time periods have been previously examined by Hughey (2014), who argues that these discursive periods are (1) the (multi)cultural wars (1987–1992), (2) the White backlash (1993–1998), and (3) the post-racial era and redemption of Whiteness (1999–2011).

Racial Discursive Time Periods: An Overview

These three discursive time periods can be also traced via reviewers' interpretations of racialized films. Before drawing the connections between the dominant racial ideologies of the times and the interpretation and review of racialized films, we briefly lay out the racial ideologies from 1990 to 2004.

During the first discursive time period (between 1987 and 1992), a culture war raged on around the idea of multiculturalism. During this period,

The Rise of the Racial Reviewer, 1990–2004 171

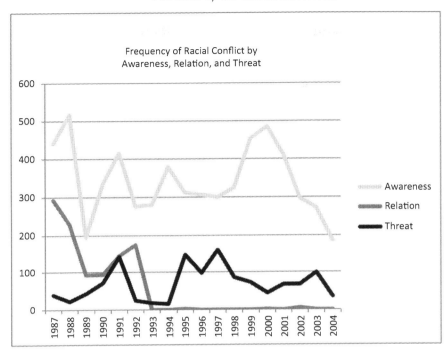

Figure 11.1 Frequency of racial conflict by awareness, relation, and threat.

the media mostly focused on relations between racial groups. The messages sent by the media to the people were of the saliency of race as a dividing category in society and the interests of particular racial groups. The latter was mostly framed either in cooperation between racial groups or racial antagonism. The discussions on race mostly focused on the future and progress of racial groups and multiculturalism (Hughey, 2014). The second discursive time period (during 1993 and 1998) is characterized by the retraction of racial progress and the perceived threat of the racial status quo being balanced in favor of people of color. The media focused its attention on the White backlash, and the racial divide between Whites and Blacks (Hughey, 2014). Whites claimed victimhood during this time period through claims of reverse racism. The third racial discursive time period (between 1999 to 2004), commonly called the "post-racial" era, was a time period characterized by the color-blindness of racial discourse. These discourses imagine a society where race no longer matters and people who claim discrimination are blamed as playing the "race card."

Reviewing Racialized Films

After analyzing the film review data, we encountered a series of themes that framed racialized films as either preachy, ahistorical, clichéd, or emotional.

172 *Bianca Gonzalez-Sobrino, Devon R. Goss, and Matthew W. Hughey*

These themes intersect with the dominant racial ideology of the relevant time period, through the attachment of meanings that either dismiss the racialized films or hail them as part of a historical past. While we identified eight themes in the data, here we focus on the three most salient themes that show the relationship between the racial discursive time periods and the ways reviewers interpreted racialized films: (1) racial clichés, (2) politically correct/sanctimonious, and (3) color-blind reviewers.

Tired of the Same: Racial Clichés in Racialized Films

The first and most dominant theme in the data was a discussion of the dominant racial clichés within films. Some of these clichés are the White Savior, stereotypical portrayals of people of color, and the harmonious portrayals of race relations in the United States. The theme of racial clichés fits well within the racial logic of multiculturalism, wherein racial inclusion is seen as more important than the racial messages that a film may be portraying.

For example, in *The Washington Post* review of the film *Cool Runnings* (1993), Desson Howe (1993) wrote, "They've pulled down the Berlin Wall. The Palestinians and the Israelis are talking peace. But they're still making comedies like [*Cool Runnings,*] in which cartoonish natives scratch their heads and try to make sense of the White world." The meanings attached to this theme create a sense of an overarching societal progress that moves toward racial equality and multiculturalism while it deems racial clichés as racists and unnecessary in this so-called time of progress.

Reviewers' themselves were split about the use of racial clichés in movies. For example, with *Cool Runnings*, *The Austin Chronicle* quipped that "[d]espite an engaging performance by Leon ..., and lovely Jamaican scenery, this movie is nothing more than a good after-school special—sweet and clean but not too fresh" (Chacona, 1993). Similarly, Roger Ebert (1993) reviews the film by noting, "Although the Jamaican bobsled team broke all the rules, the movie is content to follow them—to reprocess the story into the same formula as countless sports movies before it."

Throughout the data, ideas of racial progress were present by legitimizing racialized movies as products of the past or as pure fiction. The reviewers operated under the assumptions that the United States is a racially equal society where racialized films are products of imagination or of history. The reviewers condemned the films as racists while operating under the assumption of their racial neutrality. Other racial clichés like the White Savior and the Magical Negro were also criticized in the reviews but mostly in a comedic way, without actually problematizing them. For example, *Entertainment Weekly's* review of *Dances with Wolves* quipped:

> If you're in the mood to see a leisurely paced, three-hour hippie Western about a Union soldier who drops out of the Civil War, joins a tribe of noble and reverent Sioux, and comes to see that the Indians are

In Touch With Life in a way that White men aren't, you could probably do worse than Kevin Costner's *Dances With Wolves*.

(Gleiberman, 1990)

Although the review shows knowledge of the implementation of film stereotypes about all-knowing Native Americans, this stereotype is merely brushed off as emblematic of a "hippie" esthetic, not as racially problematic.

Another example of racial clichés in a film is *The New York Times* review of the same film. Vincent Canby (1990) writes, "Michael Blake's screenplay touches both on man alone in nature and on the 19th-century White man's assuming his burden among the less privileged." The power dynamic between the White character and the characters of color were simply ignored and the friendship developed in the movie was seen as an exemplary way that people can look past race to coexist. This is also evident in a review for the film that appeared in *The Washington Post*:

Making love, not war, with the Indians, Costner (with Michael Blake's screenplay) creates a vision so childlike, so willfully romantic, it's hard to put up a fight … You're left entirely scalped by his gentle edge, rubbing your head for liking what you saw. But there it is, and there he is, naked buns to the camera, staring at the bewildered Lakota Sioux staring back at him.

(Hinson, 1990)

The reviewer framed the bond between the White Savior and the character of color as passé but positive. The story of a White anti-hero returning back to the grace of Whiteness is presented as clichéd and overused; yet the reviewers lacked a critical analysis of the intrinsic racist storyline that accompanies any White Savior film.

The same occurs with Magical Negro (Hughey, 2009) characters, like John Coffey in *The Green Mile* (1999). In a review for the movie in the *San Francisco Chronicle*, Coffey is described as "a man who works with healing hands. There's a mythological aspect to this gentle giant … and Darabont goes to elaborate lengths to dramatize his supernatural powers" (Guthmann, 1999). The presence of a racial cliché is acknowledged by the reviewers but is simply conceptualized as part of the character's development within a multicultural society.

Even when reviewers do understand the racist undertones of John Coffey's character, they seem unable to condemn the movie, ultimately chalking up the inclusion of characters of color as a sign of a multicultural society. For example, as *The New York Times* explained, "The way in which this huge Black man, who calls the guards Boss, is given a magical capacity for self-sacrifice has its inadvertently racist undertones as well as its Christ-like ones. But as Mr. Duncan plays him, Coffey is too flabbergasting a figure to be easily pigeonholed anyhow" (Maslin, 1999). Similarly, *Salon* stated, "Even the most problematic character, the gentle giant Coffey, who sometimes borders on offensive racial caricature in King's book, becomes flesh-and-blood human being in Duncan's dignified and sensitive portrayal" (O'Hehir, 1999). Although racial stereotypes are noted by the reviewers, they ultimately do not weigh heavily into their interpretation of the merit of the film, and sometimes are instead viewed favorably as fitting into the multicultural logic of the time.

Racialized and Politically Correct: Racialized Movies as Sanctimonious

The second theme we encountered in the data stems from ideas of racial inequality as a part of the historical past. This theme highlighted how racial films are approached and understood by film reviewers in the face of the White backlash. Tolerance for multiculturalism in this era is over, and racialized films are accused of framing racial issues in politically correct or purely academic ways. For example, in the film review of *A Time to Kill* (1996), Roger Ebert (1996) called the movie out for being too "political correct":

> One might also ask if Grisham forfeits his right to moral superiority by including a subplot in [*A Time to Kill*] that gives the Ku Klux Klan prominence and a certain degenerate glamor. Yes, Klan members are the villains. But to a twisted mind, their secret meetings and corn-pone rituals might be appealing. However, if you leave out everything that might inspire a nut, you don't have a movie left—or a free society, either.

Similarly, a review in *The Austin Chronicle* accuses *A Time to Kill* of being too narrowly focused on race, explaining, "the movie 'plays the race card' by subsuming all the 'iffier' matters of jurisprudence to his direct and sole appeal to the jurors' racial biases" (Baumgarten, 1996). The focus on race in *A Time to Kill* was seen as lacking nuance and complexity. However, some reviewers felt that this perspective may be business-savvy. The magazine *Variety* argued that this political correctness could lead to box-office success, noting that the movie "stokes the political and emotional coals in ways calculated to appeal to middle-of-the-road and liberal humanist Whites as well as to Blacks, which could translate into sizable crossover business" (McCarthy, 1996).

While reviewers critiqued films for their approaches to the representations of particular events, the actual problematic nature of the films were not discussed. Racism and racial inequality are not central issues for the reviewers; the entertainment aspect of the film is of centrality in this theme when discussing *Amistad* (1997). An example of this is taken from *Entertainment Weekly's* review of the film:

> *Amistad* takes on a mass atrocity of more than comparable scope, but its approach is almost bizarrely academic. Midway through, there's a 20-minute sequence that showcases, in graphic detail, the

claustrophobic horrors of the "Middle Passage" (bloody whippings, starvation, mass drownings). Otherwise, though, the film seems all but uninterested in the psychological experience of slavery or, indeed, in the personalities of its slave protagonists. Its investment is in the issue of slavery, one that Spielberg uses to craft a courtroom drama of dull, soapbox ponderousness.

(Gleiberman, 1997)

Films are not criticized for their stereotypes or the racist ideologies present in them; they are purely measured in terms of their entertainment value or their "wow" factor. On the other hand, there were some instances where the storyline was criticized for being too simplistic and not distributing a transcending message about racial relations. For example, the *San Francisco Chronicle* opines, "In *Amistad*, an admirable but disappointing effort … Spielberg … delivers a film that veers between stoic political correctness and mushy pop-Hollywood platitudes" (Shulgasser, 1997). Simply put, reviewers understand the problematic nature of racism but chose to frame racialized films as mere entertainment artifacts that are not cultural products of the particular time and space. *Salon*'s review of *Amistad* illustrates this by explaining, "Americans never seem phonier than when we're being reverent about our past … That, I think, is part of the reason American history (particularly pre-Civil War) so fiery on the page, is usually so dully and static on screen" (Taylor, 1997).

In the case of *Boyz N the Hood* (1991), *The Washington Post* reviewer criticized the film for its un-entertaining focus on issues related to race:

When things get suspenseful, Singleton gets decidedly corny about the editing. His finger-wagging isn't as clumsily intrusive as Robert Townsend's, but it's there. The agenda in this film includes the evils of Eurocentric education, the cultural bias of SAT exams, the importance of condoms, White gentrification of Black neighborhoods, Black male mistreatment of their women, and so on.

(Kempley, 1991)

Additionally, *Variety* praises the film while at the same time criticizing it as too socially responsible, "An impressive debut by 23-year-old John Singleton, sincere pic is ultra socially responsible, sometimes to the point of playing like a laundry list of difficulties faced specifically by the urban Black community" (Variety Staff, 1991). Similarly, *The New York Times* review concludes about *Boyz N the Hood* (1991), "If Mr. [Spike] Lee felt inclined to remake George Lucas's *American Graffiti* with a more fatalistic outlook and a political agenda, the results might be very much like this" (Maslin, 1991). For reviewers, racialized movies inherently portray a political or social message, with the characters working as stand-ins for their race, whereas the same is rarely said about predominately White movies.

In sum, reviewers interpreted racialized movies as mere entertainment relegating the racialized aspect to the background. Race is simply interpreted in this theme as an element used to enliven the storyline of the films. The film reviewers framed films focusing explicitly on race as moralizing and without substance. Reviewers understood these films' purpose as not being about entertainment, but being about informing the viewers. Race is treated as non-important in a society fed up with an emphasis on multiculturalism and diversity.

The Color-Blind Reviewer

The third theme emphasized a color-blind logic by explaining the non-importance of race in today's society. In the final years of the 15-year period we observed, these logics were more apparent. Reviewers frequently would interpret racialized film as films focusing on class or human kindness instead of claiming race as a central theme in the narratives. For example, in the case of *Maid in Manhattan* (2002), the film was largely conceptualized as a film about upward mobility. The *San Francisco Chronicle* reviewer wrote:

> Of course, in a romantic comedy, star appeal is the main thing. In [*Maid in Manhattan*], Lopez and Fiennes take the old story—poor girl and rich boy meet, encounter obstacles, have the obligatory falling-out, etc.—and make it not new, definitely not new, but familiar and easy to watch. Indeed, the movie would almost qualify as pleasant, were it not for a certain condescension in its treatment of working-class life and its offhand assumption that lives not buoyed by riches or aggrandized by fame are hardly worth living.
>
> (LaSalle, 2002)

The reviewer failed to mention anything about Marisa's racial/ethnic identity as a Latina and focused only on concepts of class and upward mobility. In a similar fashion, the reviewer for *Variety* summed up the movie by stating, "In the end, *Maid* is about a working gal's dream of moving up" (Koehler, 2002). *Salon* recognizes this dynamic and notes, "There is much made of the fact that Christopher and Marisa come from 'different worlds,' although only once does Marisa speak of Christopher as White, privileged, and fortunate" (Zacharek, 2002). The lack of a discussion of the film's portrayal of race and racism is evident throughout these reviews.

Even movies that dealt with overtly racial themes in their storyline were reviewed under a color-blind logic. Racism and race are presented as unimportant while other aspects of the story are hailed as more salient. For example, in Roger Ebert's (2001) review of *Save the Last Dance* (2001), a movie about tensions with interracial relationships and friendships, he explained, "The students at Sara's high school are mostly African American, but as we notice this, we notice something else ... the students are not electrified by the arrival of (gasp!) a White girl. They have more important things to think about."

In this framework, acknowledging and considering race and the meanings of classroom diversity is focusing attention toward unimportant issues. The *San Francisco Chronicle* took a harder line on the role of race in *Save the Last Dance*, equating the film's attention to racial relations as akin to promoting racism, stating,

> Eventually, they fall in love. He gives her his culture. She gives him her heart. It hardly seems fair. But the movie never condescends to play cultural- exchange games. It's simply a bid to win Stiles the Black vote. Its pseudo- progressive stance on interracial dating is betrayed by its glaring uncoolness and formal stupidity, both of which equate to a sort of backhanded racism.
>
> (Morris, 2001)

Additionally, reviewers also embraced the presence of racial stereotypes and racist jokes in films as emblematic of society's progress with race. For example, in the culture-clash buddy movie *Rush Hour* (1998), reviewers were quick to acclaim the use of supposed harmless and funny racial stereotypes within film, which describes the working relationship between an Asian and Black cop. *Variety* praises the films' use of racial stereotypes as the hallmark of progressiveness in film, stating:

> And rather than ignore or disguise Chan's occasional awkwardness with English, *Rush Hour* uses the language barrier as a running gag, often to hilarious effect, particularly in a show-stopping song-and-dance sequence in which Carter corrects Lee's pronunciation during latter's rendition of his favorite American song, "War."
>
> (Leydon, 1998)

Similarly, Salon hails these racist jokes as the highlight of *Rush Hour*, explaining:

> In *Rush Hour*, as an LAPD detective assigned to assist his Hong Kong counterpart Jackie Chan in retrieving a kidnapped little girl, Tucker is equal parts hilarious and wearisome. I broke up when he explained that his mother was embarrassed about him working for the LAPD ("She tells everybody I'm a drug dealer") and when he tried to intimidate Chan by using what Richard Pryor once called his "best black shit. That stuff that usually scare Whitey to death."
>
> (Taylor, 1998)

The ways in which reviewers understood racialized films, particularly those near the millennium and beyond, correspond with the dominant racial ideologies of the time. These ideologies were characteristic of what is commonly called the post-racial time. Racial tensions and racial inequality are viewed as inexistent in the United States, thus racialized films cannot be interpreted as being about race. Reviewers, as social actors and part of society, are themselves a product of the times in which they live in. The reviewer's not-so-artistic interpretations of racialized films are a reflection of the dominant racial ideologies of the times.

Conclusion

Film reviewers have been commonly understood as independent social actors that exercise their artistic interpretations of racialized films. These reviews then serve as cultural artifacts that are reflective of larger social trends and meanings. In this chapter, we use film reviews to illustrate how these interpretations are not simple artistic expressions, but reflections of the dominant racial ideologies of the times. These ideologies have fluctuated across time and have an effect on how people have understood and interpreted the meanings attached to racialized content in media (in this case films) and social interactions. The three overarching frames present in the data (1) reflected a discourse of racialized movies as clichés or boring, (2) constructed racialized films as politically correct, and (3) used a color-blind lens that makes invisible the racialized structures in American society and interprets the racial as non-racial.

These three themes discussed in this chapter present a clear relationship between the dominant racial ideologies of the times and the interpretations of racialized media by reviewers and, potentially, by consumers. Future work can explore the relationship between racialized ideologies and consumptions of films, which contain racialized content. This chapter serves as an initial exploration on how racialized media content and its interpretations serve to reify and reproduce these dominant ideologies. Through the study of these cultural artifacts we continue to understand the trends in social interactions that reproduce and maintain the dominant racialized social structures and how these ideologies slowly change over time, thus changing the attached meanings with them.

Note

1. We define top news outlets as newspapers that are considered to be in the top 100 newspapers in terms of circulation, national-circulation magazines specializing in entertainment news, and review websites by famous film critics.

References

Basuroy, S., Chatterjee, S., & Ravid, S. A. (2003). How critical are critical reviews? The box office effects of film critics, star power, and budgets. *Journal of Marketing*, 67, 103–117.

Baumgarten, M. (1996, July 26). A time to kill. *The Austin Chronicle.* Retrieved from http://www.austinchronicle.com/calendar/film/1996-07-26/a-time-to-kill/.
Bonilla-Silva, E. (2010). *Racism without racists.* Lanham, MD: Rowman & Littlefield.
Bourdieu, P. (1984). *Distinction: A social critique of the judgment of taste.* Cambridge, MA: Harvard University Press.
Canby, V. (1990, November 9). Dances with wolves (1990). *The New York Times.* Retrieved from http://www.nytimes.com/movie/review?res=9C0CE6DB1338F93AA35752C1A966958260.
Chacona, H. (1993, October 1). Cool runnings. *The Austin Chronicle.* Retrieved from http://www.austinchronicle.com/calendar/film/1993-10-01/cool-runnings/.
Collins, P. H. (2000). *Black feminist thought.* New York, NY: Routledge.
Denzin, N. K. (2002). *Reading race: Hollywood and the cinema of racial violence.* Thousand Oaks, CA: Sage.
Ebert, R. (1993, October 1). Cool runnings. Retrieved from http://www.rogerebert.com/reviews/cool-runnings-1993.
Ebert, R. (1996, July 26). A time to kill. Retrieved from http://www.rogerebert.com/reviews/a-time-to-kill-1996.
Ebert, R. (2001, January 12). Save the last dance. Retrieved from http://www.rogerebert.com/reviews/save-the-last-dance-2001.
Eliashberg, J., & Shugan, S. M. (1997). Film critics: Influencers or predictors. *Journal of Marketing, 61,* 68–78.
Espiritu, Y. L. (1997). *Asian American women and men: Labor, laws, and love.* Thousand Oaks, CA: Sage.
Gemser, G., Van Oostrum, M., & Leenders, A. M. (2007). The impact of film reviews on the box office performance of art house versus mainstream motion pictures. *Journal of Cultural Economics, 31,* 43–63.
Glassner, B. (1999). *The culture of fear: Why Americans are afraid of the wrong things: Crime, drugs, minorities, teen moms, killer kids, mutant microbes, plane crashes, road rage & so much more.* New York, NY: Basic Books.
Gleiberman, O. (1990, November 16). Dances with wolves. *Entertainment Weekly.* Retrieved from http://www.ew.com/article/1990/11/16/dances-wolves.
Gleiberman, O. (1997, December 12). Amistad. *Entertainment Weekly.* Retrieved from http://www.ew.com/article/1997/12/12/amistad.
Glenn, C. L., & Cunningham, L. J. (2009). The power of black magic: The magical negro and White salvation in film. *Journal of Black Studies, 40,* 135–152.
Guthmann, E. (1999, December 10). Miles to go/At three hours, earnest prison drama starts to seem like a life sentence. *The San Francisco Chronicle.* Retrieved from http://www.sfgate.com/movies/article/Miles-to-Go-At-three-hours-earnest-prison-2891285.php.
Hinson, H. (1990, November 9). Dances with wolves. *The Washington Post.* Retrieved from http://www.washingtonpost.com/wp-srv/style/longterm/movies/videos/danceswithwolvespg13hinson_a0a9b5.htm.
Holz, J. R., & Wright, C. R. (1979). Sociology of mass communications. *Annual Sociological Review, 5,* 193–217.
hooks, b. (1995). *Killing rage: Ending racism.* New York, NY: Henry Holt and Company.
Howe, D. (1993, October 1). Cool runnings. *The Washington Post.* Retrieved from http://www.washingtonpost.com/wp-srv/style/longterm/movies/videos/coolrunningspghowe_a0affa.htm.

Hughey, M. W. (2009). Cinethetic racism: White redemption and black stereotypes in "magical negro films." *Social Problems, 56*, 543–577.

Hughey, M. W. (2010). The white savior film and reviewers' reception. *Symbolic Interaction, 33*, 475–496.

Hughey, M. W. (2014). *The white savior film: Content, critics, and consumption.* Philadelphia, PA: Temple University.

LaSalle, M. (2002, December 13). Maid marryin'/Fiennes, Lopez are the best part of condescending Cinderella story. *The San Francisco Chronicle.* Retrieved from http://www.sfgate.com/movies/article/MAID-MARRYIN-Fiennes-Lopez-are-the-best-part-2746487.php.

Leydon, J. (1998, September 21). Review: Rush hour. *Variety.* Retrieved from http://variety.com/1998/film/reviews/rush-hour-3-1200455075/.

Kempley, R. (1991, July 12). Boyz n the hood. *The Washington Post.* Retrieved from http://www.washingtonpost.com/wp-srv/style/longterm/movies/videos/boyznthehoodrkempley_a0a119.htm.

Koehler, R. (2002, December 1). Review: Maid in Manhattan. *Variety.* Retrieved from http://variety.com/2002/film/reviews/maid-in-manhattan-1200544571/.

Maslin, J. (1991, July 12). Boyz n the hood (1991). *The New York Times.* Retrieved from http://www.nytimes.com/movie/review?res=9D0CE4D7103FF931A25754C0A967958260.

Maslin, J. (1999, December 10). The green mile (1999). *The New York Times.* Retrieved from http://www.nytimes.com/movie/review?res=9501E4DA1731F933A25751C1A96F958260.

McCarthy, T. (1996, July 11). Review: A time to kill. *Variety.* Retrieved from http://variety.com/1996/film/reviews/a-time-to-kill-2-1200446194/.

Morris, W. (2001, January 12). Dance tries hard to be hip and fails miserably. *The San Francisco Chronicle.* Retrieved from http://www.sfgate.com/movies/article/Dance-Tries-Hard-to-Be-Hip-and-Fails-Miserably-2965136.php.

Motion Picture Association of America. (2014). Theatrical market statistics. Retrieved from http://www.mpaa.org/wp-content/uploads/2014/03/MPAA-Theatrical-Market-Statistics-2013_032514-v2.pdf.

Movie Research Query Engine. Retrieved from http://www.mrqe.com.

O'Hehir, A. (1999, December 10). The green mile. *Salon.* Retrieved from http://www.salon.com/1999/12/10/greenmile/.

Public Religion Research Institute. (2014, August 28). Analysis: Race and Americans' social networks. Retrieved from http://publicreligion.org/research/2014/08/analysis-social-network/.

Purkayastha, B. (2006). *Negotiating ethnicity: Second-generation South Asian Americans traverse a transnational world.* Piscataway, NJ: Rutgers University Press.

Pyke, K. D., & Johnson, D. L. (2003). Asian American women and racialized femininities: "Doing" gender across cultural worlds. *Gender & Society, 17*(1), 33–53.

Sharma, N. T. (2010). *Hip hop Desis: South Asian Americans, blackness, and a global race consciousness.* Durham, NC: Duke University Press.

Shulgasser, B. (1997). Amistad. *The San Francisco Chronicle.* Retrieved from http://www.sfgate.com/news/article/AMISTAD-3085866.php.

Taylor, C. (1997, December 12). Amistad. *Salon.* Retrieved from http://www.salon.com/1997/12/12/amistad/.

Taylor, C. (1998, September 18). Hong Kong Hollywood. *Salon*. Retrieved from http://www.salon.com/1998/09/18/reviewc_10/.
Variety staff. (1990, December 31). Review: Boyz n the hood. *Variety*. Retrieved from http://variety.com/1990/film/reviews/boyz-n-the-hood-1200428985/.
Wilson, W. J. (1980). *The declining significance of race: Blacks and changing American institutions*. Chicago, IL: University of Chicago Press.
Zacharek, S. (2002, December 13). Maid in Manhattan. *Salon*. Retrieved from http://www.salon.com/2002/12/13/maid_2/.

12 Successful Immigrants in the News
Racialization, Color-Blind Racism, and the American Dream

Jorge X. Ballinas

Recent mainstream news coverage in the United States has focused considerable attention on issues of immigration (e.g., President Obama's proposed executive order of immigration relief known as the Deferred Action for Parental Accountability). Still, U.S. media coverage of immigration since 1980 has tended to condition viewers to associate immigration with illegality, crisis, and government failure (Brookings Institution, 2008). News coverage in the summer of 2014 was dedicated to "waves of Central American children streaming across the border" (Sáenz & Douglas, 2015, p. 170). Racism has received scant coverage unless violence, unrest, or "tension" is involved (e.g., police officers murdering Non-White, mostly Black male, individuals). Overall mainstream U.S. news coverage tends to portray issues of racism and immigration as separate phenomena despite a history of racist immigration policies and the racialization of various immigrant groups in this country (Sáenz & Douglas, 2015; Sáenz, Douglas, Embrick, & Sjoberg, 2007).

Nonetheless there has been subtle coverage of immigrants in the context of racism even in a presumed color-blind era. This chapter examines two examples of the inherent rhetoric included within coverage of immigrant groups (Mexicans and Indians) in the U.S. news media, the extent to which these groups are racialized, and what this coverage helps accomplish. These two recent national news stories focused on racism and immigrants: (1) Sebastien de la Cruz (a Mexican American) singing the National Anthem at the 2013 NBA Finals, and (2) Nina Davuluri (an Indian American) winning the 2014 Miss America contest. Both individuals received racist tweets targeting their respective backgrounds. Moreover, both received considerable mainstream news coverage touting their "successes" in reference to the American Dream and overcoming racism.

In this chapter, I first briefly discuss the role of news media and introduce key analytical concepts. Next, I provide background information regarding Sebastien de la Cruz, Nina Davuluri, and their respective stories. Then, I outline my methods for this analysis. Finally, I present my analysis of these new stories and examine how coverage by FOX News, CNN, MSNBC, the *New York Times*, and *USA Today* works to disseminate some of the important frames of color-blind racism (Bonilla-Silva, 2010), while also buttressing notions of the American Dream, and Mexican and Indian American racialization. Taken together this coverage helps to maintain the racial status quo of systemic inequalities by constructing de la Cruz as a successful Mexican and Davuluri as a successful Indian who overcame racism.

News Media

In media studies, we rely on media to "portray and define those things that we have not personally experienced" (Wilson, Gutierrez, & Chao, 2013, p. 31), especially when learning about those unlike ourselves through social categories such as race (Hall, 1979). The media is a crucial part of people's daily lives because it "establish[es] a web of meanings ... of presuppositions or background assumptions within which people develop beliefs and viewpoints and in relations to which people live their lives" (Schudson, 2012, p. 19). For over two centuries the U.S. media has been vital in representing ideas about racialized groups and individuals (Wilson et al., 2013), specifically, as a cultural archive assisting to reproduce racist, and to a lesser extent anti-racist, ideas (Van Dijk, 2000).

Mainstream news is an important site to examine racism because, as many argue, post-Jim Crow racism is often subtle and symbolic. Further, many forms of "new" racism are discursive in that they are often "expressed, enacted, and confirmed by text and talk ... [including in] news reports." (Van Dijk, 2000, p. 34). Significantly, news (media) and its producers hold a systematic propensity to reflect society's dominant ideas (Gans, 1979; Hall, 1979; Schudson, 2012; Van Dijk, 2000). Hence the news is crucial in the public construction of what is important, legitimate, and common (Gans, 1979; Hall, 1979; Schudson, 2012). Moreover, Gans (1979) identified multiple enduring values in the news, of which most relevant for this research are individualism, moderatism (against extremism), social cohesion, racial integration, and the ugliness of hate and prejudice. Specifically, the violation of these values become news since the reporting of moral disorders "reinforces and relegitimates national and societal values by publicizing and helping to punish those who deviate from the values" (Gans, 1979, p. 293). The news stories analyzed in this chapter highlight some of these values: individual success, condemnation of racism and hate, immigrant integration, and validation of the American Dream.

Background

In 2013, Sebastien de la Cruz was an 11-year-old mariachi singer who was featured on TV reality show competitions like *America's Got Talent*. The San Antonio Spurs basketball team asked de la Cruz, a San Antonio native, to sing the National Anthem before Game 3 of the 2013 NBA Finals because the previously scheduled singer was unavailable. As usual de la Cruz performed wearing a Mariachi outfit. After de la Cruz's nationally televised performance, 28 tweets on the social networking site Twitter questioned why a "foreigner," "Mexican," "illegal," "wetback," and "beaner" was allowed to sing the National Anthem (Rodriguez, 2013a). All comments implied that de la Cruz was not American, since being "American" is still understood to mean "White." Consequently, the tweets were posted on the blog *Public Shaming*, which then was picked up by mainstream news outlets as the basis for their coverage (Rodriguez, 2013a). There was a strong backlash against the tweets with many more tweets supporting and defending de la Cruz (Rodriguez, 2013a). The next night, the Spurs invited de la Cruz to sing the National Anthem before Game 4; again he accepted and donned his mariachi outfit.

On September 15, 2013, Nina Davuluri was crowned Miss America 2014, the first winner who is second-generation Indian American. Although competitors in the pageant must be U.S. citizens and Davuluri was born in Syracuse, New York, the blog *Public Shaming* noted that there were 28 tweets labeling her a "terrorist," "Miss Al Qaeda," "Muslim," "Camel Jockey," "Foreigner," "Arab," "Sand Nigger," and associating her with the Muslim Brotherhood, Egypt, September 11th, and bombings. Ironically, Davuluri's platform for the pageant was "celebrating diversity through cultural competency."

Methods

For the de la Cruz story, I analyzed news stories from 2013. These stories came from MSNBC's *Politics Nation* hosted by Al Sharpton, three separate CNN.com articles, a short CNN *Newsroom* story, a 10 o'clock Fox News San Antonio broadcast, a June 15 *New York Times* article, and a June 18 *USA Today* article. For the Davuluri story, I analyzed various news segments from 2013, including Fox News' *Fox and Friends*, CNN's *Erin Burnett OutFront*, *MSNBC Live*, articles from MSNBC.com and Today.com, a September 22 *New York Times* article, and a September 18 *USA Today* article.

In this chapter, I use the examples of de La Cruz and Davuluri for several reasons. First, each story involved a different immigrant group covered by mainstream news outlets with established audiences in the millions. Second, as of mid-2015 there have been few, if any, other national stories covered that deal with racism where individuals are explicitly labeled racist and immigrants. Last, these stories occurred in a short time span, June 2013 through September 2013, so it is plausible that individuals may have seen coverage of multiple stories, but at the very least one of the stories. This last point is important insofar as viewers are presented with similar coverage of immigrants and racism, regardless of story, network, or platform (whether online or offline) they tuned into. Media outlets were chosen for analysis because of their presumed distinct ideological positions. I take an ethnographic content analysis approach (Altheide, 1987) emphasizing the documentation and comprehension of the meaning behind social products and a reflective and interactive relationship between the researcher, data collection, and analysis.

For each story I searched the websites of MSNBC, FOX, CNN, the *New York Times*, *USA Today*, and YouTube entering relevant terms for each story and titles of network shows. I focused on prime-time shows as much as possible. If stories were unavailable on these websites, I searched on CBS and NBC news websites. For each newspaper, I searched LexisNexis Academic using key terms and dates. Videos and articles were selected based on proximity to the initial date of each story to gauge each story's initial framing and in order to simplify the selection process.

Findings

Throughout the coverage analyzed, two color-blind racism frames are present: abstract liberalism and minimization of racism. Color-blind racism is noted as an ideology that upholds an unequal racial hierarchy using seemingly race-neutral terms. Abstract liberalism is the belief that everyone should have equal rights and opportunities regardless of race. Minimization of racism is the idea that racial discrimination is no longer significant in minorities' lives (Bonilla-Silva, 2010). Adherence to equal opportunity for all has been the basis of one of the U.S.'s central ideologies, the American Dream, where everyone is capable of upward mobility if they work hard enough (Delgado, 2007; Hochschild, 1995; Putnam, 2015). Although the American Dream has never been available to everyone (Hochschild, 1995), especially racial minorities, (Delgado, 2007) it has persisted among a majority of Americans until recently (Putnam 2015). In 2014, 42% of Americans said that the American Dream still holds true today (Jones, Cox, & Navarro-Rivera, 2014). As discussed later, coverage of de la Cruz and Davuluri validated the American Dream.

Throughout the coverage, usually within the same story, aspects of liberalism—individualism, egalitarianism, and meliorism (the idea that people and institutions improve over time)—were present in conjunction with the minimization of racism. Following scholars like Bonilla-Silva (2010) and Feagin (2014), I understand racism as a social structure or system, rooted in European traditions, on the bestowing of economic, political, and other resources and privileges to those deemed White over those deemed Non-White, which continues to be reproduced through the present.

Minimization of Racism

Sebastien de la Cruz

On June 14 *Politics Nation* with Al Sharpton aired a segment on the tweets against de la Cruz with guests University of Texas professor Victoria DeFrancesco-Soto and *Chicago Tribune* columnist Clarence Page. De la Cruz is portrayed as an individual victim of racism who in Sharpton's words is "standing up against hate." Sharpton started the segment by labeling the negative tweets directed at de la Cruz as "racism and hate," which after going viral de la Cruz received "a huge outpouring of support." Sharpton added, "In the year 2013, the true minority are people who preach intolerance and hate." Here racism is minimized since Sharpton first labeled the tweets "racism," lauded the "huge" support de la Cruz received buffering against it, and decreed these racists as the "true minority."

Later in the segment DeFrancesco-Soto, addressed the support for de la Cruz. "On a personal level, I feel that the backlash against that intolerance speaks of the larger feeling in the [U.S.] of the acceptance of [our] changing demographics." Moreover, she views changing demographics resulting in blended families, like President Obama's, and eventually increased racial tolerance. In effect, she argues that increasing demographic diversity is a buffer against racism. Similarly, Page equated support for de la Cruz with the marginalization of racism and hate:

> What really encourages me Reverend, I know you and I have come a long way, to see so many people, uh, rising up to show their indignation for that kind of behavior and to show don't associate me with that kind of hatred is a wonderful thing. (MSNBC, 2013a)

On CNN and Fox News, de la Cruz is again portrayed as successfully resisting racism. In a June 14 CNN.com article San Antonio Mayor Julian Castro commended de la Cruz for his "composure" in light of the "negative voices" (Rodriguez, 2013b). In the June 12 article, the author stated that "the racist comments have not fazed [de la Cruz]" (Rodriguez, 2013a) and in the June 13 *Newsroom* segment the narrator described de la Cruz as "resilient." On CNN.com, racism is minimized through the use of similar language used on MSNBC: "tweets supporting and defending Sebastien and vociferously denouncing his critics" (Rodriguez, 2013a) took over and "the support of Sebastien outweighed the criticism" (Rodriguez, 2013b). Likewise, in the CNN *Newsroom* segment the following tweet directed at de la Cruz was highlighted: "Please do not pay attention to the negative people."

A few days after the incident a San Antonio FOX affiliate aired a short segment during its 10 p.m. news show where one anchor shared similar thoughts "It's ridiculous ... the things [the tweeters] said. A lot of people commenting positively on this story ..." De la Cruz himself is also interviewed about the reaction he received:

> I knew that one day when I sing that people were going to judge me and that, that's why I've, over the time that I've grown I've learned that you don't really care what people think about you. It's what, it's what you think about yourself.
>
> (Fox, 2013)

Here the anchor's comments, and the interview with de la Cruz, minimize the effects of racism on minorities' life chances given the implication that opposing racist comments is enough to counteract structural forces. De la Cruz's comments go further in reifying the importance of self-reliance in the face of adversity, in this case racism, when pursuing goals and attaining success.

Coverage of this story is also similar in the newspapers analyzed. A June 14 *New York Times* article, "Spurs Defend 11-Year-Old Anthem Singer," focused on how the Spurs "defended" de la Cruz. De la Cruz is portrayed as a victim given support by San Antonio Mayor Castro and Spurs coach Greg Popovich; with de la Cruz quoted as saying, "I want to thank Coach Popovich and all the Spurs for helping me keep my head up" (Taylor, 2013). Hence, again, racism is downplayed since de la Cruz, a victim and child, through the support of adults, is able to overcome it.

On June 18, *USA Today* covered this incident with reporter Josh Gad sympathizing with de la Cruz and denouncing the tweets. Gad (2013) dryly praised the tweeters, or "pricks" as he called them, for being creative and fearless enough to "courageously disparag[e] an 11-year-old Mexican boy." De la Cruz is encouraged to "learn to take this tidal wave of criticism and hatred like a man" (Gad, 2013). Moreover, Gad equated de la Cruz's situation to online bullying in general and to Gad's 13-year-old bully neighbor who daily makes fun of Gad for being "fat, untalented, worthless, and a hack." This coverage of the event works to minimize racism as Gad normalizes racism through implying that it is something to get used to "like a man," that tweets are just words not to be taken "personally," and that racism only comes from "sad sociopaths" like his young neighbor (Gad, 2013).

Nina Davuluri

Coverage of the Davuluri story followed the same frames as the de la Cruz story—where racism is both marginalized and individualized. A *Today.com* article discussed how other tweeters came to Davuluri's "defense" and expressed "support" for her against racists, portraying Davuluri as a victim of racism (Kim, 2013). An article from *MSNBC.com* referred to the tweets as a "controversy online as some lashed out at the new Miss America for her ethnicity" (Lee, 2013). Although Kim (2013) directly addressed the "racist comments," both articles minimize racism.

When asked about the tweets, Davuluri reinforces the minimization of racism. On *MSNBC Live,* Davuluri's opinion is to "not pay attention to those comments." Lee (2013) stated that Davuluri "shrugged off the negative backlash" by responding to the tweets with, "I have to rise above that ... I always viewed myself as first and foremost American." Moreover, Lee focused most on Davuluri being the first Indian American winner and portraying this as a "success story" for Asian Americans. On *MSNBC Live* Davuluri's win is also framed as a success for Asian Americans. In these

188 *Jorge X. Ballinas*

particular examples, like in de la Cruz's case, racism is minimized in that Davuluri, and by implication others of similar racial/ethnic backgrounds, can *choose* to accomplish her goals without limits, simply by ignoring racism.

On September 18, 2013, Nina Davuluri visited Fox News' *Fox & Friends*. Throughout the interview the following banners appeared on the screen "Newly Crowned Miss America Promotes Diversity," "Beauty, Brains & Racism? Miss America Victim of Social Media Attack," "All American Girl: Social Media Hating on Davuluri's Heritage," "Circle of Unity: Program to Celebrate Cultural Diversity," "Beauty Inside and Out: Newly Crowned Miss America Promotes Diversity," and "Royal Diversity: Davuluri: Happy Organization Embraces Culture." Two of the banners and one of the cohosts implied that Davuluri was a victim of an "attack," "hating," and "tirade" on social media—reflecting the notion that only a few "bad apples" on the Internet are racist. One banner showed racism with a question mark attached, which leaves the impression that there is doubt whether or not the slurs directed at Davuluri are racist. In addition, another banner labeled Davuluri an "All American Girl" and told viewers that Davuluri's "heritage," (i.e., culture), was the target of "hating." Similar to de la Cruz, Davuluri, while being interviewed on Fox News and CNN, downplayed the situation by calling it "unfortunate" and referenced how she received much more support than negativity "from people across the country and from the world ..."

Taking minimization even further, Davuluri discussed diversity, which appeared in the other four banners, and the slurs by stating "a lot of that [the slurs] stem from ignorance and that's why my platform is so timely ... I am promoting the cause celebrating diversity through cultural competency." Through Davuluri's emphasis on diversity and the four banners pairing diversity with "celebrate," "promotes," "embraces," "happy," and "unity," we are led to believe that racism can be vanquished simply by being made aware of increasing cultural differences and our own biases. Once more, this obfuscates how racism operates in our society. Specifically, how systemic and embedded dimensions of racism continue to denigrate Non-Whites across various social domains (Bonilla-Silva, 2010; Feagin, 2014; Omi & Winant, 2014). Davuluri also discussed the importance of her platform "celebrating diversity through cultural competency" on MSNBC and CNN. Further, CNN's Erin Burnett minimized racism when she termed the tweets against Davuluri as "hateful" and "shocking." Not only is racism reduced to messages of hate, but also it is presumed so rare that the utterance of these phrases is completely unexpected. Burnett also labeled those who sent out the tweets as "critics," to which Davuluri was on her show to address and "take on." Thus racism is best dealt with, like in de la Cruz's case, by "standing up to hate" and denouncing it.

Newspaper coverage of this story is comparable. On September 18, 2013, "Miss America Rises Above Negative Web Comments" appeared in the "Your Say" section of *USA Today*:

> The negative comments are something that South Asians, Arabs (not just Muslim ones) and Muslims of other ethnicities face daily in America.
>
> It's what life has become for us since a handful of evil people perpetrated the events of Sept. 11, 2001. The insults, threats and occasional violence hurt, but one builds moral strength to brush off the comments, actions and their sources, as ignorant and/or intolerant. Those people deserve more pity than fear.

Here racism is minimized in three ways. First, Davuluri's denigration is reduced to negative comments that "other ethnicities" face daily. While such incidents may occur daily, the statement renders such language directed against Indians and others normal and part of their everyday experiences. Second, the author labeled the individuals behind the messages as ignorant, intolerant, but also immoral and pitiful. Again, racism is marginalized to a few who are to be felt sorry for and who do not represent broader society. Last, the apparent antidote to "insults, threats, and occasional violence" and racism itself is building the moral strength to "brush" it off. In other words, manifestations of racism are best left ignored.

In the September 22 *New York Times* article "Beauty Pageants Draw Social Media Critics," Alex Williams compared different beauty pageants around the world that have attracted controversy. Davuluri's victory is described as "a sign of cultural progress until racist messages popped up on Twitter" and the reaction to it as a "furor [that] erupted" (Williams, 2013). Here Williams implicitly evoked the backwardness of "racists" given their lack of cultural awareness, competency, and tolerance that has derailed the racial progress represented by Davuluri's victory. Laura Beck, a writer on the blog Jezebel, is quoted describing the tweeters:

> Idiot racists got so mad, they started mixing up Indian, Indian-American, Arab, Muslim, and everything in between … It's (literally) a most impressive display of dumb mixed with intolerance and even more stupidity.

Beck, like Williams, minimized racism in attributing its totality to individuals. Unlike Williams, Beck explicitly labeled these individuals as idiots, dumb, intolerant, and stupid. Similarly Sharpton and his guests labeled those tweeting against de la Cruz as cowards, ignorant, and pinheads. In both cases racism is reduced to people who do not know any better, are unintelligent, and lack a backbone. As a result, these incidents, like racism, are presented as anecdotes rather than systematic.

Williams also minimized racism and obfuscates its broader dimensions by terming the situation "a furor" and by comparing this incident to others that have attracted "controversy." Furor is associated with other terms like rage, frenzy, craze, and outburst that all convey some level of irrationality and render the individuals behind the messages as marginal. Davuluri being denigrated because of her Non-Whiteness is briefly likened to Vanessa Williams, the first Black Miss America who received death threats in 1984. However, it is also likened to a 2009 Miss America contestant opposing same-sex marriage, the 2013 Miss Universe remaining in Russia despite LGBT protests, and Davuluri being accused of prejudice for allegedly calling a former winner "fat." Terming Davuluri's incident as controversy implies that there is some disagreement over whether the Twitter messages are racist. Further minimizing racism is the broad comparing of Davuluri's incident with the other incidents that attracted "controversy." This is especially the case where the possibility that Davuluri called a former winner fat negates her denigration because of her Non-Whiteness.

Abstract Liberalism

Sebastien de la Cruz

Also present throughout coverage of both stories are aspects of the abstract liberalism frame. The *Politics Nation* discussion addressed backlash against a 2013 incident where a White woman posted a video of herself using racist language against a South Asian Dunkin Donuts employee[1] in conjunction with the de la Cruz incident:

> Sharpton: We're seeing that there's a lot people, still out there, trying to hate but it seems to be a backlash that they don't understand a lot of attitudes in this country have changed.
>
> DeFrancesco-Soto: Reverend, these people are still living in the 1950s, even in the early 1960s, we're a very different country today even than we were 10 years ago, 15 years ago. But I think as we start to see [more diversity] spread across the country, these people will become more and more the exception and they will understand that they are not in the right, that these comments are no longer acceptable. Not just politically incorrect, but morally incorrect. (MSNBC, 2013a)

In this exchange, both commentators evoke meliorism regarding individual attitudes toward racial difference in the past. Thus increasing diversity, changing racial attitudes, and opposition against overt racist terminology are portrayed as antidotes to racism.

Later on, Sharpton and Page exemplify the principle of egalitarianism:

> Sharpton: You know Clarence, we see these attitudes around race around gender, around those lesbian and gay, the tolerance level, is this the climate that leads toward more of a progressive legislative and a progressive institutional shift in this country where we are still faced with the challenge?

Page: ... That's a heavy question, but I think yes is the short answer. Uh, we are seeing several things happen at once, you know, but I look at how attitudes toward gay marriage for example have changed over the last decade, much faster than I ever expected, and most people I know ... And I think now, uh, that race does not mean what it used to mean, mixed families are becoming more common ... (MSNBC, 2013a)

In this short exchange, rapidly improved attitudes regarding same-sex marriage are equated with improved attitudes toward race and gender, implying not only egalitarianism at the individual level but somehow as a precursor for institutional egalitarianism as well. Here too racism is minimized. Somehow mixed families "becoming more common" are taken as a sign of structural egalitarianism and an improvement in what race "means." In the continuation of the preceding statement, Page discusses how race is changing in the U.S.:

... And we are seeing as the population shifts, it's going by state and region, we're seeing in the South that traditionally the most conservative area is still so, but at the same time you've got, what, a South Asian governor and Republican in two states, I could go on and on about the changes happening there. So you know it's like, I think we are going to see changes happen, we've seen them already, by region and state and uh that is going to be the new area of conflict, as we go through these changes I think. (MSNBC, 2013a)

In this statement Page invokes meliorism, in the present and future, regarding racism in the South through the elections of Bobby Jindal (as governor of Louisiana) and Nikki Haley (as governor of South Carolina). However, similar to President Obama's election, the election of these minorities has done little, if anything, to positively affect the life chances of minorities (Bonilla-Silva, 2010). Although attitudes regarding race and racism may have changed, this country's structure continues, generally, to advantage Whites over Non-Whites across social domains.

On CNN, individualism and egalitarianism are evoked. In the *Newsroom* segment and the June 12 article a tweet by de la Cruz's is cited, "I am American living the American Dream. This is part of the American life." Such a statement provides "evidence" that it is still possible to achieve the American Dream—a belief of egalitarianism and individualism that, despite racism, all you have to do is work hard. A stronger statement evoking egalitarianism appeared in the June 17 article: "The [U.S.] looks out for the powerless, the downtrodden and the oppressed. Our ... constitutional republic—protects the minority because majorities can protect themselves" (Navarette, 2013). The same article called the San Antonio Spurs "a classy outfit that boldly took a stand against bigotry and ignorance" after inviting de la Cruz back for Game 4, which "naturally [is] the American thing to do." In this case with the Spurs organization we see egalitarianism and the American Dream being upheld at the structural level, and that overt racism is deemed un-American. Overall this author argues that de la Cruz is more American than "an angry mob filled with hatred and racism" because he showed "his love for [the U.S.] where dreams come true" (Navarette, 2013).

Nina Davuluri

Coverage of this story also contained aspects of the abstract liberalism frame. On *Fox & Friends,* one cohost asked Davuluri about her heritage: "What does it mean to you in terms of pride in your background [to be crowned Miss America and] represent your heritage? What kind of response have you had?" Davuluri replies with a mixture of meliorism, egalitarianism, and individualism:

> Absolutely, it's been amazing so positive, I have always viewed Miss America as the girl next door. But for me the girl next door is evolving as the diversity in America evolves ... Its not who she was 10 years ago, and she is not going to be the same person come 10 years down the road. And to finally be that new face for this organization and reach out to younger demographics and let them know that they can truly become anything that they want and not only Miss America, regardless of their you know, race, or socioeconomic status, their religion, because I am living my American Dream right now. (Fox News, 2013)

Regarding meliorism, Davuluri connects increased racial/ethnic diversity and the "girl next door" trope to convey acceptance of this diversity where differences in race and religion, itself highly racialized for South Asians and others, over time become more tolerable among Whites. Moreover, the latter portion of Davuluri's statement, echoing some of de la Cruz's statements, reinforces the dominant individualistic myth (Delgado, 2007) known as the American Dream. Thus when one faces racism or discrimination—whether based on race, class, or religion—if one works hard enough it should not matter because U.S. society is fundamentally meritocratic.

Later this same day, Davuluri appeared on CNN's *Erin Burnett OutFront* and repeated, almost verbatim, the statement quoted earlier. Two days later, Davuluri visited *MSNBC Live* and again repeated the statement but added that being able to become anything an individual wants are "the ideals that this country was founded on," thus reinforcing individualism and egalitarianism. The host, Richard Liu, drew strong parallels between Davuluri's incident and Vanessa Williams's incident 30 years earlier. Both are said to have faced racism, broken barriers, and inspired many. When asked about spending time with Williams, Davuluri's response espoused meliorism: "Thirty years ago she received a very similar response, it just goes to show that yes we've evolved as a country, but how much further we have to go" (MSNBC, 2013b). Although Davuluri received racist tweets, she tells viewers things have improved and will only continue to improve.

Yet, some coverage does contextualize Davuluri's story. Besides the Vanessa Williams comparisons, Kim (2013) linked Davuluri's incident to Miss USA 2010 Rima Fakih, whose family is from Lebanon, and how attempts were made "to link her with the military terrorist group Hezbollah." Still, the coverage analyzed obscures the violence and other actions, ultimately rendered normal, directed at South Asian, Middle Eastern, and Arab peoples as well as followers of Islam, Hinduism, and Sikhism by U.S. citizens as a consequence of the "War on Terror" (Omi & Winant, 2014) and other U.S. governmental actions against these groups and specific countries in the Middle East.

Through all of this coverage, audiences are encouraged to believe several things. First, de la Cruz and Davuluri, as individuals, not the "Mexicanness" or "Indianness" each represents, are the targets of the tweets. In de la Cruz's case, this is despite the tweets exemplifying a constructed worldview where Mexican Americans and Latinos are racialized as an inferior "race" to be considered among other things "foreign" and "un-American" (Feagin & Cobas, 2014, p. 29). Moreover, none of the coverage discussed how being American continues to mean being White given that U.S. citizenship has and continues to exclude Non-Whites (Glenn, 2002; Hughey, 2012). Second, derogatory language directed at an individual's culture or heritage constitutes racism in totality. Thus, there is no need to acknowledge the systemic nature of racism and how it still constrains Mexicans, Indians, and others in the U.S. Third, increasing diversity, changing racial attitudes, support from others, and opposing racist language are antidotes to racism. Fourth, there are few actual racists still left, since U.S. society is not racist, and there is a much larger nonracist group that does not tolerate racists. Fifth, because individuals and institutions have changed or can change, and because "working hard" still allows one to achieve success, racism has little impact on minorities' and immigrants' lives. Importantly, none of this news coverage addressed the racialized assumptions behind the tweets against either de la Cruz or Davuluri. These assumptions are discussed next.

Conclusions

Regardless of the story covered and the outlet that this coverage is coming from, the continuing significance and systemic nature of racism in these incidents is downplayed. From the news media's perspective, slurs and other derogatory language directed at an individual's background represent racism in its totality. However, even this conception of racism is minimized. Through most of this coverage, it was implied that there are very few actual racists still left compared to the majority who are nonracist. Specifically, all coverage evoked both the minimization of racism and the abstract liberalism frames outlined by Bonilla-Silva (2010). In this regard, news media coverage of immigrants and overt forms of racism reproduce color-blind racism given that each news outlet has established audiences in the millions, presumed distinct ideological positions, and takes similar stances that minimize racism. At the very least, U.S. news media is promoting a sanitized interpretation of racism.

This news coverage also reinforced the dominant ideology of the American Dream. Although de la Cruz and Davuluri are native born citizens of this country, almost all news coverage referred to them as representatives of various groups. For instance, they are simultaneously: Mexican and Indian immigrants; Mexican Americans and Indian Americans; Latino Americans and Asian Americans; and, more implicitly, people of color. As immigrants, these individuals represent the "good" and successful immigrants who come to this country to work hard and achieve the American Dream. As Mexican Americans and Indian Americans, and both as Non-Whites, de la Cruz and Davuluri have overcome racism simply by dismissing or minimizing it in the public eye. Thus the portrayal of de la Cruz and Davuluri as members of these various groups, who have achieved their American Dream and have overcome racism, serves to uphold the notion that this country is meritocratic and open for all. More specifically, this portrayal also serves to hold those Mexicans and Indians, both immigrant and U.S. born, as well as other people of color accountable for any negative social status they may have. This potentially reinforces and legitimates any racial inequalities in this country in the minds of viewers.

Further, since these individuals' heritage is said to be the focus of racist onslaught, by implication Mexicans and Indians constitute distinct and perhaps inferior "races." Mexicans are racialized as "illegal" mariachi music enthusiasts and Indians are racialized as Bollywood dancing doctors. Consequently, the underlying premises within these stories—being American is premised on Whiteness, all Mexicans are "illegal," and that all brown people from the "Middle East" are "terrorists"—are not acknowledged nor challenged. Since 2004, less than 1% of U.S. network news coverage has focused on Latinos; even less coverage is positive (Santa Ana, 2012). Additionally, recent coverage of other Indians in the U.S. has focused on the 2014 and 2015 winners of the Scripps National Spelling Bee where Indians' innate "intelligence" and "foreignness" are referenced.

Overall, even though the news coverage discussed here conveys positive representations of Mexicans and Indians, it still obfuscates how racism operates in our society. Davuluri and de la Cruz are portrayed as being able to achieve their "American Dream" despite facing overt forms of racism. Viewers are encouraged to believe that racism has little impact on minorities' life chances. Such implications lead to a view that racial minorities who are unable to achieve their "American Dream" fail because of their own, or their group's, shortcomings. Therefore the color-blind representation of successful immigrants in the news media helps to uphold our society's ongoing social structure that bestows economic, political, and social resources and privileges by Whites over those deemed Non-White.

Note

1. For more information on this incident, see P. Caulfield, "Dunkin' Donuts workers hailed for keeping cool heads during racist rant; Texas man aims to raise $10K," *New York Daily News*, June 12, 2013, http://www.nydailynews.com/news/national/dunkin-workers-hailed-grace-face-racist-rant-article-1.1370639.

References

Altheide, D. L. (1987). Reflections: Ethnographic content analysis. *Qualitative Sociology, 10*(1), 65–77.

Bonilla-Silva, E. (2010). *Racism without racists: Color-blind racism and the persistence of racial inequality in America.* Lanham, MD: Rowman & Littlefield.

Brookings Institution. (2008, September 25). Democracy in the age of new media: A report on the media and the immigration debate. Retrieved from http://www.brookings.edu/research/reports/2008/09/25-immigration-dionne.

CNN. (2013, September 18). *Erin Burnett OutFront* [Television broadcast]. New York, NY: CNN.

CNN. (2013, June 13). *Newsroom* [Television broadcast]. Atlanta, GA: CNN.

Delgado, R. (2007). The myth of upward mobility. *University of Pittsburgh Law Review, 68*(4), 879–913.

Feagin, J. R. (2014). *Racist America: Roots, current realities, and future reparations.* New York, NY: Routledge.

Feagin, J. R., & Cobas, J. A. (2014). *Latinos facing racism: Discrimination, resistance, and endurance.* Boulder, CO: Paradigm Publishers.

Fox. (2013). *Fox 29 10 o'clock news* [Television broadcast]. San Antonio, TX: KAAB.

Fox News. (2013, September 18). *Fox and friends* [Television broadcast]. New York, NY: Fox News.

Gad, J. (2013, June 18). O'er the land of the free to spread insults online. *USA Today.* Retrieved from http://www.lexisnexis.com/lnacui2api/auth/checkbrowser.do;jsessionid=DB7A2F3BBE1F660C821E569107EB20F6.42jftcQ5qbwV8IdUo5r8pg?ipcounter=1&cookieState=0&rand=0.32106146768952537&bhcp=1.

Gans, H. J. (1979). *Deciding what's news: A study of CBS Evening News, NBC Nightly News, Newsweek, and Time.* New York, NY: Pantheon.

Glenn, E. N. (2002). *Unequal freedom: How race and gender shaped American freedom and labor.* Cambridge, MA: Harvard University Press.

Hall, S. (1979). Culture, media, and the "ideological effect." In J. Curran, M. Gurevich, & J. Woollacott (Eds.), *Mass communication and society* (pp. 315–348). Beverly Hills, CA: Sage.

Hochschild, J. L. (1995). *Facing up to the American dream: Race, class, and the soul of the nation.* Princeton, NJ: Princeton University Press.

Hughey, M. W. (2012). Show me your papers! Obama's birth and the whiteness of belonging. *Qualitative Sociology, 35,* 163–181.

Jones, R. P., Cox, D., & Navarro-Rivera, J. (2014). Economic insecurity, rising inequality, and doubts about the future: Findings from the 2014 American value survey. Public Religion Research Institute. Retrieved from http://publicreligion.org/site/wp-content/uploads/2014/09/AVS-web.pdf.

Kim, E. K. (2013, September 16). New Miss America's Indian heritage sparks racist comments. *Today.com*. Retrieved from http://www.today.com/style/new-miss-americas-heritage-evokes-racist-comments-twitter-8C11167234.

Lee, T. G. (2013, September 16). Miss America crown goes to an Indian American for first time. *MSNBC.com*. Retrieved from http://tv.msnbc.com/2013/09/16/miss-new-york-nina-davuluri-first-indian-american-woman-miss-america/.

Miss America rises above negative web comments. (2013, September 18). *USA Today*. Retrieved from http://www.lexisnexis.com/lnacui2api/api/version1/getDocCui?lni=59CV-8SY1-DYRR-92MK&csi=8213&hl=t&hv=t&hnsd=f&hns=t&hgn=t&oc=00240&perma=true.

MSNBC. (2013a, June 14). *Politics nation with Al Sharpton* [Television broadcast]. New York, NY: MSNBC.

MSNBC. (2013b, September 20). *MSNBC live with Thomas Roberts* [Television broadcast]. New York, NY: MSNBC.

Navarette, R. (2013, June 17). The mariachi singer is more American than his critics. *CNN.com*. Retrieved from http://www.cnn.com/2013/06/17/opinion/navarrette-mexican-american-singer/index.html?hpt=hp_t4.

Omi, M., & Winant, H. (2014). *Racial formation in the United States*. New York, NY: Routledge.

Putnam, R. D. (2015). *Our kids: The American dream in crisis*. New York, NY: Simon & Schuster.

Rodriguez, C. Y. (2013a). Mexican-American boy's national anthem sparks racist comments. *CNN.com*. Retrieved from http://www.cnn.com/2013/06/12/us/mexican-american-boy-sings-anthem/index.html?iref=allsearch.

Rodriguez, C. Y. (2013b). Mexican-American boy returns for NBA encore in famous mariachi suit. *CNN.com*. Retrieved from http://www.cnn.com/2013/06/14/us/mexican-american-boy-encore/index.html?iref=allsearch%20Cindy%20Rodriguez.

Sáenz, R., & Douglas, K. M. (2015). A call for the racialization of immigration studies on the transition of ethnic immigrants to racialized immigrants. *Sociology of Race and Ethnicity*, 1(1), 166–180.

Sáenz, R., Douglas, K. M., Embrick, D. G., & Sjoberg, G. (2007). Pathways to downward mobility: The impact of schools, welfare and prisons on people of color. In H. Vera & J. Feagin (Eds.), *Handbook of the sociology of racial and ethnic relations* (pp. 373–409). New York, NY: Springer.

Santa Ana, O. (2012). *Juan in a hundred: The representation of Latinos on network news*. Austin, TX: University of Texas Press.

Schudson, M. (2012). *The sociology of news*. New York, NY: W. W. Norton.

Taylor, N. (2013, June 15). Spurs defend 11-year-old anthem singer. *New York Times*. Retrieved from http://www.nytimes.com/2013/06/15/sports/basketball/spurs-defend-11-year-old-anthem-singer.html?_r=0.

Van Dijk, T. A. (2000). New(s) racism: A discourse analytical approach. In S. Cottle (Ed.), *Ethnic minorities and the media* (pp. 33–49). Buckingham, UK: Open University Press.

Williams, A. (2013, September 22). Beauty pageants draw social media critics. *New York Times*. Retrieved from http://www.nytimes.com/2013/09/22/fashion/beauty-pageants-draw-social-media-critics.html?_r=0.

Wilson II, C. C., Gutierrez, F., & Chao, L. M. (2013). *Racism, sexism, and the media: Multicultural issues into the new communications age*. Thousand Oaks, CA: Sage.

13 Black Studies in Prime Time
Racial Expertise and the Framing of Cultural Authority

Seneca Vaught

In 1903, writing nearly 50 years before the advent of television, W. E. B. Du Bois wrote in his widely read *Souls of Black Folk* of Blacks "born with a veil, and gifted with second-sight in this American world,—a world which yields him no true self-consciousness, but only lets him see himself through the revelation of the other world" (Du Bois, 1999, pp. 10–11). Du Bois's metaphor foreshadows the ongoing predicament of the ability and authority of Blacks to engage in systematic critiques of their own social dilemmas. The veil became a metaphor not only for how Blacks came to see themselves, but for the inability of a broader American society to truly see African Americans as they really were.

Since mainstream analyses of Black issues are almost always channeled through Non-Black gatekeepers, Black and Non-Black audiences are often confronted with racial crises through the filter of White interpretations of legitimate inquiry. This is complicated by the so-called lack of "qualified" minority journalists who enter the profession due to structural barriers (Meyers, 2013; A. Williams, 2015). However, many credentialed and qualified Black experts in academia and alternative media exist who can, and have, challenged these sanctioned interpretations (Jacobs, 2000; Moody-Ramirez & Dates, 2014). More than 100 years after Du Bois originally wrote on the problem of perception, Black Americans have become ubiquitous in media venues and are increasingly called on as interviewees and contributors to stories on Black issues. However, despite these historical changes, a veiled assessment of race continues to inhibit a contextualized understanding of the Black experience (Markovitz, 2011) through the marginalization of Black academic input—particularly from the perspectives of Black Studies intellectuals. Black analysts, commentators, and strategists are visible in the political economy of cable network news, but intellectually sophisticated news media-driven discussions of racial issues remain scarce (Markovitz, 2011). The presence of Black "talking heads" should give us pause about how expertise on racial matters are defined and what this means for our understanding of race in the "post-racial" era (Lewis, 2016; Moody-Ramirez & Dates, 2014).

This chapter explores an extension of Du Bois' concern in the age of mass media by analyzing the results of incorporating Black analysts, employed in network and cable news, into panel discussions of three recent racialized events: the discrimination lawsuit against Paula Deen, the George Zimmerman trial, and the grand jury verdict of Darren Wilson in the Michael Brown shooting. No area is more valuable in tracing the problem of racial expertise than the post-crisis coverage window following major racial incidents. In recent years, modern news organizations have lacked the intellectual depth of analysis to make meaningful contributions to advance the public's understanding of racially contentious events. The average American viewer's understanding of contemporary social issues has certainly evolved in the last 50 years to be more inclusive, but the critical factors that precipitate racial crises seem to be more mysterious today than they were 100 years ago. Even during the height of urban unrest during the 1960s, the Kerner Commission in 1969 concluded that the outbreak of violence had roots in causes deeper than isolated episodes of police misconduct—a holistic analysis that seems almost entirely absent from the framing of racial crises in the present (Byerly & Wilson, 2009; Jacobs, 2000, pp. 5–7). While audiences cannot blame contemporary news media alone for the decline in the public's understanding of the complexity of racial matters, critical viewers must critique the way media organizations have undermined critical dialogues on race through their framing of expertise.

Overview of Relevant Literature

Previous discussions by scholars have considered issues surrounding the selection of expertise in the news but do not attempt to address how these questions relate to discussions of race (Albaek, Christiansen, & Togeby, 2003; Kruvand, 2012; Libit, 2008; Steele, 1995). Entman and Rojecki (2000) explored Black representations in network news, and found that networks have used certain traits to characterize and frame Black subjects and their relevance to certain topics. They argued that Blacks could provide useful perspectives—when not "ghettoized as experts" on topics of drugs, gangs, Martin Luther King, Jr., and "Black issues"—if networks chose to include them. Perhaps most relevant to questions raised in this chapter, Entman and Rojecki found that of stories concerning Black issues in a 1990–1991 sample, some 33 Black experts were consulted in addition to some 27 Whites. Blacks were called on as experts on matters outside of the "race beat" less than 15 times, compared to White experts quoted more than 700 times (Entman & Rojecki, 2000, pp. 67–68).

In addition to the problem of the expert, one sees how the idea of the news panel itself could pose problems for the critical examination of racial themes. The news panel format has emerged amid a broader trend of blatant partisanship in cable network news. Its presence prompts us to inquire about the "nature and effects" of news in all of its forms (Coe et al., 2008). Gans (2004) examined the impact of these new developments in their formative stages, and pointed out that the news panel format was problematic due to its emphasis on argumentation over elucidation. Furthermore, different perspectives gleaned from different sources and levels of authority are necessary to the functioning of a democracy (Gans, 2011).

Additionally, recent criticisms have collectively argued against the validity and relevance of Black Studies professionals as racial subject matter experts (McWhorter, 2009; Riley, 2012). Black Studies are often disregarded as being pitifully parochial, brazenly polemical, and persistently pessimistic. The public's caricature of the discipline as being trapped in the 1960s and unqualified or irrelevant to current social conditions also poses a serious problem. While many of these arguments are based in a lack of familiarity with the diverse aims, impact, and literature of the discipline (Rojas, 2011), these perceptions are compounded by the aforementioned concerns regarding the problem of the Black expert, the isolation of Black expertise on racial matters, and the challenge of finding a proper format for in-depth news analysis.

These varying challenges also frame an important paradox. Major U.S. news networks have increasingly turned to the race beat during and following the election of Barack Obama as president of the United States. Two highly cited works in the *Journal of Black Studies* (Teasley & Ikard, 2010; Walters, 2007) critically interrogated the new politics of race and what the expertise of Black Studies could contribute to the so-called post-racial commentary. On the other hand, as Squires and Jackson (2010) contend, news media suppressed coverage of racial dynamics in campaign tactics, a decision that foreshadowed a serious lapse in later political analysis and precluded the advent of a post-racial state of affairs.

How is racial expertise determined in these matters and why? Given the increase of specialists with academic expertise in the discipline of Black Studies (Bailey, 2000; Wilson, 2005), has this resulted in more research-driven discussions of racial issues in major media outlets? Or, have major news networks elected to use non-authoritative Black perspectives on racial issues from other vantage points? In this chapter, I argue that the coverage of Black issues but the exclusion of "certain kinds" of racial experts for others contributes to the "ghettoization" of racial scholarship and underscores the power of dominant values and ideologies in constructing public discourse on Black life. Critical appraisals of the historical, cultural, political, and economic assumptions on these issues have been thoroughly examined and documented in Black Studies literature, yet are ignored by the mainstream media—even as the authority of other so-called experts is invoked (Bailey, 2000; Reed, 2010; Rojas, 2011; Teasely & Ikard, 2010; Thomas & Blackmon, 2015; Walters, 2007).

Piercing the Veil while Colorblind: Is Inclusion Enough?

Black academicians rooted in the Black Studies tradition often employ an epistemological framework that directly challenges colorblind ideologies of popular opinion. Allen (2001) raised important questions about the kind of criticisms leveled at Black Studies and the broader context of their significance in society. Brown's (2007) assessment of Black Studies is, on one level, about the disappearance of Black Americans and Black Studies from university life. Another equally important argument of the essay contends that the absence of critical Black voices on college campuses has seriously limited the ability of universities to deliver an authentic educational experience to *both* Black and White students.

As a warning to news organizations, simply substituting a Black person as a placeholder for the same intellectually bereft "color-blind" assumptions of the American mainstream undermines journalistic norms of professionalism and the responsibility to educate viewers with accurate information. While a color-blind approach to news stories may be the default framework for mainstream audiences, it most certainly does not adequately reflect the material conditions and insights of racially adept viewers and most Black Americans (Bonilla-Silva, 2010). Regardless of schools or disciplinary approaches, the vast majority of Black Studies professionals view race as a central and defining characteristic of the American experience.

A less sophisticated discussion of race is taking place on mainstream network and cable news than even a decade ago. Black scholars in academia have also bemoaned a parallel phenomenon in higher education. For example, Curry (2010) has explored a similar phenomenon in American philosophy that helps us to better understand challenges with race in the media. According to Curry, a theoretical engagement of race from Black perspectives was sorely lacking in American philosophy and continues to undermine critical comprehension of the Black experience. The default approach, in Curry's assessment, has been underscored by "random reflections of White thinkers on race" and environmental stances that reinforce epistemological overlap rather than engaging concepts well developed and established "within the cultural genealogy of their own thought" (p. 44, 58).

Similarly, news outlets are engaging less in discussing the politics of power in substitution for the practice of representation. In other words, some media institutions have discovered that they can sidestep critical discussions about power and privilege if they showcase culturally diverse talent. In doing so, many have reverted to an intellectually impotent multicultural intervention that pauses racial progress to reinforce existing stereotypes and inequalities. These practices are not new, but they are particularly frustrating given the racial optimism and transcendence of Black political candidates in the so-called post-civil rights era (Zilber & Niven, 2000). The journey to get more Blacks in front of newsroom cameras has been a long struggle that should not be downplayed. Chappell (2007) found a period of decline of African Americans in the broadcast news workforce from 1990 to 2006. The decline was so precipitous that it prompted Jesse Jackson and the Rainbow PUSH Coalition to call for more Black TV News anchors at their 2006 conference.

In 2008, the research center Media Matters published a study on the lack of gender and ethnic diversity during prime time. In 2014, a new study found that Blacks in newsrooms were in decline overall, with exceptions in leadership spots in television news directorships (Anderson, 2014; L. Williams, 2013).

The politics behind the search for qualified Black anchors and journalists were probably less related to the quest for well-rounded and multifaceted perspectives for audiences but more governed by the numbers game. Like other organizations, news agencies recruit Black talent to head off public criticism during vital news events, especially when a cultural angle is necessary.

Taken at face value, one would assume that the diversification in politics and media are representative of a shift in the racial climate of the nation but this is far from the truth. In reality, the kinds of representatives chosen—in media and in politics—are representative of the politics of racial contention in the United States. Paradoxically, as there is increasing news coverage of Black issues in American politics, discussions of race have become less sophisticated. By less sophisticated, I am referring to a precursory conclusion on the public consensus regarding racial matters without critically interrogating the short and long-term rationale behind these positions. For instance, coverage of racial issues tends to emphasize color-blind notions of egalitarianism without critically engaging what justice means in specific regional, cultural, and historical contexts.

A Certain Kind of Expert: The Black Studies Scholar in the News

What does the presence of Black journalists and anchors in the so-called post-racial era tell us about structural issues in mass media and its impact on ideas of expertise and racial knowledge? Clearly, given the broader political resonance of race in rather complicated ways, there must be an equally compelling message that the news media present. Perhaps one key lesson is that the exclusion of particular racial experts and the inclusion of others are indicative of corporate attitudes, public shifts in media consumption, and the political economy of news media. Is it enough for networks to simply cover racial events in the news? Are there broader questions about curatorial and editorial processes that are neglected in media analyses of racial crises?

One of the issues that make this study so relevant are the many different types of panels that news programs use. If the purpose of panels is to provide greater analysis and in-depth discussions on a topic from a variety of perspectives, it appears than many of the panels fall short of this goal. Kovach and Rosenstiel have argued that as the reportorial aspects of news have shrunken, viewers are increasingly subjected to a type of speculative discussion commandeered by "activist experts" (2010, p. 85). The expansion of punditry in cable news has increasingly turned to the business of "analysis," using expert panels to both escape and challenge the interview and single-expert-based coverage of traditional news programming (Jacobs & Townsley, 2011). Producers may have discovered that they can appeal to a certain type of audience by framing controversial issues through an expert panel—often selected much more for their charisma and viewer appeal than professional credentials.

Jacobs and Townsley (2011) have also found that the rising role of academics, especially from elite institutions, has contributed to the diversity of political commentary in print media. What does their data hint about the role of racial expertise in the space of opinion? How can panels present audiences with a certain level of analysis when so many of panels are comprised of self-declared experts on racial affairs without the academic credentials to validate such claims? But how is racial expertise validated? Some might argue that panel experts are valued because of their proximity to the event; that their closeness grounds the legitimacy of their argument. As this relates to racial analysis, who would be in the best position to articulate the complex and seemingly contradictory developments of the racial conflagrations that have so often characterized this nation?

To approach these questions, this study examines three high-profile racial incidents from 2013 and 2014 on six major news outlets (ABC, NBC, CBS, Fox News, CNN, and MSNBC), to better understand the racial dynamics at play in evaluating the role of race experts in news media. This study selected particular events that represented the apex of coverage for breaking news stories in which critical race literacy would play a key role in both the coverage and analysis of the story. The samples focus primarily on coverage during the prime-time news slot (7:00–11:00 p.m. Eastern Standard Time). However, some early daytime and morning shows that emphasize the expert panel format in their coverage have also been included to provide a broader exploration of racial commentary. Eighteen unique shows with 32 Black appearances as experts, analysts, or discussants out of some 66 discussants appeared in the sample.[1] Out of the 34 Black discussants (excluding anchors and hosts) who appeared on the six network shows examined, only 4 experts of the 34 panelists (11.8%) possessed academic expertise in racial subject matter. Out of those 4 Black Studies scholars, two of the same experts appeared three or more times on other panels. In other words, two Black academic experts accounted for more than half of the appearances of all scholarly Black experts on television during this period.

Although the public is getting broader exposure to Black insights in moments of racial crises, it is receiving a limited view with regard to Black academic expertise. The lack of public exposure to Black expertise on news panels not only inhibits racial dialogue, but it also indirectly undermines academic expertise in a racially distinct way. This is not to say that non-scholarly voices on racial matters are unimportant, but rather certain types of voices account for much more of the airwaves on these issues than others.

Expert panelists on legal issues, law enforcement, and public relations may yield important professional insights on racial matters, yet the scope of analysis in these panels often forays into frontiers well beyond their authority. This is particularly troubling because of the widespread availability of Black scholars with deep expert knowledge regarding the areas in question. Table 13.1 illustrates this by outlining the major coverage of race crises stories in 2013 and 2014. Of note is that network channels offer little coverage during prime time as it relates to issues of race in the panel format. On the other hand, cable news programming offers a substantial amount of panel discussion during the prime-time viewing hours.

Table 13.1 Overview of Selected Expert Panels during Coverage of Racial Events in 2013 and 2014

	ABC	NBC	CBS	FOX	CNN	MSNBC
Paula Deen, June 2013	*The View* June 26, 2013 **Whoopi Goldberg,** Barbara Walters, Elizabeth Hasselback, **Star Jones,** Joy Behar	*Today* with Matt Lauer June 26, 2013 (no comparable panel)	No comparable panel identified	*On the Record with Greta Van Sustern* June 25, 2013 (H) Greta Van Sustern, Ted **Williams,** Gloria Allred	*CNN Live* with Don Lemon June 29, 2013 Buck Davis, Wendy Walsh, **Kelly Goff,** *Tim Wise, * **Marc Lamont Hill**	*All In* with Chris Hayes June 23, 2013 (H) Chris Hayes, **Seaton Smith, Nancy Giles,** *Jelani Cobb
Zimmerman verdict, July 14, 2014	*This Week* July 14, 2014 Dan Abrams, **Pierre Thomas,** Paul Gigot, **Tavis Smiley**	*Meet the Press* July 14, 2014 David Gregory, Rich Lowry, **Al Sharpton, Bill Richardson**	*Face the Nation* July 14, 2014 Bob Schieffer, **Ben Jealous,** *Michael **Eric Dyson, Daryl Parks, Mark** Strassman, Mario Diaz-Balart, Mike Kelly, Dick Durbin	*Hannity* July 1, 2014 **Rod Wheeler,** Anna Yum *Hannity* July 16, 2014 Live panel *Hannity* July 17, 2014 Juan **Williams,** Leo Terrell	*Piers Morgan Live* July 12, 2014 Alex Ferrer, * **Marc Lamont Hill,** Jo-Ellan Dimitrius, Jayne Weintraub *CNN*(A) Don Lemon, * **Marc Lamont Hill, Wynton Marsalis**	*Jansing and Company* July 16, 2014 * **Marc Lamont Hill, Alexis Stodghill**
Darren Wilson grand jury, November 24, 2014	*This Week* Martha Raditz, November 30, 2014 **Donna Brazile,** Bill Kristol, Cokie Roberts, Bret Stephens	*Meet the Press* November 23, 2014 Rudy Giuliani, * **Michael Eric Dyson** *Meet the Press* 11/30/2014 **Deval Patrick, Helene Cooper,** Andrea Mitchell, **Sherrilyn Ifill,** David **Brooks,** *Charles **Ogletree, Ben Carson**	*Face the Nation* August 17, 2014 (H) Bob Schaeffer, **Cornell William Brooks,** *Michael **Eric Dyson, Ruth Marcus,** Michael Gerson	*Hannity* November 18, 2014 **Derk Brown, Bill Johnson,** Bo Dietl	*Situation Room* November 10, 2014 (H) Wolf Blitzer, (A) Don Lemon, Tom Fuentes, **John Gaskin, Sunny Hostin**	No comparable panel identified

Notes: Panelists with names in **bold** indicate a person racially identifiable as Black in an American context. The notations (H) and (A) are abbreviations for the following: (H) head anchor, (A) anchorperson. An asterisk (*) denotes a scholar holding Black Studies credentials by training, association, or appointment.

Summary of Panel Coverage of Racial Episodes

The Paula Deen Incident: Heartfelt Apology or Coded Appeal

In August 2013, months following a deposition where it emerged that the food mogul admitted to using racial slurs, Paula Deen embarked on an apology tour to salvage her wounded public image, which prompted many sponsors to cancel partnerships and endorsements (Macht, 2013). Ironically, MSNBC's *NOW with Alex* reported a favorability poll conducted by Public Policy Polling (PPP) that found Deen rated more favorable than Martin Luther King, Jr., among Georgia Republican voters (Kim, 2013). News networks employed the panel format to probe for deeper meaning.

Panelists on ABC's *The View* discussed whether Deen should be forgiven. The Black panelists, Whoopi Goldberg and Star Jones, accepted the notion of forgiveness but Jones repeatedly mentioned that the use of the n-word did not make one a racist but rather the context and one's life history. Previous comments by Deen regarding a plantation-styled wedding and her urging of accusers "to cast the first stone" if they had never said anything they regretted raised skepticism about the sincerity of the apology (Macht, 2013).

The prime-time panels turned to the experts to probe for deeper meaning. MSNBC's *All in With Chris Hayes* hosted an all-Black guest panel that included commenter/writer Nancy Giles; comedian Seaton Smith; and Jelani Cobb, an African American Studies professor at the University of Connecticut. The panel varied in sentiments from Smith urging for forgiveness and focus on substantive racial matters like policing, to Giles emphasizing the dilemma that Black-on-Black usage of the n-word caused, to Cobb discussing the historical and geographical context for White–Black relations in the South. Though no particularly poignant analysis emerged, the spectrum of Black views on the crisis was clearly demonstrated.

Two days after the story gained traction on MSNBC, Fox News opted for a lawyer's panel that pitted civil rights attorney Gloria Allred against a Black defense attorney, Ted Williams. Williams took up the side of Deen, arguing that the use of the word may have been a bad choice but that the context and her cultural background should be considered. Allred emphasized that Deen had not really apologized enough and that too many Blacks had died on account of that term in the past to take this case lightly.

The Paula Deen fiasco brings many of the concerns of racial expertise to the fore. The increasing public perception that a degree from the sciences, law, or a medical profession is a "trump card" over degrees in the humanities and social sciences (Kohn, 2011) is certainly noted in the exchanges on this issue. Out of all the panels examined, the most informed analysis of the Paula Deen incident was when Black Studies public intellectuals such as Jelani Cobb and Marc Lamont Hill appeared on CNN and MSNBC. Viewers were able to gain critical insights into not only opinions of what happened, but explanations for why people felt betrayed, angered, or outraged by Deen's comments.

206 Seneca Vaught

Additionally, the inclusion of a variety of experts with academic expertise in Black Studies illustrated that there is no singular Black perspective on these issues, but a spectrum of vantage points, each with a distinct rationale. Conversely, the Fox panel tended to focus on the nuances of argumentation and the public relations side of Deen's comments, further demonstrating why racial misunderstanding persists even amid intensified race coverage.

Post-Verdict Zimmerman Panels: Debating Justice or the Disregard for Black Life

In mid-July 2013, the news cycle was punctuated by high-profile coverage of the Zimmerman trial. George Zimmerman was a man patrolling the neighborhood of Twin Lakes as a self-appointed watchman following a burglary in the community. On the night of February 26, 2012, he sighted Trayvon Martin walking through the community around 7:00 p.m. He approached the youth and the series of events that followed are still debated to this day. Zimmerman allegedly attempted to stop Martin after being told by authorities to stay in his car. Shortly afterward a struggle ensued. We will never know the full story because we only have Zimmerman's account to rely on; yet we do know that Martin was shot and killed as Zimmerman pleaded self-defense based on a controversial statue known as "Stand Your Ground." According to Reuters (2013), more than 10.6 million viewers tuned in to watch the jurors return a verdict of not guilty on charges of second-degree murder and manslaughter.

CNN developed a special program titled "The N-Word: Is it Ever Okay?" to help viewers process the racial language that had become such a key issue in interpreting the broader meaning of the Zimmerman case, as well as the previous Paula Deen incident. The network included African American Studies professor Marc Lamont Hill, jazz musician Wynton Marsalis, journalist Safiya Songhai, and actor Levar Burton. Most of the panels relied on legal expertise to justify or explain the verdict and relied on Black panelists and Black Studies experts such as Hill to clarify why African Americans responded so differently to the verdict. Analyses of what this instance meant for Black lives in America and its parallels in a racial past were largely absent from all these discussions. Recent research from scholars with subject matter expertise in Critical Race or Black Studies present a deeper understanding of the Martin episode than most Americans audiences were exposed to via televised panels. For example, Thomas and Blackmon (2015) presented an introspective analysis of the influence of Martin's shooting on the racial socialization practices of African American parents. While most audiences are unaware of what racial socialization practices are, the structured and systematic analysis provided by these authors revealed an intricate knowledge of the workings of race and its impact in measurable ways.[2] Importantly, the authors show the complex challenges of African American parenthood that were almost entirely absent from discussions in the news but very relevant in providing context for the incident.

Michael Brown Shooting: Cops under Pressure or People under Siege

Shortly after the intensity of the Zimmerman panels had subsided, another crisis appeared on the national news cycle out of Ferguson, Missouri. An adolescent by the name of Michael Brown had been shot dead in the streets of Ferguson by police officer Darren Wilson on August 9, 2014. At the time, unconfirmed reports relayed that Brown had been shot even though he had his hands up in the air at the time of shooting. The event escalated over several weeks through social media, especially Black Twitter,[3] as hashtags #handsupdontshoot and #Blacklivesmatter became a rallying cry to online activists.

The network television channels in this sample struggled to cover the event with an adequate level of analysis. On the one hand, ABC and CBS attempted to characterize what seemed to be an outbreak of police violence directed toward young Black men. Yet they also insinuated that certain aspects of Black youth culture provoked, if not encouraged, these lethal episodes. NBC pitted Rudy Giuliani against academician Michael Eric Dyson on the problem and misconceptions of Black-on-Black violence. In all of the cases selected, the Mike Brown panels seemed the most constrained either by format or by limitations of panelists to engage deeper meaning from the developments in question. Black Studies perspectives provided by Michael Eric Dyson and Charles Ogletree provided broader social and legal context for the incident while most of the other panelists opted for elucidation of emotions of respect for police authority or disbelief at the mounting number of racial crises in the past two years.

Perhaps more so than any of the other cases, the coverage of Michael Brown revealed how relevant the perspectives derived from Black Studies are to news coverage. Had media outlets turned to a cadre of African American Studies experts, who specialize in race and criminal justice, they would have benefited from a well-developed and thoroughly documented body of literature that has examined the racial tension between policing and African American youth. What makes the Black Studies research emphasis somewhat different than other perspectives offered in criminal justice, law, and the social sciences is the ability for scholars to offer an interdisciplinary critique on the Black experience in which race rises as a central and fundamental issue rather than a peripheral one. Legal scholarship written from a Black Studies paradigm (e.g., Butler, 2004; Mauer, 2006; Miller, 2010) demonstrates that racial context is not a spurious factor in criminal justice as so many experts claim, but that it is central to decoding the meaning of policing and punishment within the context of the Black community.

Branding Racial Crises

The mere inclusion of Black voices in mainstream media is not enough. Excluding racial experts from a Black Studies paradigm risks diminishing the complexity of racial matters and perpetuating existing power structures built off racial hierarchies. A relationship exists between the types of racial experts who are invited to panel discussions regarding racial matters and the underlying messaging of the news "brand." This matter is not only relevant to assessing the viewer demographics of a given network but also in examining how pundits influence public discourse. Previous studies have explored the phenomena of cable news and its impact on partisanship, but perhaps we need to consider more carefully the role of panels in shifting, informing, and channeling the public perception and discourse of racial incidents in particular. Jacobs and Townsley note that the single-host format engages panels with "a more diverse range of media intellectuals" but often use predetermined points of view to arrange inquiry that underscores the political views of the host (2011, pp. 241–242). This is further complicated by the exclusion of certain types of experts who may challenge the moral certitude of the hosts—such as academics and other purveyors of complex historical narratives (Jacobs & Townsley, 2011).

As more students graduate with degrees in Black Studies we seldom hear the critical and highly relevant perspectives that scholars trained in these interdisciplinary approaches can provide in mainstream media. Instead, these critical voices are exiled to alternative media and the blogosphere. Patton (2012) illustrated the new approaches and interdisciplinary perspectives that have characterized the rise of new stars within Black Studies. The article focused specifically on Northwestern University doctoral candidates but became somewhat of a bellwether article for the field. Far from one-dimensional racial ideologues, the article painted a picture of cooperative and multi-racial coalition builders willing to tackle serious social issues, such as the difficult dialogues on race and ongoing challenges to justice in the wake the Trayvon Martin shooting.

MSNBC appears to have a clear edge in employing Black Studies academic expertise in racial matters. Its inclusion of Melissa Harris-Perry and other high-profile Black academics reveals a commitment to analysis beyond the politics of representation. Fox News, on the other end of the spectrum, relied more so on legal analysis with no academic expertise on racial matters during panel sessions of these racial crises. These decisions on expertise align more or less with the dominant themes in the Fox brand and the expectations of its audience.[4] Perhaps the most troubling are the networks in between (CNN, ABC, NBC), whose inclusion/exclusion of racial experts seemed to follow no clear pattern. It is one thing for racial issues to be discussed *ex parte* in an arrangement that is explicitly understood by a viewer base, but it is another thing altogether for the constellation of authority to be configured in a way that appears completely random.

Entman and Rojecki (2000) found that "the news embodies the effects of tacitly obeying norms and following cultural patterns of which journalists are only imperfectly aware, and of responding to pressures from elites and markets which news organizations are disinclined to challenge" (p. 77). What this means for the deployment and employment of the Black expert is complex. As news organizations follow established norms and cultural patterns, they become complicit in reinforcing and commoditizing the very racial attitudes at the core of their coverage (Cashmore, 1997; Lewis, 2016; Rome, 2004). In each of these cases, we can see how Blacks experts are called upon to be racial representatives; but specifically in the coverage of Michael Brown, we can see how deep contextual knowledge and academic expertise can transform the meaning of a particular crisis.

Conclusion

From this analysis, it can be concluded that despite the presence of minorities, particularly African Americans, in the mainstream news media, major news organizations seem reluctant to seek perspectives from African American specialists with Black Studies credentials as an authoritative voice on racial issues. Despite criticisms of a full-blown "race hustle," from various positions on the political spectrum, the academic expertise of Black Studies specialists remains marginalized as an irrelevant voice on major racial issues of the day (Crouch, 1995). Some would argue that the inclusion of greater numbers of Black Studies academicians would further undermine objective analysis because these experts have a particular cultural and political ax to grind.

However, this is one of the major problems with the coverage of racial crises. By preempting the discussion of these issues from an empirically grounded Black vantage point, one actually validates prevailing norms in race relations that are far from objective. As Allen (2001) criticized the academy for purporting to be neutral while advancing racial agendas, we can make similar criticisms of the news media during the years of Obama's presidency. A desire for race-neutral analysis does not make it a post-racial reality.

The inclusion of Black voices and the coverage of racial crises by major news networks are certainly a welcome trend but have proven to be quite paradoxical. In many cases, an uninformed Black guest or anchor can reinforce normative racial ideologies rather than challenge implicit racial biases and structured inequalities. While viewers cannot ascertain how or why race experts are selected, they can understand how the inclusion of certain types of Black opinion and the exclusion of other forms of racial expertise contributes to an increasingly polarized racial climate.

The lack of academically qualified Black expert panels reflects an explicit disregard for the intellectual dimensions and seriousness of racial issues. Many of the prime-time news shows that would never use entertainers, athletes, or comedians as an authority for legal analysis, medical commentary, or science coverage, consistently do so for issues centered on race. By transforming every racial crisis into a sound off for uninformed public opinion, they contribute to a discourse evaluated by the level of loudness over the degrees of intellect. This is not to say that only experts have something meaningful to contribute to discussions on race; but given the professionalism and accuracy implied in the practice of journalism and the high standards applied to other topics (such as foreign policy, legal cases, election coverage, and science and medicine), it appears that the gift of the veil and second-sight remains yet to be truly understood.

Notes

1. Black Studies scholarship has long challenged dominant paradigms for a biological basis of Black identity (Diop, 1991; Du Bois, 1999; Smedley & Smedley, 2005). Instead engaging self-disclosed criteria that presume static catergories based on genetic or ethnic heritage—as many casual observers of race tend to emphasize—scholars advocating a Black Studies paradigm have emphasized the commonality of unique forms of oppression in the racial experiences of African-descended people. In this tradition, "Blackness" among Black Studies scholars has not historically been based soley upon complexion, lineage, and phenotypical characteristics but a commonality of experiences and culture stemming from an external imposition of otherness. Using a distinctly American approach to Black racial identity based on historical and popularly perceived characteristics rather than self-disclosed critieria, I categorized each of the panelists as Black or Non-Black. The criteria for inclusion as a person with adequate expertise in racial matters were determined by the following: (1) professional training or academic credentials from a program in Black Studies or a comparable unit (Africana Studies, Africology, Pan-African Studies, African American Studies, Critical Race Studies, etc.), (2) a current or past academic appointment in a departmental or programmatic unit or Black Studies, or (3) a body of research or engaged scholarly community work that includes peer-reviewed interdisciplinary critiques of the role of racism in Black communities.
2. According to Thomas and Blackmon, "Racial socialization is defined as the process by which African American parents raise children to have positive self-concepts in an environment that is racist and sometimes hostile and includes exposure to cultural practices, promotion of racial pride, development of knowledge of African American culture, and preparation for bias and discrimination …" (2015, p. 76).
3. "Black Twitter" is the cultural and technological eponym for the disproportionally large number of African Americans who discuss cultural and political events on the social media platform Twitter. Black Twitter, as it is called, has come to be an important source for analyzing trending topics of interest in Black America. For more information, see work by Brock (2012), Sharma (2013), and Florini (2014).
4. Works that have discussed the Fox News brand and its implications are too numerous to explore in this study. For further reading consult Iyengar and Hahn (2009), Chan-Olmsted and Cha (2007), and Morris (2005).

References

Albaek, E., Christiansen, P. M., & Togeby, L. (2003). Experts in the mass media: Researchers as sources in Danish daily newspapers, 1961–2001. *Journalism & Mass Communication Quarterly, 80*(4), 937–948.

Allen, R. L. (2001). Politics of the attack on Black Studies. In N. Norment (Ed.), *The African American studies reader*. Durham, N.C.: Carolina Academic Press.

Anderson, M. (2014, August 1). *As news business takes a hit, the number of Black journalists declines*. Retrieved from http://www.pewresearch.org/fact-tank/2014/08/01/as-news-business-takes-a-hit-the-number-of-Black-journalists-declines/.

Bailey, R. W. (2000). Black studies in the third millennium: Reflections on six ideas that can still (and must) change the World. *Souls, 2*(3), 77–90.

Bonilla-Silva, E. (2010). *Racism without racists: Color-blind racism and the persistence of racial inequality in the United States*. Lanham, MD: Rowman & Littlefield.

Brock, A. (2012). From the Blackhand side: Twitter as a cultural conversation. *Journal of Broadcasting & Electronic Media, 56*(4), 529–549.

Brown, C. (2007). *Dude, where's my Black studies department?: The disappearance of Black Americans from our universities*. Berkeley, CA: North Atlantic Books.

Butler, P. (2004). Much respect: Toward a hip-hop theory of punishment. *Stanford Law Review, 56*(5), 983–1016.

Byerly, C. M., & Wilson, C. (Eds.). (2009). Journalism as Kerner turns 40: Its multiculticultural problems and possibilities. *Howard Journal of Communications, 20*(3), 209–221.

Cashmore, E. (1997). *The Black culture industry*. London: Routledge.

Chan-Olmsted, S. M., & Cha, J. (2007). Branding television news in a multichannel environment: An exploratory study of network news brand personality. *International Journal on Media Management, 9*(4), 135–150.

Coe, K., Tewksbury, D., Bond, B. J., Drogos, K. L., Porter, R. W., Yahn, A., & Zhang, Y. (2008). Hostile news: Partisan use and perceptions of cable news programming. *Journal of Communication, 58*(2), 201–219.

Chappell, K. (2007). The big newscasts and the Black anchors who deliver them. *Ebony, 62*(10), 84.

Crouch, S. (1995). The Afrocentric hustle. *The Journal of Blacks in Higher Education, 10*, 77.

Curry, T. J. (2010). Concerning the underspecialization of race theory in American philosophy: How the exclusion of Black sources affects the field. *The Pluralist, 5*(1), 44–64.

Diop, C. A., Salemson, H. J. (Ed.), & de Jager, M. (Ed.). (1991). *Civilization or barbarism: An authentic anthropology*. Brooklyn, NY: Lawrence Hill Books.

Du Bois, W. E. B., Gates, H. L. (Ed.), & Oliver, T. H. (Ed.). (1999). *The souls of Black folk: Authoritative text, contexts, criticism*. New York, NY: W.W. Norton. (Original work published 1903).

Entman, R. M., & Rojecki, A. (2000). *The Black image in the White mind: Media and race in America*. Chicago, IL: University of Chicago Press.

Florini, S. (2014). Tweets, tweeps, and signifyin': Communication and cultural performance on "Black Twitter." *Television & New Media, 15*(3), 223–237.

Fox News. (2013, June 25). *On the record with Greta Van Sustern* [Television broadcast]. New York, NY: FOX.

Gans, H. J. (2004). *Democracy and the news*. Oxford University Press.

Gans, H. J. (2011). Multiperspectival news revisited: Journalism and representative democracy. *Journalism, 12*(1), 3.

Iyengar, S., & Hahn, K. S. (2009). Red media, blue media: Evidence of ideological selectivity in media use. *Journal of Communication, 59*(1), 19–39.

Jacobs, R. N. (2000). *Race, media, and the crisis of civil society: From Watts to Rodney King.* Cambridge, UK: Cambridge University Press.

Jacobs, R. N., & Townsley, E. (2011). *The space of opinion: Media intellectuals and the public sphere.* New York, NY: Oxford University Press.

Kim, C. (2013, August 7). Georgia Republicans like Paula Deen more than Martin Luther King, Jr. Retrieved from http://www.msnbc.com/the-last-word/georgia-republicans-paula-deen-more.

Kohn, A. (2011, February 16). STEM sell: Are math and science really more important than other subjects? Retrieved from http://www.huffingtonpost.com/alfie-kohn/the-stem-sell-are-math-an_b_823589.html.

Kovach, B., & Rosenstiel, T. (2010). *Blur: How to know what's true in the age of information overload.* New York, NY: Bloomsbury.

Kruvand, M. (2012). "Dr. Soundbite": The making of an expert source in science and medical stories. *Science Communication, 34*(5), 566.

Lewis, L. (2016). *The myth of post-racialism in television news.* New York, NY: Routledge.

Libit, D. (2008, June 24). Meet the make-believe strategists of TV. *Politico.* Retrieved from http://dyn.politico.com/printstory.cfm?uuid=BC9D1553-3048-5C12-00F5BE5F28096DD0.

Macht, D. (2013). Paula Deen: I'm not a racist. Retrieved from http://www.nbcnewyork.com/entertainment/entertainment-news/Paula-Deen-Today-Show-Race-Controversy-213096531.html.

Markovitz, J. (2011). *Racial spectacles: Explorations in media, race, and justice.* New York, NY: Routledge.

Mauer, M. (2006). *Race to incarcerate.* New York, NY: The New Press.

McWhorter, J. (2009, October 1). What should African-American studies students learn? *The New Republic.* Retrieved from http://www.newrepublic.com/blog/john-mcwhorter/what-should-african-american-studies-students-learn.

Media Matters. (2008). *Gender and ethnic diversity in prime-time cable news.* Retrieved from http://cloudfront.mediamatters.org/static/pdf/diversity_report.pdf.

Meyers, M. (2013). *African American women in the news: Gender, race, and class in journalism.* New York, NY: Routledge.

Miller, J. (2010). *Search and destroy: African-American males in the criminal justice system* (2nd ed.). New York, NY: Cambridge University Press.

Moody-Ramirez, M., & Dates, J. L. (2014). *The Obamas and mass media: Race, gender, religion, and politics.* New York, NY: Palgrave Macmillan.

Morris, J. S. (2005). The Fox News factor. *The Harvard International Journal of Press/Politics, 10*(3), 56–79.

Patton, S. (2012, April 12). Black studies: "Swaggering into the future." *The Chronicle of Higher Education.* Retrieved from http://chronicle.com/article/Black-Studies-Swaggering/131533/.

Reed, I. (2010). *Barack Obama and the Jim Crow media: The return of the nigger breakers.* Montreal, CA: Baraka Books.

Reuters. (2013, July 15). Zimmerman verdict gives U.S. cable networks rare Saturday boost. *Reuters*. Retrieved from http://www.reuters.com/article/2013/07/16/us-usa-florida-shooting-ratings-idUSBRE96F00420130716.

Riley, N. S. (2012, April 30). The most persuasive case for eliminating Black Studies? Just read the dissertations [Web log post]. *The Chronicle of Higher Education*. Retrieved from http://chronicle.com/blogs/brainstorm/the-most-persuasive-case-for-eliminating-Black-studies-just-read-the-dissertations/46346.

Rojas, F. (2011). Institutions and disciplinary beliefs about Africana Studies. *The Western Journal of Black Studies, 35*(2), 92–105.

Rome, D. (2004). *Black demons: The media's depiction of the African American male criminal stereotype*. Westport, CT: Praeger.

Sharma, S. (2013). "Black Twitter?": Racial hashtags, networks and contagion. *New Formations: A Journal of Culture/Theory/Politics, 78*(1), 46–64.

Smedley, A., & Smedley, B. D. (2005). Race as biology is fiction, racism as a social problem is real: Anthropological and historical perspectives on the social construction of race. *The American Psychologist, 60*(1), 16–26.

Squires, C. R., & Jackson, S. J. (2010). Reducing race: News themes in the 2008 primaries. *International Journal of Press/Politics, 15*(4), 375–400.

Steele, J. E. (1995). Experts and the operational bias of television news: The case of the Persian Gulf War. *Journalism & Mass Communication Quarterly, 72*(4), 799–812.

Teasley, M., & Ikard, D. (2010). Barack Obama and the politics of race: The myth of postracism in America. *Journal of Black Studies, 40*(3), 411–425.

Thomas, A. J., & Blackmon, S. M. (2015). The influence of the Trayvon Martin shooting on racial socialization practices of African American parents. *Journal of Black Psychology, 41*(1), 75–89.

Walters, R. (2007). Barack Obama and the politics of Blackness. *Journal of Black Studies, 38*(1), 7–29.

Williams, A. (2015, July 22). Why aren't there more minority journalists? *Columbia Journalism Review*. Retrieved from http://www.cjr.org/analysis/in_the_span_of_two.php.

Williams, L. (2013). Newsroom diversity: Black reporters preparing for newsroom cuts. Retrieved from http://wp11.americanobserver.net/2013/05/newsroom-diversity-how-Black-reporters-are-preparing-for-newsroom-cuts/.

Wilson, R. (2005). Past their prime? *Chronicle of Higher Education, 51*(33), A9.

Zilber, J., & Niven, D. (2000). *Racialized coverage of Congress: The news in Black and White*. Westport, CT: Praeger.

14 The Good, the Bad, and the Ugly Muslim

Media Representations of "Islamic Punk" through a Postcolonial Lens

Saif Shahin

> Mary's only famous for being a virgin,
> Our Ayesha was humping like Rastas are toke'n
> Jesus ignored whores; maybe boys were his hos then?
> Muhammad would've kept Mary Magdalen Moaning.

These are lines from a song released as part of the 2008 album *Wild Nights in Guantanamo Bay* by The Kominas, a Boston-based band. They are obviously meant to be provocative, but whom do they intend to provoke? Is it Muslims, by portraying Prophet Muhammad and his wife Ayesha engaging in debauch acts? Or is it Christians, with sexualized references to Virgin Mary, Jesus Christ, and Mary Magdalene? Or is it both at once—culminating as the lines do depicting a salaciously styled coitus between sacred figures from both religions, extending the metaphor insinuated in the title of the song: "Suicide Bomb the Gap?"

The Kominas are part of an "Islamic punk" subculture that began sprouting a little over a decade ago, spreading from San Antonio to Boston, then farther north into Canada and, eventually, all the way to the United Kingdom. It has come to be known as taqwacore, derived from the Arabic word *taqwa* (consciousness of God) and the suffix *core* that is common to many "angry" punk genres (Knight, 2011). The term was first used in *The Taqwacores*, a novel written in 2003 by Michael Muhammad Knight, a White American convert to Islam. Knight created a fictitious world of young Muslim punks leading part-hallowed and part-hedonistic lives in New York, struggling to find a common ground between their Islamic and American identities in the years following the 9/11 attacks (Knight, 2004). Young American Muslims who came across the novel closely identified with Knight's characters and began to put the songs in the novel to music. Taqwacore was born (Andersen, Lingner, Ernst, Tadini, & Coelli, 2010; Hosman, 2009).

Soon, the idea of Islamic punk not only fired up the young Muslim imagination but also evoked the interest of national and international media—especially when some of these groups launched a "taqwa tour," enacting a passage from Knight's novel. It culminated in taqwacore artists attending, "disrupting," and being kicked out of an Islamic convention in Chicago in 2007 (Crafts, 2007; Knight, 2011). Several news organizations reported the event.

This chapter examines the news coverage of taqwacore in mainstream United States and United Kingdom, publications as well as ethnic newspapers and magazines in both nations. Because of their amorphous character and ambivalent identities, taqwacores defy easy representation. Yet, news coverage must necessarily give them some shape and form, some roots and some purpose. As Durham notes, "[J]ournalists are as much subject to the multiplicity of ideological meanings in their work as they are charged with rendering some order from them" (1998, p. 113). But the journalistic act of rendering order is a social and political act, and mirrors the stock of cultural assumptions and understandings upon which it is based. Examining it takes one through the looking glass into the socially constructed reality of narratives and ideologies that underpin thought and action (Berkowitz, 2010; Reese, 2001). The form that taqwacore is given in news coverage thus reflects the news media's worldview, their perception of not just Islamic punk subculture but also of "Muslims" as a racial category, and of the relationship between "Islam" and "the West."

The objective of this chapter, in line with the general purpose of this volume, is to broaden our knowledge of the U.S. media and their interactions with racial minorities, in this case, Muslims. Recent scholarship has problematized the understanding of *race* as a static notion and focused on *racialization*, "a concept [that] reflects the changing meanings of race within different political, social, and economic contexts producing a more expansive and complex discussion of race" (Selod & Embrick, 2013, p. 648). Such accounts take the discourse of race beyond skin pigmentation to look at how various other identity markers, including religion, language, and geography, can become racialized (e.g., Barth, 1969). In this vein, Kumar (2012) and Rana (2011) chart "the parallel development of Islamophobic discourses alongside other forms of racial bigotry and discrimination" and show that "Islamophobia is in fact a form of racism" (Love, 2013, p. 70; see also Stein & Salime, 2015). Taking a comparative approach and juxtaposing taqwacore coverage in the U.S., U.K., and "ethnic" news media helps place the narratives and ideologies at work in their proper historical and political context, revealing where they themselves spring from and what purposes they serve. Specifically, this study locates the coverage of Muslims in the U.S. media as a racialized "other" in White supremacist/savior narratives that have historically driven European/Western colonization projects and continue to provide ideological succor to neocolonialism. In doing so, it also lays bare the role of news media in reflecting and reproducing such narratives, thereby legitimizing the political actions they spur (Kumar, 2012).

Framing Islam

News, far from being an objective representation of the world we live in, represents journalists' and news organizations' interpretations of the world, reflected in the choices they make about *what* issues and events to cover (and what not to cover), as well as *how* to cover them. But these interpretations are not idiosyncratic (Zelizer, 1993). They are shaped by commonly shared cultural narratives and social and political ideologies (Tuchman, 1978; Zelizer, 1990). Journalism, as a social practice and an instrument of social control, coheres within these narratives and ideologies—and the structures of power they represent (Berkowitz, 2010; Shoemaker & Reese, 2013).

For at least three decades, news framing has been the theoretical umbrella under which a lot of research along these lines has been conducted. Reese defines frames as "organizing principles that are socially shared and persistent over time, that work symbolically to meaningfully structure the social world" (2001, p. 11). As this definition stresses, frames pan out through space and time: they are widely shared over long periods. Indeed, it is this shared, enduring characteristic of frames that makes them potent meaning-making devices. They constitute the fabric of knowledge in a society, of what is deemed good or bad, right or wrong by its members and its institutions, including journalists and news organizations—indeed, what is considered worth knowing itself (Durham, 1998). The act of news framing—"to select some aspects of a perceived reality and make them more salient in a communicating text" (Entman, 1993, p. 52)—thus need not be intentional or instrumentalist. It is the fallout of collectively held and deep-seated beliefs about "who we are, what we stand for, what our values are, and what our relationships are with other groups" (Van Dijk, 1998, p. 69).

A number of scholars have looked at the framing of Islam and Muslims in Western, especially mainstream U.S., media (Chuang & Roemer, 2013; Kumar, 2010; Powell, 2011; Reese & Lewis, 2009). Kumar identifies five frames that are commonly used in Western media portrayals of the religion and its followers post-9/11: "Islam is a monolithic religion, Islam is a uniquely sexist religion, the 'Muslim mind' is incapable of rationality and science, Islam is inherently violent, [and] the West spreads democracy, while Islam spawns terrorism" (2010, p. 254). Framing Islam as monolithic is a central frame as "it is only by denying the diversity of Islamic practices that one can argue that 'Islam' has certain inherent, unchanging characteristics that render it antidemocratic, violent, backward-looking, and so on" (p. 260). The remaining four frames serve the purpose of "othering" Muslims by ascribing them characteristics—such as oppression of women, irrationality, extremism and terrorism—that are different from or even the opposite of certain qualities presumed to be inherent to the West. In sum, these frames construct the Muslim as an enemy, to be reviled, feared, and fought—and thus create the justification for the colonization of Muslim lands and peoples (see also Kumar, 2012).

From Orientalism to "Good" and "Bad" Muslims

Critical studies on the framing of Muslims in Western media explicitly or implicitly draw on *Orientalism*, or "a style of thought based upon the ontological and epistemological distinction made between 'the Orient' and ... 'the Occident,' in which the West is constructed in opposition, and superior, to the Orient" (Said, 1978, p. 2). In this worldview, people of the Orient are often represented as backward and premodern; violent and oppressive of their own people (especially women); irrational; and lacking in democracy, human rights, and scientific development. When they are pitted against a "modern" West, enlightened and rational, technologically advanced, and willing to share its bounties with the "natives," colonization itself becomes a moral act—something the West does for the good of the Orient. This worldview is reflected in what Said (1978) called the *postcolonial gaze*—the colonizer's scrutiny of its colonized subject in a manner that simultaneously objectifies the colonized and identifies it as inferior, thereby elevating the status of the colonizer and justifying the colonizer–colonized power hierarchy as natural and necessary.

Said himself put U.S. media reporting of the "Islamic world" under the scrutiny of Orientalism and argued that:

> Muslims and Arabs are essentially covered, discussed, apprehended either as suppliers of oil or as potential terrorists. Very little of the detail, the human density, the passion of Arab-Muslim life has entered the awareness of even those people whose profession it is to report the Islamic world. (1981, p. 26)

Mamdani (2004) examined how Muslims are regarded under the postcolonial gaze after the 9/11 attacks and noted the emergence of a binary black-and-white perspective. Muslims who explicitly criticized the attacks and championed the U.S.'s decision to wage war to root out "Islamic terrorism" were viewed as "good Muslims," while those who questioned the violent response and pointed out that U.S. foreign policy in Central Asia and the Middle East may ultimately be responsible for the attacks were labeled "bad Muslims." The goodness and badness of Muslims had nothing to do with either the Islamic faith or Western "enlightenment" principles. Instead, it depended on their political position vis-à-vis the U.S. and its "war on terror." This was an extension of the with-us-or-against-us mentality that took over the country after the attacks, and yet had its roots in the age-old Orientalist discourse.

Taqwacore: A Brief History

Taqwacore, a subculture populated mostly by second- or third-generation immigrant Muslim youth who have been born or brought up in the West but feel a deep emotional bond with the societies their families hail from, complicates such a good–bad binary. It came into being in the years following the 9/11 attacks, a difficult time when the world appeared divided between radicalized Islamism and bloodthirsty neoconservatism. There was no middle ground, no meeting point—until some young American-Muslims began to create it (O'Brien, 2013).

Michael Muhammad Knight was born into a Catholic family in New York and converted to Islam as a teenager. He moved to Pakistan to study Islam, but soon "burned out on the demands of organized religion" and returned to the U.S. (Andersen et al., 2010). He discovered punk music through some friends and found a symphony between his spiritual and musical creeds.

> They (Islam and punk) aren't so far removed as you'd think. Both began in tremendous bursts of truth and vitality but seem to have lost something along the way—the energy, perhaps, that comes with knowing the world has never seen such positive force and fury and never would again. Both have suffered from sell-outs and hypocrites, but also from true believers whose devotion had crippled their creative drive. Both are viewed by outsiders as unified, cohesive communities when nothing can be further from the truth.
>
> (Knight, 2007)

Knight turned his ideas into a fictional account on the lives of a group of youngsters in Buffalo, New York, who weave together Islamic and punk lifestyle values and philosophies—often by defying both of them (Knight, 2004; see also McDowell, 2014). *The Taqwacores* was finished in 2003 and initially Xeroxed and hand-distributed by Knight before finding a publisher a year later (Hosman, 2009). True to the punk creed of effrontery, the novel deliberately confronts norms, such as when a character reads the Quran while smoking pot, or a riot grrrl plays the guitar in a burqa and leads mixed-sex prayers. All through the novel, the characters have to deal with difficult issues such as gender politics, drugs, and homosexuality—issues that both Islam and American punk cultures are grappling with today—as they try to make sense of who they are and how, or how not, to define themselves (Andersen et al., 2010; McDowell, 2014; O'Brien, 2013).

Soon, it was not just Knight and his characters who were putting Islam and punk together. Shahjehan Khan, a young Boston musician of Pakistani origin, had an epiphany of sorts when he read *The Taqwacores*. "I had a lot of guilt growing up about not doing the right thing or not being a good Muslim or a good Pakistani kid. And it was reading the book that was kind of an assurance that this confusion and maybe disenchantment was normal, and that other people went through it and there was nothing wrong with it," Khan said in an interview (Crafts, 2009). But that wasn't Khan's only problem. "On 9/12, the day after 9/11, I was a senior in high school and I was walking to a class or something like that and some random kid was like, 'Yo, what did your people do?' he said. And I didn't really know how to respond to that" (Crafts, 2009).

After hearing one of the poems from the novel, "Muhammad Was a Punk Rocker," set to music by an Iranian teenager from Texas (Crafts,

2007), Khan decided to team up with his friend Basim Usmani and form a punk rock band. Knight's fiction turned into fact and The Kominas were born. Gradually, similar bands started forming across the U.S. Five of them—The Kominas, Secret Trial Five, Al-Thawra, Vote Hezbollah, and Omar Waqar—came together for a "Taqwa tour" in 2007, bringing an event in the novel to life (Knight, 2011). This event led to a documentary of the tour being released that year. A feature film based on the novel was made in 2010.

Methods

This study is based on a comparative frame analysis of the coverage of taqwacore in mainstream U.S. and U.K. media, as well as "ethnic" media in the two countries. A search on the LexisNexis database for the term "taqwacore" yielded six articles from mainstream U.S. publications (*The New York Times, The Washington Post,* and *The International Herald Tribune*) and 10 articles from U.K. publications (*The Guardian* and *The Times*). A search for the same term in the Ethnic NewsWatch database yielded eight articles from *Hyphen Magazine, India Currents, International Examiner, Arab American News, News India Times* (all U.S.-based), and *Eastern Eye* (U.K.-based). The frame analysis focuses on three issues: (1) the representation of taqwacore, (2) the representation of Muslims, and (3) the representation of the Islam–West relationship in media coverage. While the corpus is small in size, the sharpness of the similarities and differences found between the U.S., U.K., and ethnic media samples lends validity to the findings—as does their interpretation within the broader canon of critical and postcolonial literature. Like all cultural analysis, however, this effort is "not an experimental science in search of law but an interpretive one in search of meaning" (Geertz, 1973, p. 5).

Framing Taqwacore

United States Media

The U.S. media attribute two main characteristics to taqwacore. The first is its representation as intentionally provocative. Both Knight and the taqwacore artists he inspired are supposed to intentionally shock Muslims out of their traditional/conventional thinking and way of life. An article in *The New York Times* noted that "[Knight] often satirizes his fellow Muslims, pricking the traditionalists. He is a court jester to the Islamic world, a provocateur in a kufi" (Oppenheimer, 2011). *The Washington Post* published an article by Knight himself, in which he, while referring to a couple of songs by The Kominas, said: "Unfortunately, neither song title can be printed in a family newspaper—which gives you a sense of the liberties that some taqwacore groups take with social convention" (Knight, 2014).

Related to this framing, taqwacore is also portrayed as a revolutionary movement—a brave rebellion by second- and third-generation immigrants against the first. As stated in another article in *The Washington Post*:

> Deep in the woods of this colonial town boils a kind of revolutionary movement. From the basement of this middle-class home tucked in the woods west of Boston, the Kominas have helped launched a small but growing South Asian and Middle Eastern punk rock movement that is attracting children of Muslim and Hindu immigrants.
>
> (Contreras, 2010)

United Kingdom Media

In the British media, taqwacore artists were initially portrayed as rebels against traditional/conventional Islam. An article in *The Times* suggested, "Rebellion is certainly key to the Kominas and their angry, funny, iconoclastic music reflects the complexities and contradictions of growing up both Muslim and American" (Dalton, 2010). The same trope was also present in *The Guardian*. Describing taqwacore artist and playwright Sabina England, the newspaper said,

> There can't be that many female playwrights who are deaf, punk and Muslim, so Sabina England is something of a find. With a lurid Mohawk and leather jacket slathered with slogans, she looks every inch the rebel and has an attitude to match.
>
> (Butt, 2007)

Some later coverage implied that the idea behind taqwacore as a subculture was inauthentic, even unreal. Another *Guardian* article, for instance, reported,

> "There never really was a scene," says Imran Malik, of the Kominas, a so-called Taqwacore band from New Jersey ... "A few bands came together for that documentary, but the film crew was paying for it, so it was fabricated and forced by someone who was trying to sell a narrative, a sexy narrative. Since then, a lot of those bands have either ceased to exist, or said they're not Taqwacore after all."
>
> (Bhattacharya, 2011)

The article went on to note that, "Similarly, the characters of The Taqwacores movie seem confused. Their revolution is compromised ... a rebel who doesn't know what to rebel against begins to veer into the realm of comedy" (Bhattacharya, 2011). In British coverage, thus, taqwacore became a caricature of itself.

Ethnic Media

Ethnic media differed sharply from mainstream American and British media representations of taqwacore. First, they decried mainstream media's portrayal of taqwacore artists as young rebels trying to shock the traditionalist Muslim community. This, the reports suggested, took the attention away from music. A *News India Times* article noted,

> "No one actually gave us an album review; it was always, 'Oh, look at this, it's shocking,'" [Shahjehan] Khan said. "It's cool something I created is getting attention, and then you sit back and think, "Well, is the attention getting out the message that I want?'"
>
> (Abdulrahim, 2009)

The report quoted taqwacore artist Omar Waqar as saying, "It's been less about the music than about who we are and how we're dressed" (Abdulrahim, 2009). On similar lines, *India Currents* observed, "The Taqwacores [film] looks not to alienate, but to provide a space for Muslim youth that has not been provided before" (Maiwandi, 2011).

Second, ethnic media framed taqwacore as not inauthentic but against the very notion of authenticity—refusing to fit under any label or category, including the "taqwacore" label. An *Arab American News* report noted,

> [The filmmakers] deal with anti-Muslim racism on the one hand—the deep stares from passing motorists and a Detroit show at Small's canceled because of 'the Muslim thing.' On the other hand, they deal with intolerance from conservative Muslims, culminating at the Islamic Society of North America conference, which ends in a ruckus as cops tell one of the bands to either leave or be arrested.
>
> (Moossavi, 2009)

India Currents took the issue head-on, asking taqwacore bands what the term means to them. The reporter wrote: "I got some friendly and informative responses, but other bands' reactions varied from suspicious to overtly hostile … I was trying to make Taqwacore represent a new Muslim ideology. Taqwacore is more interested in questioning all ideology than creating a new one" (Rockwell, 2009b). Ethnic media, in its coverage of taqwacore, thus attempted to give artists more agency in defining who they are, or aren't, rather than impose a "rebel" narrative or pass judgment upon them as inauthentic or unreal.

Framing Muslims

United States Media

The U.S. media's taqwacore coverage split the Muslim community into "good Muslims" and "bad Muslims." In this framing, good Muslims would typically be young, born and/or brought up in the U.S. and, most important, culturally Americanized. The bad ones, on the other hand, are traditional, orthodox, first-generation Muslims who remain un-American in their ways and beliefs. Punkness, as an American tradition, becomes a symbol and a measure of how good a Muslim is in this narrative.

For instance, *The Washington Post* noted that taqwacore "is drawing scorn from some traditional Muslims who say their political, hard-edged music is 'haraam,' or forbidden" (Contreras, 2010). Referring to The Kominas's visit to the 2007 Islamic convention, the article said:

> The musicians performed at several venues but were kicked off stage during an open-mike performance at the Islamic Society of North America convention in Chicago. Traditional Muslims at the convention decried the electric guitar-based music as un-Islamic, and others were upset that a woman dared sing on stage.
> (Contreras, 2010)

In a similar vein, *The New York Times* constructed Knight as a good Muslim who was challenging the orthodoxy of bad Muslims—not just in the U.S. but around the world.

> Mr. Knight has written seven books since 2002, including a memoir in which he describes his disillusionment with orthodox Islam ... His writings have perturbed many Muslims, as have his attacks on hypocrisy and fractiousness in the Muslim world.
> (Oppenheimer, 2011)

United Kingdom Media

Like the American media, the British media also relied on the binary good Muslim–bad Muslim trope in its coverage. *The Guardian* quoted taqwacore artist and playwright Sabina England as saying,

> A lot of Muslim kids are tired of being told what to do, how to think, what to believe in, and how to act, by their parents. There are "the angry Muslim kids" who wanna grow beards and pray five times a day, and then there are the OTHER "angry Muslim kids" who wanna get drunk and say a huge big "fuck you" to the Muslim population.
> (Butt, 2007)

Oppressing women is deemed a common characteristic of the ordinary bad Muslims—which taqwacore artists were rebelling against. Referring to Sena Hussain, a Canadian member of the all-girl taqwacore group Secret Trial Five, the report said:

> [I]n a male-dominated culture, she thinks they will face challenges from all sides. "It's another thing that drives us," she says, "Muslim

women are seen as helpless and oppressed. We want to prove that wrong. I used to sport a mohawk, I don't now, but we will totally play up the punk thing."

(Butt, 2007)

While good Muslims, such as the taqwacore artists, are supposedly pro-West, bad Muslims are linked directly with terrorism as well as oppressive culture. *The Times*, for instance, quoted The Kominas' Basim Usmani as saying: "Everyone always asks about our struggle after 9/11, but we didn't feel that great about our culture before 2001, you know?" (Dalton, 2010).

Ethnic Media

In contrast with mainstream U.S. and British media, ethnic media outlets presented the Muslim community as a broad church within which differences in attitude and opinion were quite normal. Referring to the characters created by Knight, an *India Currents* article said,

> At one extreme is Umar, who embraces both puritanical "straight-edge" punk and orthodox Salafi Islam, but is condemned by the latter because of his many tattoos and his tendency to burst into obscenities when his housemates smoke dope in his pick-up truck. At the other extreme is Jehangir, who repeatedly declares that "Islam can take any shape you want it to" … There is Rabeya, whose face no one has ever seen because she always wears a burqa. She also sings Iggy Pop songs, reads Betty Friedan and Simone de Beauvoir, and blacks out passages she cannot accept in her copy of the Koran. In the middle of all of this is Yusuf, abstaining from drugs and alcohol, who is studying engineering because his parents told him to.

(Rockwell, 2009a)

Taqwacore artists are not necessarily "pro-West"—at least in any political sense—in this frame. Another *India Currents* article reported that despite being gay herself, the Secret Trial Five member Sena Hussain, "criticized [gay "Islamic reformer" Irshad] Manji for her support of 'apartheid states like Israel.'" It observed that "[r]eal-life Muslims, unlike their media caricatures, often agree to disagree, and tolerate their differences even when their disagreement is strong and passionate" (Rockwell, 2009b).

News India Times also problematized the "good Muslim/bad Muslim" narrative. For instance, The Kominas' vocalist Nyle Usmani was quoted in an article as saying, "I'd like to thank 9/11. I wouldn't be here without you" (Abdulrahim, 2009). While good Muslims are supposed to categorically view 9/11 as an act of evil, here was a purported good Muslim finding something positive in it—indeed, calling it his raison d'être. Bandmate Shahjehan Khan agreed with Usmani, saying, "Yeah, basically we wouldn't be here without [9/11]." The article later clarified that taqwacore groups' "satirical and brash lyrics and song titles criticize both fundamentalist Islam and post-September 11 ethnic and religious profiling" (Abdulrahim, 2009).

Framing the Islam–West Relationship

United States Media

Two frames dominated the representation of how the "Islamic world" and the "West" relate to each other in the U.S. media. One was a "White savior" frame, reflected, first, in the overwhelming focus on Michael Muhammad Knight in the taqwacore coverage and, second, in his portrayal as a catalyst of modernization and reform in "backward/premodern" Muslim society. *International Herald Tribune,* for instance, suggested,

> If Islamic radicals—the "fundys" in Mr. Knight's terminology—yearn to rescue what they see as authentic seventh-century Islam from the accumulated corruptions of the centuries, especially the corruptions of Western contact, Mr. Knight wants to do the inverse: save Islam by shedding antiquated and retrograde seventh-century ideas (about women and gays, for example) and making it consistent with the personal and sensual liberations of the 21st century.
>
> (Bernstein, 2010)

The second, closely related frame was that of American triumphalism. Taqwacore's ethos were deemed American ethos. As stated in *The Washington Post,* "The (taqwacore) bands are doing what American kids have done for generations: forming bands and making loud music" (Contreras, 2010). Knight, the White savior, was himself deemed an embodiment of American values that would liberate Islam.

> Knight is deeply American himself, which, for those concerned about a clash of civilizations between the Muslim world and the Judeo-Christian West, raises the question whether he could represent an amalgamation of cultures, a sort of Americanization and liberalization of Islam from within.
>
> (Bernstein, 2010)

The *International Herald Tribune* article concluded by quoting Knight himself as saying: "I very much believe … that America … on some level America can save Islam" (Bernstein, 2010).

United Kingdom Media

While the British media did not, for obvious reasons, project any American triumphalism, the White savior frame was apparent in their coverage as well—with the focus on Knight and his depiction as the man behind the movement. *The Guardian* wrote in 2007,

> Knight, who is 29 and lives in New York with his dog Sunny—"not as in Sunni Muslim"—downplays his achievement of single-handedly inspiring this subculture that has produced artists such as the Kominas, Secret Trial Five, Vote Hezbollah, Al-Thawra, 8-Bit and Diacritical.
> (Butt, 2007)

Four years later, the same trope was still prevalent in the newspaper.

> *The Taqwacores* [novel] spawned real-life Muslim punk bands. Bands such as The Kominas from Boston, the all-girl Secret Trial Five from Toronto, Al Thawra (The Power) from Chicago and even a few bands out in Pakistan and Indonesia. They took Knight's book as a manifesto for a new kind of Islamic youth culture that respects women and gay people and isn't afraid to challenge Islam.
> (Bhattacharya, 2011)

The Times claimed that Knight's influence went well beyond the taqwacore movement. It wrote,

> [Knight] argues for a "more tolerant, more gender-inclusive, social-justice-oriented" form of Islam, championing heretical ideas, including female-led prayer. Knight has inevitably made enemies, but he remains an inspirational figure to thousands of culturally conflicted young Muslims.
> (Dalton, 2010)

Ethnic Media

Once again, the coverage in American and British ethnic media often stood in stark contrast to mainstream news coverage, such as the lack of American triumphalism. *India Currents* observed, "Vote Hezbollah repeatedly point out that their name is a joke, but their song 'Poppy Fields' pulls no punches in its criticisms of American foreign policy" (Rockwell, 2009b). Nor was there any White savior to be found. Instead of painting Knight as the White guy reforming Islam, he is depicted as someone who chose Islam over Christianity and is deeply faithful to it. One article noted, "Knight, a convert to Islam, exhibits extensive knowledge and compassion for the religion, and that spirit is brought to life in [filmmaker] Zahra's work" (Maiwandi, 2011).

Even when ethnic media give credit to Knight, Islam and the West remain on a much more equal footing in their coverage, evident in passages such as this:

> In 2004, Michael Muhammad Knight wrote an extraordinary novel called *The Taqwacores,* which proposed that Islam and Punk Rock "aren't so far removed as you'd think. Both began in tremendous bursts of truth and vitality but seem to have lost something along the way ..."
>
> (Rockwell, 2009a)

News India Times pointed out the presence of extremists on both sides: "The (taqwacore) groups' satirical and brash lyrics and song titles criticize both fundamentalist Islam and post-Sept. 11 ethnic and religious profiling" (Abdulrahim, 2009). *India Currents* also, to a certain extent, problematized the Islam–West dichotomy by highlighting the complexities within Muslim societies in the U.S. and elsewhere. One article noted, "It is not always a peaceful relationship, but the Taqwacore sensibility is an integral part of modern Muslim culture, and not just in America" (Rockwell, 2009b).

Conclusion

Studying frames comparatively reveals that (1) journalism is an interpretive process rather than an objective representation of reality and (2) journalistic interpretations are themselves derived from dominant cultural narratives as well as hegemonic social and political ideologies (Tuchman, 1978; Zelizer, 1993). This study has presented a comparative frame analysis of the taqwacore coverage in mainstream U.S. and U.K. media as well as English-language "ethnic" media in both countries. The main object of the analysis, in line with the agenda of this volume, is the U.S. media. But looking at U.S. news frames juxtaposed with British and ethnic news frames allows us to better understand the narratives and ideologies at work, where they spring from, and what purposes they serve.

Mainstream U.S. news outlets that covered taqwacore, including *The New York Times, The Washington Post*, and *International Herald Tribune*, followed the narrative that Muslims, as a rule, are primitive and out of sync with the modern world. Their backward mentality is at least partly responsible for breeding radicalism, even terrorism, in Muslim society. Most Muslims, in this narrative, are "bad Muslims" (Mamdani, 2004). Taqwacore, on the other hand, is "good" and is consciously attempting to reform Muslim society. All of taqwacore's goodness is, however, *American* in origin—the subculture comprises American-born or American-bred youth, steeped in American cultural values. Moreover, it has been given life by a White American. In this manner, the U.S. news media simultaneously demonize Muslims as violent and ugly primitives, celebrate their own social progressivism by conceding the possibility of "reform" in Muslim society, and eulogize America by suggesting that all that is good and praiseworthy happens to come from this country. America itself is represented through Knight as White and inclined to—indeed meant to—change the world in its own image. Such a change, in this worldview, constitutes progress and modernization—a change from bad to good. In their taqwacore coverage, the U.S. media thus vilify and marginalize Muslims while patting their own back and rallying around the metaphorical flag of American exceptionalism.

The British media follow the same trope to a large extent, except for replacing "America" with "the West" wherever possible. So Muslims as a rule remain primitive and bad in their coverage, while taqwacore members are good because they are modern and Western. Even the later framing of taqwacore as inauthentic reflects an underlying belief that there is much that is wrong with Muslim society and it is in need of reform—coupled with a realization that taqwacore is failing in this purpose. But such a purpose only exists within the narrative that the media weave, and the "inauthentic" framing of taqwacore only betrays the inauthenticity of the media narrative itself.

Just like the U.S. media, the U.K. media's taqwacore coverage thus objectifies the Muslim community as primitive and oppressive, and naturalizes the need for Muslims to become more "West-like." The trans-Atlantic prevalence of these frames suggests that the ideological underpinnings of U.S. media framing go deeper than mere American exceptionalism. It indicates the presence of what Said (1978) called the *postcolonial gaze*—the objectification of the colonized in the view of the colonizer that serves to relegate the colonized into an inferior and submissive position and naturalizes the power that the colonizer wields over them. It makes colonization a moral act. The presence of this gaze reveals just how deeply this colonialist sensibility pervades U.S. (and U.K.) media, suffusing even the coverage of a musical subculture.

However, the contrasting coverage in ethnic media shows this is not the only possible way of writing about taqwacore. In their coverage, there is no conflation of good with America or the West and bad with Muslims. America and Muslims are represented as complex social categories with not one or two but a variety of undercurrents running across and even against each other. Furthermore, their coverage suggests taqwacore is as much about challenging bigotry and oppression within Islam as it is about questioning the racism and hypocrisy prevalent in the U.S. and the West in general, especially the hypocrisy apparent in their relationship with Islam. By stressing that taqwacore is primarily a musical phenomenon, they uncover even deeper layers of its colonialist objectification in mainstream U.S. and U.K. media—indicating that taqwacore may not have been covered at all had it not been perceived as a modernist rebellion against a monolithic, premodern Islam (Kumar, 2010).

This chapter demonstrates that the racialized "othering" of Muslims in the U.S. media is not limited to coverage of acts of "terrorism" or other instances of perceived Muslim radicalism, as previous research has noted (Chuang & Roemer, 2013; Kumar, 2010; Powell, 2011; Reese & Lewis, 2009). Even the coverage of a hybrid, immigrant, musical subculture related to Muslims and Islam takes the same shape and form, suggesting the presence of a deeper cultural instinct—an instinct that impels White Europe/America to view itself as superior to the Orient and justifies the conquest of other races as the White man's burden. News media share this broader social and political ideology as the natural order of things—and they serve to reproduce it across space and time. To be sure, such cultural impulses are neither instrumental nor deterministic. Subtle differences between British and U.S. coverage are evident even within the small sample of articles studied here. The presence of "ethnic" publications in these countries further complicates the trans-Atlantic public sphere. But the broad patterns of coverage in mainstream media cohere with the colonialist logic of White supremacy, Western modernity, and the naturalness of the Orient's subjugation.

References

Abdulrahim, R. (2009, August 21). Yeah, they're Muslim, but what about the music? *News India Times*, p. 16.

Andersen, A., Lingner, B., Ernst, N., Tadini, N., & Coelli, T. (2010). *Looking for cultural space discourses of identity formation on the case of taqwacore*. Roskilde University, Denmark.

Barth, F. (1969) *Ethnic groups and boundaries: The social organization of culture difference*. Boston, MA: Little Brown.

Berkowitz, D. A. (Ed.) (2010). *Cultural meanings of news: A text-reader*. London, UK: Sage.

Bernstein, R. (2010, January 28). Givin' it to the man, Islamic style. *The International Herald Tribune*, p. 2.

Bhattacharya, S. (2011, August 5). Never mind the burqas. *The Guardian*, p. 6.

Butt, R. (2007, April 27). Islamic street preachers: From Boston to Lahore and beyond, the tentacles of taqwacore—aka Islamic punk rock—are spreading. *The Guardian*, p. 10.

Chuang, A., & Roemer, R. C. (2013). The immigrant Muslim American at the boundary of insider and outsider: Representations of Faisal Shahzad as "homegrown" terrorist. *Journalism & Mass Communication Quarterly*, 90(1), 89–107.

Contreras, R. (2010, January 9). An unlikely hotbed of hard rock. *The Washington Post*, p. B02.

Crafts, L. (2007, December 14). Muhammad rocked the casbah. *The Texas Observer*. Retrieved from http://www.texasobserver.org/2653-muhammad-rocked-the-casbah-san-antonios-muslim-punk-scene-goes-national-and-europe-is-next/.

Crafts, L. (2009, July 25). Taqwacore: The Real Muslim Punk Underground. *National Public Radio*. Retrieved from http://www.npr.org/templates/story/story.php?storyId=107010536.

Dalton, S. (2010, June 14). Never mind the burkas. *The Times*, p. 55.

Durham, F. S. (1998). News frames as social narratives: TWA flight 800. *Journal of Communication*, 48(4), 100–117.

Entman, R. M. (1993). Framing: Toward clarification of a fractured paradigm. *Journal of Communication*, 43(4), 51–58.
Geertz, C. (1973). *The interpretation of cultures*. New York, NY: Basic Books.
Hosman, S.S. (2009). *Muslim punk rock in the U.S.: A social history of the taqwacores*. Greensboro, NC: University of North Carolina.
Knight, M. M. (2004). *The Taqwacores*. New York, NY: Autonomedia.
Knight, M. M. (2007). *The Taqwacores*. London, UK: Telegram.
Knight, M. M. (2011). Taqwacore. In E. E. Curtis (Ed.), *Encyclopedia of Muslim American history* (pp. 547–548). New York, NY: Infobase Publishing.
Knight, M. M. (2014, May 11). Hip-hop's global role in Muslim youth cultures. *The Washington Post*, p. E17.
Kumar, D. (2010). Framing Islam: The resurgence of Orientalism during the Bush II era. *Journal of Communication Inquiry*, 34(3), 254–277.
Kumar, D. (2012). *Islamophobia and the politics of empire*. London, UK: Haymarket Books.
Love, E. (2013). Beyond "post 9/11." *Contexts*, 12(1), 70–72.
Maiwandi, N. (2011, May). "The Taqwacores" tears it down. *India Currents*, p. 20.
Mamdani, M. (2004). *Good Muslim, Bad Muslim: America, the cold war and the roots of terror*. New York, NY: Pantheon Press.
McDowell, A. (2014). Warriors and terrorists: Antagonism as strategy in Christian hardcore and Muslim "taqwacore" punk rock. *Qualitative Sociology*, 37(3), 255–276.
Moossavi, A. (2009, November 28). Taqwacore: The birth of punk Islam. *Arab American News*, p. 15.
O'Brien, J. (2013). Muslim American youth and secular hip hop: Manifesting "cool piety" through musical practices. *Poetics*, 41, 99–121.
Oppenheimer, M. (2011, October 29). Convert straddles worlds of Islam and Hip-Hop. *The New York Times*, p. A16.
Powell, K. A. (2011). Framing Islam: An analysis of U.S. media coverage of terrorism since 9/11. *Communication Studies*, 62(1), 90–112.
Rana, J. (2011). *Terrifying Muslims: Race and labor in the South Asian diaspora*. Durham, NC: Duke University Press.
Reese, S. D. (2001). Prologue—Framing public life. In S. D. Reese, O. H. Gandy, Jr., & A. E. Grant (Eds.), *Framing Public Life* (pp. 7–31). Mahwah, NJ: Lawrence Erlbaum.
Reese, S. D., & Lewis, S. C. (2009). Framing the War on Terror: The internalization of policy in the US press. *Journalism*, 10(6), 777–797.
Rockwell, T. (2009a, May). Muslim punk rock? *India Currents*, p. 38.
Rockwell, T. (2009b, July). Taqwacore 2. *India Currents*, p. 34.
Said, E. (1978). *Orientalism*. New York, NY: Vintage Books.
Said, E. (1981). *Covering Islam*. New York, NY: Pantheon.
Selod, S., & Embrick, D. G. (2013). Racialization and Muslims: Situating the Muslim experience in race scholarship. *Sociology Compass*, 7(8), 644–655.
Shoemaker, P. J., & Reese, S. D. (2013). *Mediating the message in the 21st century: A media sociology perspective*. New York, NY: Routledge.
Stein, A., & Salime, Z. (2015). Manufacturing Islamophobia: Rightwing pseudo-documentaries and the paranoid style. *Journal of Communication Inquiry*. Advance online publication.
Tuchman, G. (1978). *Making news: A study in the construction of reality*. New York, NY: The Free Press.

Van Dijk, T. A. (1998). *Ideology: A multidisciplinary approach*. Thousand Oaks, CA: Sage.

Zelizer, B. (1990). Achieving journalistic authority through narrative. *Critical Studies in Media Communication, 7*(4), 366–376.

Zelizer, B. (1993). Journalists as interpretive communities. *Critical Studies in Media Communication, 10*(3), 219–237.

Conclusion
Looking Ahead

Bhoomi K. Thakore and Jason A. Smith

In this book, we have set out to complicate the intersection between race and media. To date, there has been limited focus on the role of critical race theory in the world of media, which we have attempted to address here. We are at a moment in time in the United State where we are moving forward socially and navigating our experiences through these myriad media lenses.

In September 2015, the *New York Times* published an article called "Move Over, Millennials, Here Comes Generation Z" (Williams, 2015). This article compares Millennials (born between 1980 and 2000) to the next generation of Americans currently being born. These individuals, who are the teens and tweens of today, are experiencing the most technologically advanced society to date. Not only are they the ones being most targeted by industry through media and advertising, but they are also the ones who are interacting and shaping media as we know it. As a result, this next generation is the most technologically connected group in our society. Their everyday experiences are also heavily mediated through social media like Tumblr, Instagram, Twitter, and Facebook, and are the generation to almost exclusively access all of their media through a smartphone or similar device. They also have an extremely short attention span, evident in the popularity of short bursts of text and images like those in Snapchat and other messenger apps. As reported in the article, many in Generation Z have lived in our post-9/11 reality of fear. Thus, in many ways, they are more conscientious of the problems in the world.

This generation is also the most diverse we have ever seen. According to data the article quoted from the 2010 U.S. Census, the number of individuals who identify as mixed White-and-Asian grew by 84%. Additionally, the number who identify as mixed Black-and-White grew by 134% (Williams, 2015), which is exceptionally notable considering the long-rooted inequality and desegregation practices by Whites against Blacks in the United States. In this report, the U.S. Census also noted that the number of individuals who identify as "two or more races" has increased by over 2 million. No doubt that many of these are the young people who will make up our forthcoming society. The racial landscape is indeed changing. However, what remains to be seen is the extent to which these racialized ideologies change and form, and the relationship between our new society and its many forms of media.

At the structural level, our ability to access media will be influenced by media policies and procedures, as well as new media adaptation and use. As Randy D. Abreu noted, our access to critical information by way of diverse media outlets is necessary for us as a society, but will be inevitably tied to the bureaucratic political process. As Leah P. Hunter and Jennifer M. Proffitt discussed, while niche broadcast outlets such as Bounce TV serve an important outlet for African American audiences, this is not sufficient in changing the status quo from the major media networks. The structural makeup of new media, as discussed by Nathan Jamel Riemer, highlights more accessible media to a generation of Black youth, which serves as a platform to address and promote important social issues. These new structural parameters for media come into tension with the preexisting structures before them.

At the production level, opportunities for directors and performers of color have long been limited, and will likely continue to be limited without a change to the inherent system of White privilege. Maryann Erigha notes how directors of color are limited to niche opportunities due to the faulty perception of audiences of color as non-marketable. The role and power of actors from minority backgrounds remains limited as well, despite the increased visibility they might have through successful media projects. Both Maritza Cárdenas and Salvador Vidal-Oritz demonstrate this contention for Latino/a actors through their case studies on Carlos Mencia and Sofía Vergara. Minority actors face competing with limited stereotypes rooted at intersections of race, gender, class, sexuality, and nationality, which hinder both opportunities and potential avenues to reframe White-centered narratives. Additionally, Sheena Sood highlights this trend through her analysis of Indian American Mindy Kaling, whose performances serve to cement her in a "honorary White" position within her *own* show for the purposes of appealing to a mainstream audience on a mainstream television network.

The same inequalities that inform the structure and production of media also inform its visual content and the representations that audiences see onscreen. As John D. Foster wrote, even though the number of films with Asian characters has increased, they continue to reinforce a White patriarchal system. As Jennifer Mueller and Rula Issa found, even representations of overt racism and physical violence in the film *12 Years a Slave* fail to critically examine the social structure of slavery and reinforce a White hegemonic ideology for its majority White viewers. Visual representations also play a key role in the maintenance of White spaces of leisure, as David L. Brunsma, Nathaniel G. Chapman, and J. Slade Lellock demonstrate in their analysis of promotional videos for electronic dance music festivals.

As our final section demonstrates, these ideologies are reproduced at the level of mainstream news coverage, which has larger implications among mainstream consumers of news. As Bianca Gonzalez-Sobrino, Devon R. Goss, and Matthew W. Hughey contend, even though film reviewers are seen as independent journalists and arbiters of cultural taste, they indeed reproduce the normative White ideologies of their news outlets.

As Jorge X. Ballinas argued, news media outlets perceive outspoken xenophobia on Twitter as exceptional, and spin the story to emphasize the American Dream success story of Non-White children of immigrants. As Seneca Vaught emphasized, Black Studies scholars are important to conversations surrounding racial crises, yet fail to successfully be included in news coverage of those crises. As Saif Shahin found, the ways in which U.S. and U.K. news media cover subcultural Muslim identity emphasizes the benefits of the "American/Western" identity of these individual social performers.

In conclusion, the future of media representations will be heavily influenced by many social factors for the next generation of consumers, including the increasing technological advances, along with the increasing multi-racializing of our society. As more and more individuals will identify outside of the normative racial identity, it will become even more important to include them in these normative media structures. These issues speak to continually revisiting the need for assessing the ways that media and race intersect in new and interesting ways.

Reference

Williams, A. (2015, September 18). Move over, Millennials, Here comes Generation Z. *New York Times*. Retrieved from http://www.nytimes.com/2015/09/20/fashion/move-over-millennials-here-comes-generation-z.html.

Editors and Contributors

Editors

Jason A. Smith is a PhD Candidate in Public Sociology at George Mason University, currently working on his dissertation involving media policy and diversity. Jason's primary research interests lie at the intersection of race and the media. He recently completed a co-edited section in the *International Journal of Communication* (2015) entitled, "Communication in Action: Bridging Research and Policy." Past work has been featured in the *Journal of Black Studies, International Journal of Media and Cultural Politics, Sociation Today*, and the edited volume *Agenda for Social Justice: Solutions 2012*.

Bhoomi K. Thakore is visiting Assistant Professor and Director of the Sociology Program at Elmhurst College (IL). Her research interests broadly cover structural inequality, with particular focus on race/ethnicity/gender and media. In her forthcoming book, *South Asians on the U.S. Screen: Just Like Everyone Else?* (Lexington Books, 2016), she examines the ways that South Asian characters and actors in popular entertainment reinforce a racialized hierarchy on Screen and in society.

Contributors

Randy D. Abreu is a graduate of Thomas Jefferson School of Law in San Diego, California, and current Law Fellow with the Congressional Hispanic Caucus Institute. As a law student, Abreu focused his studies on Critical Race Theory, Cyber Law, and Media Policy. As a Congressional Fellow, Abreu focuses his work in Washington, DC, on the legislative process as well as the intersections of media and technology policy and its effects on low-income, rural, and people of color. His current interests and work focus on digital technology adoption among the more vulnerable members of society.

Jorge X. Ballinas is a doctoral candidate in the Department of Sociology at Temple University. He examines the overlap of race, racism, immigration, as well as media portrayals of these topics. More specifically, Ballinas looks at the racialization of Latinos, particularly Mexicans, within U.S. institutions. Currently he is investigating how Mexican Americans make sense of their experiences while in college in nontraditional settlement destinations with a focus on the difficulties they have faced and the identities that are salient for them.

David L. Brunsma is Professor of Sociology at Virginia Tech and founding co-editor of *Sociology of Race and Ethnicity*. He does research on racial identity, racialization, and human rights.

Maritza Cárdenas is an Assistant Professor of English at the University of Arizona. Her research interests focus on U.S. Central Americans, Latina/o cultural productions, Latina/o subjectivities, and U.S. American ethnicities. A recipient of the Woodrow Wilson fellowship for her research on U.S. Central Americans, her most recent essay has been published in the journal *Studies in 20th and 21st Century Literature*. Currently she is working on completing her book manuscript, which highlights the historical, socio-political, and economic processes that have facilitated the construction of a pan-ethnic transnational cultural identity (U.S. Central American) to emerge in the U.S. diaspora.

Nathaniel G. Chapman is Assistant Professor of Sociology at Arkansas Tech University. His research focuses on craft beer and the production of culture in the United States. He recently completed research on the Grateful Dead.

Maryann Erigha is an Assistant Professor of Sociology at the University of Memphis. Her work on race and contemporary media has appeared in *Sociology Compass, The Du Bois Review: Social Science Research on Race*, and *The Black Scholar*. She holds a PhD in Sociology from the University of Pennsylvania.

John D. Foster is Associate Professor of Sociology at the University of Arkansas at Pine Bluff. He is the author of *White Race Discourse: Preserving Racial Privilege in a Post-Racial Society* (Lexington Books, 2013), as well as several articles published in academic journals, including *Discourse & Society* and *Ethnic and Racial Studies*. He studies the different methods used to rationalize and perpetuate social inequalities.

Bianca Gonzalez-Sobrino is a doctoral student in Sociology at the University of Connecticut. She previously received a MS in Sociology from Mississippi State University. Her research examines racial and ethnic competition and threat, racial identity formation, and media constructions of racial identity. She particularly focuses on the Puerto Rican diaspora as a site of ethno-racial experiences.

Devon R. Goss, MS, MA, is doctoral candidate in Sociology at the University of Connecticut. She previously received a MA in Sociology from the University of Connecticut (2014) and a MS in Psychological and Cultural

Studies from Lewis & Clark College (2012). Her research examines the color line, particularly in relation to instances of boundary crossing in typically racialized institutions; and the impact of racialization in family formation and processes, through an examination of transracial adoption. Goss's work has appeared in *The ANNALS of the Academy of Political and Social Science* and *Sociology Compass*.

Matthew W. Hughey is Associate Professor of Sociology at the University of Connecticut. He examines the relationship between racial inequality and collective understandings of race. His research has been published in journals such as *The ANNALS of the American Academy of Social and Political Science*, *American Behavioral Scientist*, *Social Problems*, *Social Psychology Quarterly*, *Du Bois Review*, *Ethnic and Racial Studies*, *Ethnicities*, and *Sociology of Race and Ethnicity*. He is also the author of *The White Savior Film: Content, Critics, and Consumption* (Temple University Press, 2014) and *White Bound: Nationalists, Antiracists, and the Shared Meanings of Race* (Stanford University Press, 2012).

Leah P. Hunter (PhD, Florida State University) is a visiting Assistant Professor in the School of Journalism & Graphic Communications, Florida A&M University. Her research interests include political economy of media and the intersection of diversity and class, popular culture, race and representation in media, and minority media ownership.

Rula Issa is an undergraduate student double-majoring in Sociology and International Affairs at Skidmore College. She is particularly interested in education as a social institution and how education can be used to address social issues.

J. Slade Lellock is a graduate research assistant and PhD student in the Department of Sociology at Virginia Tech. His current research interests broadly include the examination of symbolic and expressive elements of culture.

Jennifer C. Mueller is an Assistant Professor of Sociology and Assistant Director of the Intergroup Relations Program at Skidmore College, in upstate New York. Mueller's research centers on the interplay between racialized structures and everyday, cultural processes involved in racial reproduction. Her work targets this synergy across two lines: one examining racial differences in the intergenerational transmission of wealth and capital; and a second centered on everyday, cultural practices and ways of knowing, as well as aspects of material culture.

Jennifer M. Proffitt (PhD, Pennsylvania State University) is an Associate Professor in the School of Communication, Florida State University. Her research interests include political economy of media, specifically broadcast history and regulation, popular culture, and news coverage of labor.

Nathan Jamel Riemer is a doctoral student in the Department of Sociology at the University of Chicago. His current research focuses on the civic and political engagement of young Black people and the ways in which new media affords new means for types of engagement.

Saif Shahin is a doctoral candidate in journalism at the University of Texas at Austin, chief editor of *Sagar: A South Asia Research Journal*, and research fellow at Muslim Public Affairs Council, Washington, DC. He studies news, culture, and politics in both U.S. and global contexts, focusing on issues of identity and power. His research has been published in refereed journals including *Journalism, Journalism Practice, Global Media and Communication,* and *Journal of Communication Inquiry*. He earlier worked as a journalist in India, England, and the Middle East, covering domestic and international politics, diplomacy, and diasporic cultures.

Sheena Sood is a doctoral candidate in Temple University's Sociology department. Her research interests focus on racism, immigrant experiences, social movements, and political alliances. Sood's dissertation research explores how South Asian American organizations define their political agendas and with whom they construct alliances and coalitions. She works as a Gender and Sexuality Inclusion coordinator at Temple's Wellness Resource Center where she organizes holistic programming for the LGBTQIA+ community. As a healer, she enjoys sharing wellness practices such as yoga and meditation with everyone, especially with individuals who are marginalized from accessing these healing modalities due to cost, stress, and burnout.

Seneca Vaught is a jointly appointed Assistant Professor of African and African Diaspora Studies at Kennesaw State University in the Departments of History and Interdisciplinary Studies. He uses his expertise in the intersections of race, policy, and technology to address contemporary issues. He has been awarded the William Wells Brown Award for his innovative and project-oriented approach to framing community problems in policy terms for scholars, activists, and community leaders seeking to creatively apply historical knowledge.

Salvador Vidal-Ortiz (PhD) is Associate Professor in the sociology department at American University, in Washington, DC. He co-edited *The Sexuality of Migration: Border Crossings and Mexican Immigrant Men* (NYU Press, 2009) and *Queer Brown Voices: Personal Narratives of Latina/o LGBT Activism* (University of Texas Press, 2015). He is working on a manuscript tentatively titled *An Instrument of the Orishas: Racialized Sexual Minorities in Santería*. While his past research focused on U.S. Latino studies, two recent projects (one on internal displacement and LGBT Colombians; the other, transgendering human rights, lessons from Latin America) have turned his focus to the region.

Index

Academy for Television Arts and Sciences 91
advertising: *see also* 'media'
African Americans: as audience 198; as news experts 198, 200–203, 207, 209; as magical negro 137, 167; Black studies scholarship 200–03, 206–07; in prison system 138; racialization of African Americans in the media 199, 207; victimization 135–37; *see also* 'directors'
American Dream ideology 95, 104, 111, 123, 183, 185, 191–92, 194
Arab Americans: on television 102–03
Asian Americans: as model minorities 123, 125, 129; as perpetual strangers 118; in film 117–18; *see also* 'directors'
audiences: narrowcasting 28, 30, 232; worth 27; *see also* 'African Americans'

Blacks: *see also* 'African Americans'
Black Youth Project 100 41, 42, 44–52
Bonilla-Silva, E.: *see also* 'racial theory - Color-blind ideology and racism'
Bounce TV 26, 32–36; political connections 32; programming 35
Brown, M. 207, 209

Clyburn, M.: *see also* 'Federal Communications Commission'
Cohen, C. 45–46
color-blind racism: *see also* 'racial theory'
Communication Policy Research Network 18
Critical information needs 16, 18–22; aims and purpose 22; opposition to 21–22; shortcomings 20; *see also* 'Federal Communications Commission'

Deen, P. 205–06
directors: budgets and genres by racial category 63–65; demographics 61; female and minority 65–66
dramaturgy 105, 109
Du Bois, W. E. B. 198

Feagin, J.: *see also* 'racial theory - systemic racism,' 'racial theory - white racial frame'
Federal Communications Commission 15, 21, 18–22, 33–34
Ferguson, Missouri: *see also* 'Brown, M.'

Hollywood: exclusion of minority groups 60; film reviewer 165, 168, 178; racialized industry 60–62, 67, 165, 167, 172–176; *see also* 'directors'

Knight Commission on Information Needs of Communities 17
Kaling, M. 100; *see also* 'South Asian Americans'

Latino/a Americans: and accent 86, 89, 91, 94–95; Central Americans 70, 72, 76–81; Colombianidad 86, 90, 91, 95–96; ethnoracial subject 74; Honduran identity 70, 72, 76–81; in Hollywood 88–90, 94–95; *Latinidad* 70, 72, 76, 85–88; Latino imaginary 70; racialization of Latinos in the media 73–74, 76–77, 88–89, 166; *see also* 'directors'
Lear, N.: *see also* 'sitcoms'

male gaze 92, 104
Martin, T. 41, 43, 51–52

McArthur Research Network on Youth and Participatory Politics 45
media: advertising 27; and race 7, 17, 36, 67, 166, 172; and social movements 41–43; as social practice 199–202, 208–09, 216, 226; concentration of 3, 16, 23, 34; digital switch, impact of 32–33; Ethnic media 215, 221, 223, 225, 227; media ecology 19, 23; news media 183, 199, 203, 215; online media 3, 41; ownership diversity 34; social media 42, 48–52, 79, 81, 231; sociology of 1–2; stereotypes 167, 172, YouTube 70; *see also* 'African Americans,' 'directors,' 'Hollywood,' 'Latino/a Americans,' and 'Muslims'
Media Action Network for Asian Americans 120
Mencia, C.: fued with J. Rogen and G. Lopez 78–79; *Mind of Mencia* 71, 74–77; internet backlash 79–80; *see also* 'Latino/a Americans - Honduran identity'
methods: content analysis 105–06, 153–54, 168, 184–85; discourse analysis 71; frame analysis 219; qualitative analysis 20, 170, 219
Muslims: on television 103–04; racialization of Muslims in the media 215–16, 221–27

new media: *see also* 'media - online media'

Omi, M. and H. Winant: *see also* 'racial theory - racial formation'
oreintalism 216–17, 226–27

Pai, A,: *see also* 'Federal Communications Commission'
presentation of self 105
public interest 26, 33

racial theory: anti-racism 141–43; cinethetic racism 124; colonialism 217, 227–228; Color-blind ideology and racism 5, 104–05, 108–09, 112, 148, 152–53, 157–58, 167, 176–78, 182, 185–94, 200–02; intersectionality 60, 65–66, 232; new racism 124; racial formation 5, 87; racialization 4–5, 86–87; racialized social system 118–19; systemic racism 6, 16–18, 167; tri-racial social system 118, 123–24, 127, 129; White racial frame 5, 28, 104–05, 156, 174
Racial crises 198–199, 203, 207–209; *see also* 'Brown, M.,' 'Deen, P.,' and 'Zimmerman, G.'
Raves 150–52
Republican party 21
Rock, C. 59

sitcoms: historical look at 28–30; Lear, N. 28–29; *see also* 'racial theory - White racial frame'
social epistemologies 132
South Asian Americans: on television 103–04; as model minorities 104, 111

Taqwacore 214, 217–19, 227
Telecommunications Act of 1934 21, 26
Telecommunications Act of 1996 21

United States Census 87

Vergara, S. 85; cultural resistance 91; *see also* 'Latina/o Americans'

Wheeler, T.: *see also* 'Federal Communications Commission'
White Americans: White savior 124–26, 128, 159, 167, 173, 224–25; White supremacy 132–35, 139–40, 144–45; Whiteness 148; *see also* 'directors,' 'racial theory – White racial frame'

Zimmerman, G. 41, 47, 50, 206